Private Intergenerational Transfers and Population Aging

Contributions to Economics

Further volumes of this series can be found at our homepage
http://www.springer.de/cgi-bin/search_book.pl?series=1262

Frank Riedel
Imperfect Information and Investor Heterogeneity in the Bond Market
2000. ISBN 3-7908-1247-1

Kirsten Ralf
Business Cycles
2000. ISBN 3-7908-1245-5

Michele Bagella/
Leonardo Becchetti (Eds.)
The Competitive Advantage of Industrial Districts
2000. ISBN 3-7908-1254-4

Frank Bohn
Monetary Union and Fiscal Stability
2000. ISBN 3-7908-1266-8

Jaime Behar
Cooperation and Competition in a Common Market
2000. ISBN 3-7908-1280-3

Michael Malakellis
Integrated Macro-Micro-Modelling Under Rational Expectations
2000. ISBN 3-7908-1274-9

Stefan Baumgärtner
Ambivalent Joint Production and the Natural Environment
2000. ISBN 3-7908-1290-0

Henri Capron, Wim Meeusen (Eds.)
The National Innovation System of Belgium
2000. ISBN 3-7908-1308-7

Tobias Miarka
Financial Intermediation and Deregulation
2000. ISBN 3-7908-1307-9

Chisato Yoshida
Illegal Immigration and Economic Welfare
2000. ISBN 3-7908-1315-X

Nikolaus Thumm
Intellectual Property Rights
2000. ISBN 3-7908-1329-X

Max Keilbach
Spatial Knowledge Spillovers and the Dynamics of Agglomeration and Regional Growth
2000. ISBN 3-7908-1321-4

Alexander Karmann (Ed.)
Financial Structure and Stability
2000. ISBN 3-7908-1332-X

Joos P. A. van Vugt/Jan M. Peet (Eds.)
Social Security and Solidarity in the European Union
2000. ISBN 3-7908-1334-6

Johannes Bröcker/Hayo Herrmann (Eds.)
Spatial Change and Interregional Flows in the Integrating Europe
2001. ISBN 3-7908-1344-3

Kirstin Hubrich
Cointegration Analysis in a German Monetary System
2001. ISBN 3-7908-1352-4

Nico Heerink et al. (Eds.)
Economic Policy and Sustainable Land Use
2001. ISBN 3-7908-1351-6

Friedel Bolle/Michael Carlberg (Eds.)
Advances in Behavioral Economics
2001. ISBN 3-7908-1358-3

Volker Grossmann
Inequality, Economic Growth, and Technological Change
2001. ISBN 3-7908-1364-8

Thomas Riechmann
Learning in Economics
2001. ISBN 3-7908-1384-2

Nicole Pohl
Mobility in Space and Time
2001. ISBN 3-7908-1380-X

Claus Brand
Money Stock Control and Inflation Targeting in Germany
2001. ISBN 3-7908-1380-X

Erik Lüth

Private Intergenerational Transfers and Population Aging

The German Case

With 19 Figures and 53 Tables

Physica-Verlag
A Springer-Verlag Company

Series Editors
Werner A. Müller
Martina Bihn

Author
Dr. Erik Lüth
International Monetray Fund
700, 19th Street, N.W.
20431 Washington, D.C.
USA
E-mail: elueth@imf.org

ISSN 1431-1933
ISBN 3-7908-1402-4 Physica-Verlag Heidelberg New York

Cataloging-in-Publication Data applied for
Die Deutsche Bibliothek – CIP-Einheitsaufnahme
Lüth, Erik: Private intergenerational transfers and population aging: the german case; with tables / Erik Lüth. – Heidelberg; New York: Physica-Verl., 2001
(Contributions to economics)
Zugl.: Freiburg (Breisgau), Univ., Diss., 2000
ISBN 3-7908-1402-4

Physica-Verlag Heidelberg New York
a member of BertelsmannSpringer Science+Business Media GmbH

Softcover Design: Erich Kirchner, Heidelberg

SPIN 10835504 88/2202-5 4 3 2 1 0 – Printed on acid-free paper

Preface

First and foremost, I'd like to thank my parents for investing in a risky project. My chief and supervisor Prof. Dr. Bernd Raffelhüschen for suggesting the subject of this thesis and always having patience with me. My colleague Holger Bonin for fruitful discussions. My colleague, housemate, and friend Christoph Borgmann – I'll miss our buttermilk breaks. Peter Cypra for his friendship, humor, and advice. And Ursula Seeger.

Washington, D.C. January 2001 *Erik Lüth*

Contents

1. Introduction

In the forthcoming decades the industrialized countries as well as, to a lesser extent, developing countries will experience a demographic transition which is unprecedented in history. Within the next 40 years the German population being 65 years and older will increase from 15 to 27 percent, the median age will raise by 10 years, and the dependency ratio – the ratio of pensioners to workers – will almost double.

Coping with the fiscal consequences of population aging is generally perceived as one of the central challenges of the decades to come. With generous pay-as-you-go schemes in place in most countries, policy makers as well as the general public are particularly concerned about the demographic transition's impact on intergenerational distribution. Most of the programs are of a defined-benefit type. Consequently, an increasing ratio of retirees to workers will impose a formidable fiscal burden on the young and yet unborn.

However, apart from public intergenerational transfers in the form of Social Security, health care, and old-age care programs, generations are linked by a variety of private intergenerational transfers such as bequests, in-kind services, interest-free loans, shared living arrangements, or investment in the children's human capital. These transfers' impact on the distribution of generational welfare has gone almost unnoticed by the literature.

The virtual neglect of the role of private transfers during a demographic transition is somewhat astonishing. Alike their public counterpart private transfers will be markedly affected as the relative size of donor and recipient generations changes. Admittedly, it is possible for the average transfer *per* donor or the average transfer *per* recipient to remain unchanged in the course of population aging. It is, though, logically impossible for both of these magnitudes to stay constant as the population grows older.

In addition, the volume of private intergenerational transfer is considerable. In a widely noticed article Kotlikoff and Summers [1] estimate that 80 percent of US wealth is inherited from preceding generations. While this estimate is commonly viewed as too high, there exists a broad consensus that inherited wealth accounts for at least one third of observable wealth. For Germany we find that bequests amount to 75 percent of pay-as-you-go pensions, both calculated on an annual basis. Assuming transfers *inter vivos* of the same order of magnitude as supported by US data [2] would suggest private intergenerational transfers in excess of Social Security transfers.

This study attempts to make up for the gap in the literature by investigating the consequences of population aging for private transfers and intergenerational distribution, in general. The cornerstones of the analysis are the overlapping generations model as developed by Samuelson [3] and Diamond [4] as well as the generational accounting framework put forward in a series of articles by Auerbach et al. [5, 6] and Kotlikoff [7]. In the empirical part of this study our focus lies on Germany with data obtained from the Income and Expenditure Survey 1993 and the German Socio-Economic Panel. On the other hand, the overlapping generations model, while being calibrated to German data, is general enough to fit most industrialized economies.

To our knowledge for the first time this study gives a comprehensive overview of private transfer patterns in Germany. Earlier studies confine their analysis to parent-child transfers (Juerges [8]), bequests (Schlomann [9], Reil-Held [10]) or remittances of guest workers to their home countries (Merkle and Zimmermann [11]). Apart from Reil-Held, these studies exclusively draw from data of the Socio-Economic Panel.

By means of an accounting framework our study further permits a direct comparison of the volume of private and public intergenerational transfers in Germany. This approach determines the volume of private intergenerational transfers as a residual and is therefore particularly suited for monitoring transfers *inter vivos*, which otherwise are hard to observe. Principal goal of this exercise is to establish, whether private transfers can make up for the fiscal burden incurred on the young and yet unborn by population aging. So far a similar study has only been undertaken by Ablett [12] for Australia. Our study owes considerably to this pioneering work.

Finally, the computable general equilibrium model presented in this study for the first time allows to analyze various bequest motives in a unified framework. Earlier studies investigating the impact of population aging on intergenerational distribution usually restrict their attention to a single transfer motive (cf. [13] and [14]). Lacking empirical evidence in favor of a predominant bequest motive, this approach seems somewhat tenuous.

The proceeding of the study is as follows. Given the critical nature of the underlying transfer motive, any study concerned with the implications of private transfers must depart from those motives. Chapter 2 therefore reviews the most prominent motives proposed in the literature, namely altruism, precaution against longevity (in combination with imperfect annuity markets), exchange, and joy-of-giving. In particular, we elaborate the models' main predictions that serve to discriminate empirically between different motives. Subsequently, the chapter gives a survey of the empirical research undertaken so far to establish a predominant bequest motive.

Chapter 3 comprises an empirical investigation of private transfers in Germany based on two micro data sets, the Income and Expenditure Survey 1993 and the Socio-Economic Panel. While private transfers are hard to observe in general, German data on transfers are of even poorer quality than comparable US sources, which to date have served for most empirical studies. The two major shortcomings are either small sample size or the lacking linkage of transfer recipients and donors, both being a prerequisite of econometric tests for alternative transfer motives. As a consequence this chapter, rather than providing rigorous empirical evidence in favor of specific transfer motives, contents itself with identifying transfer patterns for Germany. We, thus, further evidence on size, direction, composition, and distribution of transfers, characteristics of donors and recipients, as well as particulars on wealth holdings. Not only do these stylized facts give a sense for the corresponding figures and magnitudes in Germany, which is indispensable for calibrating the general equilibrium model to reality. In addition, the plausibility of the different transfer models can be evaluated in the light of this evidence.

The following two chapters address the central question of whether private intergenerational transfers can ease the fiscal burden induced by population aging. As the study proceeds along these lines the degree of abstraction increases, turning from mere demographic and accounting exercises in Chapter 4 to a general equilibrium model with sound economic basis in Chapter 5. Chapter 4 is particularly suited for the applied economist or policy maker concerned with the specific extent of intergenerational imbalance. Section 4.1 discusses the determinants of the demographic transition, the assumptions underlying the population projection, and the degree of prospective population aging. Section 4.2 then proceeds by inspecting into what demographics reveal about the development of intergenerational transfers. Specifically, an index for private intergenerational transfers is constructed and over the coming decades contrasted with the dependency ratio, the corresponding index for public intergenerational transfers. Private transfer can only make up for higher contributions to social insurance, if the transfer *per* recipient increases in the course of population aging. Whether this is the case under the common transfer motives is investigated in Section 4.3. The accounting framework is introduced in Section 4.4. First, the method and results of conventional generational accounting are reviewed. Subsequently, this method is extended to include both public and private intergenerational transfers.

Of course, various forces determining generational welfare during a demographic transition can not be captured in a mere accounting framework. Chapter 5 therefore introduces a dynamic general equilibrium model suited for analyzing different transfer motives, price effects, and excess burden. After introducing the model in Section 5.1, Section 5.2 investigates the distributive consequences of population aging under different transfer motives and a defined-benefit pay-as-you-go scheme, while still abstracting from distortionary taxes. In Section 5.3 we use the general equilibrium model as a benchmark for assessing the accurateness of our earlier accounting exercise. In particular, we show in which direction the accounting results will be biased and whether this bias is likely to be significant. Section 5.4, finally, introduces an endogenous labor supply and in this way allows for labor disincentive effects induced by social insurance. Not only does this measure give a more comprehensive account of the fiscal burden and in this way improves our understanding of the distributive implications of population aging. At the same time, the inclusion of distortionary taxes permits to inspect into whether there is scope for efficiency gains. In particular, we investigate whether financing part of the pay-as-you-go scheme by inheritance rather than payroll taxes can reduce excess burden and in this manner alleviate the fiscal burden of the young and yet unborn. The study's main findings are summarized in Chapter 6.

This study can also be read selectively. Those merely interested in empirical evidence on transfer patterns are referred to Section 2.5 and Chapter 3 for a general and Germany-specific survey, respectively. The reader primarily concerned with generational accounting may confine his attention to Sections 4.4 and 5.3, with the former presenting the methodology and results for Germany and the latter laying the theoretical foundations. The welfare analysis in general equilibrium, finally, is confined to Sections 5.1, 5.2, and 5.4. Beforehand, those not acquainted with private transfer motives, however, are recommended the reading of Sections 2.1 through 2.4 as well as Section 4.3, where the micro-foundations of the general equilibrium model are unfolded in detail.

2. Motives for Private Intergenerational Transfers

2.1 Altruistic Transfers

Altruism is the most prominent among the motives for private intergenerational transfers and was first introduced by Barro [15] and Becker [16]. In order to understand, what is meant by altruism in economic theory take a look at the following stylized model. An individual lives for one period, say period t, during which he earns a labor income w_t. There exists only one good in the present economy, the price of which is assumed to equal unity. During his life the individual consumes c_t units of the good and leaves the remaining resources as a bequest b to his offspring. The latter is born immediately before the parent dies and lives through period $t+1$. Since by means of the bequest resources can be transferred from one period to another it is assumed to bear interest at rate r. Also the child works during his life. Consequently, the child's resources comprise the bequest, interest earned on the bequest, and labor income w_{t+1}. All of these resources are spent for consumption c_{t+1}.

Altruism is incorporated into the model by letting the child's utility enter the parent's utility function. If u_{t+1} depicts the offspring's utility and both individuals derive utility from consumption, the parent's utility can be expressed as $u_t(c_t, u_{t+1}(c_{t+1}))$, where both u_t and u_{t+1} are monotonous and concave. Furthermore, it is assumed that $\partial u_t / \partial u_{t+1} = \psi > 0$ with ψ denoting the degree of altruism. The parent's maximization problem can then be stated as follows:

$$\max_{c_t, c_{t+1}} \; u_t(c_t, u_{t+1}(c_{t+1}))$$

$$\text{s.t.} \quad c_t = w_t - b \tag{2.1}$$

$$c_{t+1} = (1+r)\, b + w_{t+1} \tag{2.2}$$

$$b \geq 0\,, \tag{2.3}$$

with the inequality constraint precluding negative bequests. Assuming, for the moment, that the inequality constraint does not bind, the first two constraints can be combined to $c_t + c_{t+1}/(1+r) = w_t + w_{t+1}/(1+r)$, which states that family consumption must equal family resources. Maximizing the parent's utility function subject to this constraint, one derives the Euler equation:

$$\frac{\partial u_t}{\partial c_t} = \psi \frac{\partial u_{t+1}}{\partial c_{t+1}} (1+r) \; . \tag{2.4}$$

A useful reference is complete altruism, where the offspring's consumption is weighted less only because it lies in the future, i.e. $\psi = 1/(1+r)$. In this case Equation (2.4) states that the testator allocates family resources across individuals until their marginal utility of consumption corresponds. In analogy to the life-cycle model this implies consumption smoothing over time and individuals, given the concavity of the utility functions.

Next, the implications of altruistic bequests will be discussed by further exploring the analogy to the standard life-cycle model. Unless stated differently, these implications in the same manner apply to transfers *inter vivos*. Note, that the following exposition is limited to so-called operational bequests, meaning that the inequality constraint does not bind. For a formal treatment please refer to Appendix A.1. First, bequests depend positively on parents' earnings, since an increase in parents' labor income is partly directed towards children's consumption: $\partial b/\partial w_t > 0$.[1] Furthermore, the elasticity of bequests with respect to testators' earnings is usually greater than unity: $\eta_{b,w_t} > 1$. To see this, assume homothetic preferences on the part of the parents. As parents' earnings only account for a fraction of family earnings an increase in w_t by 1 percent translates into an increase of parents' consumption c_t by less than one percent. According to Equation (2.1) bequests must therefore increase by more than one percent. It is for this reason, that bequests are sometimes called a 'luxury good' (cf. [17]).

From consumption smoothing it also follows, that altruistic bequests are inversely related to heirs' earnings: $\partial b/\partial w_{t+1} < 0$. This has far-reaching implications. Specifically, one would not expect to observe equal division of the bequest among offspring, unless required by legal norms. Instead, one would suppose parents to level out earnings differences among their children by means of bequests. Contrary to common belief, bequests then would not increase but alleviate inequality, at least within family lines.

Apart from the incomes of testators and heirs, the degree of altruism determines the size of bequests. The more altruistic the parents the more they bequeath: $\partial b/\partial \psi > 0$. One can also draw conclusions about the impact of altruistic bequests on intergenerational immobility (cf. [18]). Intergenerational immobility is a property of society and denotes the extend to which children's circumstances depend on the economic, social and genetic background of their parents. It is usually measured as the correlation between offspring's

[1] Anything that holds for labor income in the present model can be extended to life-cycle income in a model, where individuals live and work for more than one period. Thus, bequests also depend positive on parents' wealth; cf. Appendix A.1.

wealth and their fathers' wealth at a corresponding age. In order to infer this correlation in the present model, one has to link the wealth of subsequent generations at their time of death. This is done, by slightly modifying Equation (2.1) to include a bequest b_{t-1} left to the parent by his predecessors. Additionally taking into account accrued interest on the bequest, Equation (2.1) is changed to

$$c_t = b_{t-1}(1+r) + w_t - b \tag{2.5}$$

and family resources increase to $b_{t-1}(1+r)+w_t+w_{t+1}/(1+r)$. Now presume once more that the parent exhibits homothetic preferences. In this case the parent has a constant propensity to spend on own consumption which is denoted by e. Hence, his demand function for own consumption reads $c_t = e[b_{t-1}(1+r) + w_t + w_{t+1}/(1+r)]$ and from Equation (2.5) it follows that

$$b = (1-e)(b_{t-1}(1+r) + w_t) - e\frac{w_{t+1}}{(1+r)} . \tag{2.6}$$

Obviously, the correlation between parents' and offspring's wealth depends on the magnitude of bequests relative to live-cycle earnings. One would therefore expect to observe intergenerational immobility predominantly among the very well-to-do. For the majority of families, though, bequests are small relative to live-cycle income and, according to the altruistic model, do not account for intergenerational immobility.

Altruistic bequests further have strong implications for the effectiveness of public intergenerational transfers, such as public debt or pay-as-you-go Social Security. Imagine the government finances a tax cut in period t by issuing bonds on international capital markets. In the following period it repays principal and interest by raising taxes. Thus, while the parent faces lower taxes, the child is hit by a tax increase. In the absence of operational altruistic bequests, this fiscal policy will result in a one-by-one increase of c_t and a one-by-one decline in national saving. It can therefore be called expansionary. Now suppose the two generations are linked by operational bequests. As illustrated above, c_t and c_{t+1} then depend on the present value of family income. From the government's intertemporal budget constraint it follows, that the present value of tax changes is zero. Consequently, also the present value of family income remains constant and consumption is unaffected by fiscal policy. Bequests will therefore increase by the amount of the tax cut, as well as private saving, which equals bequests in the model at hand. The latter implies that national saving remains unchanged. This result is known as 'Ricardian Neutrality' and was first shown by Barro [15] to hold for altruistic agents with finite lives. With the same line of argument a pay-as-you-go Social Security system will have no real effects. Any public transfer from young to old agents will be offset by private transfers in the opposite direction.

It should be emphasized again that, even under the altruism hypothesis, Ricardian Neutrality only holds, if bequests are operative.[2]

A final implication of altruism refers to the timing of intergenerational transfers. Since individuals in the economy at hand only live for one period, this issue is actually beyond the model's scope. Nevertheless, it shall be briefly presented for reasons of completeness. Without capital market imperfections children are indifferent to the timing of intergenerational transfers. All that matters to them is the present value of received transfers. This changes, however, when young individuals face binding liquidity constraints. In this case the utility of a Dollar received is highest in the period where constraints bind. If the child's utility enters the parent's utility function, the latter will take this into account. Stated differently, a parent will transfer resources, when they are needed most. From this reasoning it follows that if intergenerational transfers are motivated by altruism and if, in addition, offspring face binding liquidity constraints during some years of their life, the bulk of transfers should occur *inter vivos*. There is another argument, why altruistic parents should prefer transfers *inter vivos* to bequests. Altruistic parents seek to maximize family resources. Since gifts are, in general, taxed at a lower rate than bequests, they better suit this aim (cf. [20]).

So far the exposition has exclusively focused on operational bequests. Of course, non of the above implications holds, when the non-negativity constraint is binding. When is this likely to happen? The smaller the degree of parent's altruism and the higher children's resources relative to parental resources, the higher the probability, that parents wish negative bequests. Due to Equation (2.3) this results in zero bequests. This suggests that parents, who themselves received a large bequest, will leave something to their children. On the other hand one would suppose few bequests in the lower tail of the wealth distribution, as children, owing to productivity growth, are in general better off than their parents (cf. [21]).

In the remainder of this section, two objections to the altruism hypothesis will be outlined. For one thing, some authors claim that children might act as free-riders in view of their parents' altruism. In particular, they assume that children do not take their parents' transfer as given, but realize, that the transfer depends inversely on their own effort (cf. [22], [23], [24], chapter 3). This phenomenon, known as 'Samaritan's Dilemma', leads to a sub-optimal effort on the part of the children and might induce parents to behave in a way not consistent with altruism as defined above.

For another thing, Bernheim and Bagwell [25] have demonstrated, that altruism leads to implausible results, if one takes into account that distinct family lines are linked through marriage of their adult children. In this case altruism not only implies neutrality with respect to redistribution *across* generations but also *within* generations. To see this imagine a couple, that receives transfers from both the husband's and the wife's parents. The par-

[2] For a comprehensive survey on Ricardian Neutrality see [19].

ents are only altruistic towards their own child. However, because the married couple pools their resources, the transfers of the two parents become interdependent. It can be shown, that if the government redistributes an amount T from the husband's parents to the wife's parents, the former will reduce and the latter will increase their transfer by exactly T, leaving children's as well as their own consumption unaffected. This reasoning, though, abstracts from non-negativity constraints. Furthermore, Laitner [26] has demonstrated that, when making allowances for assortative mating, the Bernheim-Bagwell neutrality ceases to hold. Thus, according to Laitner, highly stylized models with one parent and one child per family only serve to mimic more elaborate models with two parents, two children, and assortative mating.

2.2 Accidental Bequests

As was first shown by Yaari[27] and further explored by others (cf. [28], [29], [30], [31], [32], [33], [34]) intergenerational transfers need not be intentional. Thus, lifetime uncertainty in conjunction with imperfect annuity markets can result in so-called accidental bequests. To understand the forces at work, first consider a scenario with lifetime uncertainty when annuity market imperfections are absent. An individual has a maximum life expectancy of two periods, the first of which he survives with certainty and the second with probability $0 < \pi < 1$. His utility function reads

$$u_t = u(c_t) + \pi u(c_{t+1}) \; , \tag{2.7}$$

with $u(.)$ being concave and monotonous and c_t and c_{t+1} denoting first and second period consumption, respectively. This is a common formulation in the uncertain lifetime literature. It states that preferences are independent over time and that utility is the expectation of the utility from consumption. Further note, that the individual has no concern for his offspring.

In the first period of life the agent earns a wage w_t, a part of which is consumed and the remainder saved for possible second period consumption. In principle, the agent has two possibilities of transferring resources into the second period of life: bonds and annuities. While a bond can be resold upon bearing interest, the purchaser of an annuity acquires the entitlement to a pension, which expires with the holder's death. For reasons that become obvious in due course it is assumed that the agent buys solely annuities. The present analysis is restricted to actuarially fair annuities. As this implies that the issuing company makes no profit, the entire revenue of period t plus accrued interest is distributed to its surviving clients in period $t{+}1$. Accordingly, for any dollar invested in annuities, a surviving agent receives $(1{+}r)/\pi$ dollars in the subsequent period. Let q depict the quantity of purchased annuities. The agent then maximizes (2.7) subject to the following budget constraints:

$$c_t = w_t - q \tag{2.8}$$

$$c_{t+1} = \frac{(1+r)}{\pi} q \,. \tag{2.9}$$

The resulting Euler equation reads $(1+r)u'(c_{t+1}) = u'(c_t)$. If for the present the interest rate is set to zero, it follows from the concavity of $u(.)$, that $c_t = c_{t+1} = w/(1+\pi)$. Obviously, in a model with lifetime uncertainty and annuities agents consume more than in a certainty life-cycle model, which corresponds to $\pi = 1$. This hinges on the fact, that annuities bear a higher gross return than bonds, namely $(1+r)/\pi$ as opposed to $(1+r)$.

To sum up, agents can make provisions for old age by means of bonds or annuities. Annuities will pay them more during lifetime, since agents relinquish any claim upon their death. Bonds, on the other hand, are less profitable while still alive, but can be left to potential heirs. Since, in the present model, agents do not derive utility from leaving bequests they will exclusively purchase annuities, as was suggested above. Consequently, in the presence of perfect annuity markets one would never observe accidental bequests.

While well-developed annuity markets exist, few people make use of them. Hubbard and Judd[32], for example, cite evidence, that only about 1 percent of U.S. households surveyed in 1962 held annuities, with holdings of less than 0.1 percent of household net worth for those who did. According to Friedman and Warshawsky [35] the Retirement History Survey indicates that as few as 2 percent of U.S. elderly own individual annuities of any sort. In addition, they mention the example of a large insurer, that is especially active in the field of annuities. While the company sold an average of 18.1 *billion* of life insurances each year during 1980 – 1983, the sales of annuities in the same period averaged only 18.5 *million*. One obvious explanation for the disinterest in annuities certainly is concern for ones children. People might derive utility from leaving bequests, which they weigh against the higher returns from annuities. Nevertheless, this factor seems to account only partially for the missing annuities demand. Besides, economists have identified imperfections on annuity and insurance markets as likely causes (cf. [35]). In particular, adverse selection seems to drive the return from annuities below that of bonds. Thus, Friedman and Warshawsky proof that annuity purchasers exhibit greater life expectancy than the general population. Since companies *ex ante* have few information with respect to individual mortality risks, they have to demand a uniform price which makes annuities unattractive for the majority of people. People may also want to hold liquid assets to provide for the risk of severe and costly illnesses in old age. While bonds are liquid, annuities are not. Note however, that this argument requires imperfect markets for health insurance (cf. [36], chapter 6).

If annuities are less profitable than bonds, even elderly who are not altruistic towards their children – or just childless – will invest in bonds. Let this investment be denoted s. An agent then maximizes (2.7) subject to

$$c_t = w_t - s \tag{2.10}$$
$$c_{t+1} = (1+r)s \ .^3 \tag{2.11}$$

For illustrative purpose once more assume that $r = 0$, the Euler equation can then be stated as

$$\pi = \frac{u'(c_t)}{u'(c_{t+1})} \ . \tag{2.12}$$

Let us first consider the two polar cases $\pi = 1$ and $\pi = 0$. If the agent lives for two periods with certainty, he will consume half of his life-cycle income in each period. If, on the other hand, he is certain that life will end after period t, all resources will be consumed in the first period. In both cases the agent leaves no bequests to his successors. However, if one allows for lifetime uncertainty the agent will make provisions for second period consumption, which accrue to his children as a bequest, in case he actually dies.

Now have a look at the implications of accidental bequests. Due to the income effect, they are positively correlated with testator's life-cycle income. They exhibit a unitary earnings elasticity, if testator's preferences are homothetic. They are, per definition, independent of children's income or wealth, and they depend positively on the survival probability, as was shown above. In short:

$$\frac{\partial b}{\partial w_t} > 0 \quad , \quad \eta_{b,w_t} = 1 \quad , \quad \frac{\partial b}{\partial w_{t+1}} = 0 \quad , \quad \frac{\partial b}{\partial \pi} > 0 \ . \tag{2.13}$$

Also note that, while altruistic transfers can take place both as bequests and *inter vivos*, unintended transfers only occur upon the donor's death.

Finally, consider the impact of Social Security on accidental bequests. Both fully funded and pay-as-you-go Social Security programs smooth the profile of after-tax-income. This depresses private saving and, as a consequence, accidental bequests (cf. [30]). For a detailed treatment, please refer to Appendix A.2.

2.3 Transfers as Exchange

Not surprisingly, economists believe that a great deal of intergenerational transfers are payments in exchange for services provided by the extended

[3] Usually the problem of optimal consumption over time requires an additional constraint $s \geq 0$, if lifetime is uncertain (cf. [27]). The intuition is, that no one would give credit to someone, who is likely to die next period. In the present example, however, the agent does not wish to borrow, since he has earnings only in the first period of life. Consequently, the constraint can be safely ignored.

family. There is an abundance of models, which have in common that the family can provide services which the market can not supply at all or, at least, only at a much higher cost (cf. [37], [38], [39], [40], [41], [42], [43], [44], [45], [46], [47], chapter 3). The models differ in the kind of services (attention, insurance, loans), the timing of transfers (*inter vivos, post mortem*), and the enforcement mechanism of the implicit contracts (altruism, strategic interaction). Unfortunately, the implications of bequests-as-exchange are as numerous as the models. In order to contrast exchange with the other motives of intergenerational transfers, we will therefore restrict our attention to the basic and relatively general model of Cox [41]. While the model incorporates both altruism and exchange, with the latter only becoming effective when altruistic transfers cease being operational, we highlight the exchange motive by entirely abstracting from altruism.

Imagine a parent, that derives utility from consumption c_t and a service provided by his child, say attention a. As usual the utility function $u_t(c_t, a)$ is assumed to be concave and monotonous. Furthermore, the parent is endowed with a fixed income, which is split between own consumption and a transfer to his child: $w_t = c_t + b$. For the child, providing attention is costly in terms of forgone time and income. Accordingly, if a denotes the fraction of child's time spent with his parent, the child's budget constraint can be stated as $c_{t+1} = (1-a)\, w_{t+1} + b$. His utility function simply reads $u_{t+1}(c_{t+1})$. Note, that, although the present model is not intertemporal in nature, we maintain the indices t and $t+1$ for reasons of comparability. In the present context they should consequently be interpreted as generation rather than time indices. The components can now be arranged to yield the parent's maximization problem:

$$\max_{c_t, a}\; u_t(c_t, a)$$

$$\text{s.t.} \quad c_t = w_t - b \tag{2.14}$$

$$u_{t+1}((1-a)w_{t+1} + b) \geq u_{t+1}(w_{t+1}) \tag{2.15}$$

$$0 \leq a \leq 1\,,^{4} \tag{2.16}$$

with constraint (2.16) assumed to be non-binding. Constraint (2.15) states that the child must be at least as well off in exchange as in being independent. If one assumes, following Cox, that the parent reaps off all gains from the exchange, constraint (2.15) holds with equality.[5]

[4] In modeling the child's cost of providing attention in terms of time, we use a variant of the Cox model, put forth by Davies [18]. Instead, Cox models the cost by including attention in the child's utility function, with $\partial u_{t+1}/\partial a < 0$. While the Cox approach is more general, the implications are not altered by using the analytically more convenient procedure of Davies.

[5] As Cox remarks, the exchange may just as well be formulated in a Nash-bargaining framework. While letting the child participate in the gains from trade, this approach would, in essence, produce the same results.

Obviously, the intergenerational transfer compensates the child for spending time with his parent. In particular, one can perceive the child as supplying a service with a specific price. The supply price for a unit of attention in terms of transfers can be derived by totally differentiating Equation (2.15): $db/da = w_{t+1}$. Consequently, parental transfers equal child's forgone earnings:

$$b = w_{t+1} a \ . \tag{2.17}$$

If this relationship is substituted into Equation (2.14), Equation (2.15) becomes abundant and the parent's maximization problem boils down to

$$\max_{c_t, a} \; u_t(c_t, a)$$

$$\text{s.t.} \quad c_t + w_{t+1} a = w_t \tag{2.18}$$

$$0 \le a \le 1 \quad . \tag{2.19}$$

One is now in a position to derive the main implications of exchange motivated transfers. Important in itself, but also central for the following conclusions is the positive relation of transfers and filial attention proclaimed by Equation (2.17). Owing to the income effect, the demand for attention a increases with parental life-cycle resources w_t. In view of Equation (2.17) and in correspondence with the previous models, intergenerational transfers therefore depend positively on donor's resources, $\partial b/\partial w_t > 0$. If, in addition, homothetic preferences are assumed, the demand for services is proportional to donor's income, which, according to Equation (2.17), translates into a unitary earnings elasticity of transfers: $\eta_{b,w_t} = 1$.

How do offspring's resources affect the magnitude of intergenerational transfers? First, notice that an increase in w_{t+1} depresses the demand for services a, since income and substitution effect work into the same direction. Hence, without any additional assumptions the effect on b is ambiguous. However, as stated earlier, models of transfers-as-exchange are primarily concerned with services, for which close market substitutes do not exist. In view of this argument, one would therefore expect a highly inelastic demand for services and, contrary to the previous models, $\partial b/\partial w_{t+1} > 0$.

As to the timing of intergenerational transfers, the present model does not allow for powerful conclusions. If at all, one would, in analogy to common consumer purchases, expect immediate payment for services, that is *inter vivos* transfers. This changes, when strategic interaction between parents and offspring is taken into account, as done by Bernheim et al. [39]. While their model is in large parts identical with the Cox model, they try to explain the occurrence of bequests by explicitly modeling the bargaining process. In addition, they clarify why parents might appropriate all gains from the bargain.

Given that parents have more than one credible beneficiary, they can commit themselves to a bequest division rule. This rule states, that the bequest is shared equally, if all heirs provide the attention requested. However, any heir that defects from his obligation is disinherited. Thus, parents can play their children off against each other and, in this way, appropriate the whole surplus. Above all, this reasoning explains, why parents prefer bequests to transfers *inter vivos*. By transferring resources during lifetime they would gradually dissipate their bargaining power and consequently give up part of the surplus.[6]

2.4 Transfers for Joy-of-Giving

Although not as vigorous as the previous models in explaining intergenerational transfers, a fourth model, known as 'joy-of-giving', deserves consideration. In this model the transfer enters the donor's utility function as an argument and thus becomes an end in itself:

$$\max_{c_t, b} \; u_t(c_t, b)$$
$$\text{s.t.} \quad c_t + b = w_t \; . \tag{2.20}$$

As this formulation amounts to the tautology, that people make intergenerational transfers, because they appreciate intergenerational transfers, it does not produce many testable implications. The model does not allow any predictions about, for example, the division of bequests, the timing of transfers, or the degree of intergenerational mobility. All we can say is that, due to the income effect, transfers increase with donor's resources, $\partial b/\partial w_t > 0$, that income elasticity equals unity, given homothetic preferences, $\eta_{b,w_t} = 1$, and that transfers are independent from beneficiary's endowment, $\partial b/\partial w_{t+1} = 0$.

In spite of its lacking empirical relevance, the joy-of-giving motive has attracted much attention (e.g. [48], [49], [50], [51], [52], [53], [33]). This owes to the fact that the joy-of-giving motive can mimic the altruism motive in a number of problems related to intergenerational transfers. It should be stressed that this resemblance does not hold in any case. Thus, it was shown that altruistic transfers are inversely related to beneficiaries' endowments, while the latter have no effect whatsoever on transfers motivated by joy-of-giving. For the same reason Ricardian Neutrality prevails in the context of pure altruism, but not under joy-of-giving. Nevertheless, there are a number of theoretical and empirical problems for which the choice of bequest motive is not critical. For example, as will become clear in Section 4.3, the impact of a drop in fertility on intergenerational transfers is the same, whether transfers are motivated by altruism or joy-of-giving. The two transfer motives are

[6] For a critical evaluation of the Bernheim et al. model, cf. [18].

also qualitatively equivalent with respect to inheritance taxation (cf. [54]). Abel and Warshawsky [55] have demonstrated, that with correct parameter specifications even the quantitative implications coincide. According to the same authors, the joy-of-giving motive can be interpreted as a reduced form representation of altruistic preferences. For applied economists it is therefore tempting to use the easily tractable joy-of-giving formulation instead of the relatively sophisticated Barro/Becker model.

In that joy-of-giving is merely a generic motive for intergenerational transfers, we will not discuss its empirical validity. We will, however, make use of this model in subsequent sections, whenever convenient and reasonable.

2.5 Empirical Evidence

This section reviews what empirical work, so far, has brought to light about the motives of intergenerational transfers. In general, four strands of research can be distinguished. A first approach tries to identify transfer motives by exploring the income-transfer relationship. As has been shown in the previous sections, the three major transfer motives generate distinct predictions about the impact of recipient's income on the amount of transferred resources. Thus, transfers are inversely, positively or not at all affected by recipient's resources depending on whether they are induced by altruism, exchange or imperfect annuity markets, respectively. In addition, one can discriminate between altruistic and non-altruistic transfers by inspecting the elasticity of transfers with respect to donor's income, since only altruism generates an elasticity greater unity.

A second strand of literature assesses the importance of accidental versus intended transfers by inspecting the timing of intergenerational transfers. Some authors take an agnostic view as to whether posthumous transfers are intentional or not, but identify the volume of transfers *inter vivos* as a lower-bound estimate for the magnitude of intentional transfers. However, recall from the previous sections, that apart from strategic behavior of the Bernheim et al. type [39], there is no reason to expect intentional transfers to occur upon the donors death. Depending on how convincing one finds the arguments for strategic behavior, one can even claim, that transfers among living are the only intentional transfers. Some authors therefore infer the importance of intended versus unintended transfers by comparing the relative magnitude of transfers *inter vivos* and bequests.

Data on intergenerational transfers are scarce. For this reason a third set of papers seeks to discriminate between transfer motives by observing saving patterns over the life-cycle. To see the link between saving and bequests, note that resources earmarked for bequests are not consumed and consequently saved. Finally, economists have tried to provide evidence for the exchange model of transfers by exploring the positive relationship between services and transfers set out by Equation (2.17). Empirical studies, related to the four procedures, will be presented in turn.

Income-transfer relationship

Adams [56] estimates the elasticity of bequests with respect to testator's income using data collected by Sussman et al. [57]. As will be explained in due course, these data seem to be of poor quality. Furthermore, they do not contain direct information on testator's income compelling Adams to use a proxy for this variable. The evidence provided by Adams is mixed. While one estimation, based on cross-sectional data, yields an elasticity greater unity, a time series regression produces a value smaller unity. Menchik and David [58] match Wisconsin income tax and probate record data of about 1400 individuals and in this manner obtain direct information on donor's income. Regressing the sum of bequests and transfers *inter vivos* (discounted forward to time of death) on donor's life-cycle resources, the authors find an elasticity smaller unity for parents with wealth below the 80th percentile and greater unity for the top 20 percent. Hence, according to this study altruism only seems to be operational among the very rich.

Investigating the impact of recipient's income on transfers *inter vivos* Cox [41] finds a positive correlation, which is inconsistent with altruism. Besides he observes, that received transfers decrease with a household's number of children. Since children induce additional needs, this evidence as well contradicts the altruism hypothesis. At the same time it lends support to the exchange motive, given that raising children is time-consuming and most likely reduces services supplied to other family units. In another study Cox and Rank [59] try to cure a major shortcoming of the previous article, namely its reliance on a crude proxy for donor's income. Note, that, if not controlled for donor's income, a correlation of donor's and recipient's income due to genetic or cultural factors, might generate a positive relation between transfers and recipient's income regardless of the underlying motive. For this reason it is crucial to control for donor's income on the basis of exact data. However, also with direct data on donor's income the findings of the previous study are confirmed.

Altruism as a motive not only implies, that parents smooth consumption intergenerationally but also among their offspring. Given that income inequality among siblings is almost as pronounced as in the population as a whole (cf. [60]), altruism would therefore induce unequal division of bequests. This line of reasoning is exploited by Menchik [61], who inspects a highly stratified sample of 1050 probate records including net estates of $ 40,000 or more (in dollars of the day). It is important to note, that the tax law of the State Connecticut, from which the sample was drawn, does not set any incentives for equal estate division as do most other death tax laws. Specifically, the tax base is the bequest as a whole and not the inheritance received by each heir, so that the tax burden is independent of the estate division, even when the tax rate is progressive. Menchik finds approximate equality in estate division for 70 percent of two-children families, an evidence, that is at odds with the altruism hypothesis.

These findings are challenged by Tomes [62, ?] on the basis of the Sussman et al. [57] data. According to his observation only 21 percent of the overall sample reveal exactly equal division and 44 percent of two-children families reveal approximately equal division. Moreover, inheritances are compensatory since poor children get more. However note, that Tomes relies on proxies for heirs' lifetime earnings. In addition, Menchik [64] has convincingly proved that the Sussman data can not be trusted. Since estates are, by order of law, always divided equally, when an explicit will is missing, the share of cases with equal division must at least equal the proportion of intestate cases in the overall sample. The latter, however, amounts to 31 percent which is far ahead of the 21 percent reported by Tomes.[7] Menchik further draws a random sample of probate records in the same place and over the same period as the Sussman sample and finds an incidence of approximately equal division amounting to 88 percent.

Equal division is also confirmed by Wilhelm [65] employing high quality data on bequests, *inter vivos* transfers within the three years prior to death, and incomes of both heirs and testators. In particular, he reports approximately equal division in 77 percent of all cases and only a weak inverse relation between heirs' income and transfers in the cases of unequal division. Wilhelm additionally tests altruism with respect to *inter*generational distribution by regressing transfers on the average earnings of siblings. In this case the negative relation implied by altruism is rejected as well.

With respect to transfers *inter vivos* McGarry and Schoeni [66] reject equal division. Their data set is the Health and Retirement Survey, which begun in 1992 and samples individuals born from 1931 through 1941. In particular, the authors find that only 30 percent of those siblings receiving transfers, receive identical amounts. Moreover, worse-off children are more likely to receive a transfer and, in general, receive higher amounts. McGarry [67] as well as Dunn and Phillips [68] by separately inspecting bequests and transfers *inter vivos* provide evidence, that the underlying motives differ. While, in correspondence with earlier research, equal division of estates is the rule, transfers *inter vivos* seem to be compensatory in that less well-off children receive more. Thus, bequests behavior is inconsistent with both altruistic and exchange motives, whereas transfers prior to death seem to be governed by altruism.

Two papers by Altonji et al. [69, 70] have a predominantly macroeconomic focus in that they challenge the validity of Ricardian Neutrality implied by operational altruism. Both papers employ data from the Panel Study of In-

[7] Admittedly, Tomes uses a subsample, whose intestacy rate could deviate from the overall sample. Still, the difference is very large and points towards inconsistencies in the data.

come Dynamics (PSID) which allow the authors to link different households belonging to the same extended family. The first paper regresses household food consumption on both household and family resources. Given the prediction of the standard altruism model that within the extended family the distribution of consumption is independent of the distribution of resources, the coefficient of household resources should be zero when controlling for combined resources. This hypothesis is clearly rejected by the data. In their second paper Altonji et al. test the implication that a government redistribution between two households belonging to the same extended family should be offset one by one through private intergenerational transfers. While, according to the PSID data, transfer behavior is consistent with altruism in that the transferred amount is positively related to parents' resources and inversely related to children's resources, the sum of the partial derivatives falls short of one and, thus, contradicts Ricardian Neutrality.

Timing of intergenerational transfers

Horsman [71] estimates the annual flow of transfers *inter vivos* and bequests for Great Britain in the late 1960ies. According to his calculations gifts among living account for 17 percent of all intergenerational transfers. Since Horsman uses gift tax and estate tax data sources, his calculations should, however, be considered a lower bound estimate. In contrast, the weights for gifts versus bequests are almost the opposite in an investigation conducted by Cox and Raines [72]. Their data stem from the Household Survey of the President's Commission on Pension Policy, which is a representative cross-section sample of the U.S. population covering the first 8 month of 1979. It is worth noting that, besides cash transfers, respondents are asked to declare the monetary equivalent of specific in-kind transfers, for example transferred durables. On the other hand, many implicit transfers which take place in shared living arrangements are not reported. Strikingly, the authors find that inheritances amount to only 25 percent of overall transfers, the remainder being transfers *inter vivos*.

Hurd and Mundaca [73] assess the relative importance of bequests versus gifts on the basis of the 1964 Survey on the Economic Behavior of the Affluent. Admittedly, the survey comprises 957 high-income households and only 94 low-income households, but sampling weights allow to calculate population averages. In particular, respondents are asked which fraction of their assets is due to gifts and bequests, respectively. Since the question is ambiguous in that it remains unclear, whether interest gained on gifts or bequests should be included, the authors present two estimates. With accrued interest included inheritances account for 20 percent and gifts for 8 percent of 1964 private wealth. Without accrued interest, the figures reduce to 11 and 4 percent, respectively. The estimates should, however, be regarded with caution. For one thing, the survey does not include specific questions on in-kind transfers.

For another thing, the survey does not provide exact figures but only ranges of figures and, partly, even open-ended intervals.

Gale and Scholz [2] seek to determine the significance of intentional transfers with the help of the Survey of Consumer Finances, including more than 3000 households. In 1986 the household head was asked, if she or he had received or made a transfer of $ 3000 or more in the previous 3 years and, if so, what the exact amount was. Thus, in the period in question transfers *inter vivos* accounted for 31 percent, college payments for 17 percent, and bequests for 52 percent of overall transfer flows. Note, that although college payments occur among living, they are reported separately as some authors do not consider them transfers (e.g. Modigliani [74, 75]). The authors stress, that the share of 31 percent, respective 48 percent, if college expenses are included, is most likely a lower bound estimate of intentional transfers. This is attributable to the fact, that transfers below $ 3000 are not reported, concrete questions for in-kind transfers are absent, and some bequests might be intentional as well.

Poterba [76], on the basis of the same data source, assesses the potential for tax avoidance through *inter vivos* transfers. He calculates that by transferring resources prior to death 1/4 of taxable assets could be exempted from estate tax. If potential tax payers made full use of this opportunity, the annual transfer flow *inter vivos* would equal $ 443 billion. In sharp contrast to these figures stand the actual flows, which according to the Survey of Consumer Finances average only $ 32.7 billion in the period 1993–1995. These findings contradict the standard altruism model, which predicts, that parents maximize family resources. Instead, they point to strategic behavior or imperfect annuity markets as a likely driving force for intergenerational transfers.

To sum up this paragraph, evidence on the importance of intentional versus unintended transfers is mixed, even if the order of magnitude is rather 50 than 20 percent for the share of intended transfers. In any case the scale of intended transfers is such, that the standard life-cycle model without a transfer motive seems a poor description of reality.

Observation of saving patterns

A vast quantity of papers inspect saving patterns to test the standard life-cycle model of Modigliani and Brumberg [77] against a life-cycle model augmented by bequests.[8] Many of these papers ascertain that the elderly refrain from dissaving and, in this way, confirm the mayor significance of bequests. However, few have the power to discriminate between accidental and planned bequests, not to mention altruistic and exchange-motivated bequests. The papers relevant to this question are briefly reviewed.

Hurd [53] draws from the Longitudinal Retirement History Survey (LRHS), which comprises 11,000 respondents, born between 1906 and 1911 and inter-

[8] Cf., for example, [78], [79], [80], [81], [82].

viewed every two years from 1969 through 1979. By using longitudinal data, the author precludes the possibility that wealth profiles increase with age only because life-expectancy is positively correlated with wealth. Indeed, he observes dissaving for the elderly, in contrast to various cross-section studies. Next, Hurd designs a test for intentional versus accidental bequests. In doing so, he exploits a relationship, already set out in the previous sections. While accidental bequests are independent of children's characteristics, or even of children's existence, planned bequests are not.[9] Consequently, if transfers were planned, agents with living children should behave differently from childless individuals. In particular, the rate of wealth decumulation in old age should be smaller for parents with children. This is not supported by the data. On the contrary, parents with children appear to decumulate faster. If anything, this seems to be evidence in favor of precautionary saving, since agents with children can rely on filial support in case of uninsurable hardship. Hurd therefore concludes that the majority of bequests are accidental.

Bernheim [83] seeks to establish the existence of intentional bequests, be they motivated by altruism or exchange, by showing that the typical retired household refrains from fully annuitizing its resources. Using the 1975 wave of the LRHS, the author demonstrates that an increase in government provided annuities induces households, first, to reduce their demand for private annuities and, subsequently, to sell private annuities by purchasing term life insurances.[10] As emphasized by the author, the inverse relation between private and public annuities indicates, that the elderly want to hold wealth in liquid form, but does not necessarily confirm the prevalence of intentional bequests. Recall from Section 2.2 that instead of planning for bequests the motive could as well be provision for uninsurable old-age risks. In contrast, the positive relationship between life insurance holdings and public pension benefits unambiguously hints at a bequest motive. Were households concerned about the risk of severe illnesses, they would purchase medical or disability insurance rather than life insurance. At least the term component of life insurance provides no means in case of an emergency. Just as little would

[9] In Sections 2.1 through 2.3 this was demonstrated with respect to children's earnings. Thus, $\partial b/\partial w_{t+1} = 0$ in the case of accidental bequests but $\partial b/\partial w_{t+1} \neq 0$ for altruistic or exchange motivated bequests.

[10] As shown by Yaari [27], the purchase of a term life insurance in the amount of x dollars is equivalent to the sale of x dollars worth of annuities and the simultaneous purchase of x dollars worth of bonds. The sale of an annuity works in the following way. The seller is provided with money on which he pays interest during his lifetime, while he or, strictly speaking, his offspring are held free of any obligation upon his death. In that the seller of an annuity never pays back any principal, the interest on annuities must exceed the interest on bonds. The seller of the annuity can now use the received amount to purchase bonds, which after his death go to his offspring. The difference in interest between what he has to pay on the annuity and what he receives on the bonds, can be considered the insurance premium. The bonds inherited by the offspring correspond to the life insurance's amount of cover.

households invest in life insurance, were they primarily concerned about favorable interest rates. Owing to the insurance premium, life insurances, in general, pay much lower interest than bonds. Consequently, the only conceivable reason for the portfolio shift towards life insurance seems to be concern for ones offspring.

Ando et al. [84] have written a paper in the spirit of Hurd [53], using the 1989 Bank of Italy Survey of Household Income and Wealth. After correction for cross-section bias the authors find, that households with children decumulate wealth at a faster rate than childless households and, thus, confirm the results of the earlier study. However, they correctly claim that a test like the one designed by Hurd has little discriminatory power with respect to the bequest motive. Particularly, if parents anticipate bequests in the form of *inter vivos* transfers, the faster decumulation of parents with independent children could even be interpreted as evidence *in favor* of intentional transfers. In fact, the authors present evidence that these *inter vivos* transfers occur. Specifically, they show that the decumulation of wealth is greater than dissaving, defined as consumption minus income, suggests, which can only be explained in the light of transfers *inter vivos*. The authors then propose to look at the pattern of wealth accumulation and decumulation at an earlier stage of the life-cycle. If bequests or, generally speaking, transfers are intentional, working parents with dependent children should, other things being equal, accumulate at a faster rate than households without children. This, indeed, is suggested by the data. At last, the authors compare the life insurance holdings of households with independent children to those without. The holdings of the former significantly exceed the holdings of the latter, which can be interpreted as further evidence for intentional intergenerational transfers.

Hurd's [53] method is also taken up in a recent paper by Jürges [85] on saving patterns in Germany. Using the 1988 cross-section of the Socio-Economic Panel, he estimates age-wealth profiles, separately, for households with and without a bequest motive. Instead of relying on living children as indicator of a bequest motive, however, the author can exploit direct questions on saving motives, with 'saving for bequests' among possible answers. In fact, it is shown that living children are a rather crude proxy for a bequest motive. While 30 percent of childless households report a bequest motive, 40 percent of household with living children have no such motive. Using various wealth measures and econometric specifications, the author finds that households with a declared bequest motive are wealthier over the entire life-cycle and dissave significantly less after retirement – both evidence in favor of intentional bequests.

Laitner and Juster [86], finally, review a 1988 Survey of 1000 TIAA-CREF annuitants. Their findings seem to confirm the occurrence of intentional transfers, but provide only limited support for altruism. The survey contains detailed questions on respondents' 1988 net wealth (including pension equity), lifetime earnings history and their choice with respect to the annuity payment option. Furthermore, respondents are asked, how well-off they think their children will be relative to themselves and if they consider leaving a bequest as important. Among families with children 73 percent choose annuities with so-called "guarantees", meaning that the benefit payment is guaranteed for say 20 years, even if the original annuitant dies in the meantime. Since, guarantees are not free of charge, they constitute an intentional transfer. About half the sample view leaving a bequest as important, with net worth significantly in excess of those, who do not value bequests. Moreover, within this subgroup wealth holdings are inversely related to the assessment of children's well-being, which seems to hint at altruism as a motive. On the other hand, looking at the sample as a whole, there is no significant relation between parent's conjecture of children's relative well-being and their valuation of leaving a bequest, as would be predicted by the standard altruism model. The evidence with respect to altruism is therefore at best mixed.

The relation between transfers and services

Some authors have tried to confirm or reject the exchange model of bequests by observing the relationship between filial services and intergenerational transfers as predicted by Equation (2.17). More precisely, the literature generally resorts to a weaker condition, namely a positive relation between services and bequests, since the proportionality is a mere consequence of expressing the child's cost in terms of forgone time.

In his previously mentioned article, Tomes [62] regresses received inheritance on various explanatory variables, among them the frequency of contact between recipient and decedent. The latter variable enters with a significant negative coefficient in the inheritance equation and, ergo, provides evidence against the exchange model. In addition, Tomes finds support for the altruism model by identifying an inverse relationship between recipient's income and the amount inherited. Recall, however, that the author's research draws from the Sussman data, whose deficiencies were outlined above [cf. page 17].

In contrast to Tomes, Bernheim et al. [39] find strong empirical support for their model of strategic exchange, employing data from the Longitudinal Retirement History Survey (LRHS). For multiple child families the authors establish a significant positive relationship between parents' bequeathable wealth and the intensity of contact between parents and children, measured by the number of telephone calls and visits. In the case of single child families, however, the number of contacts enter negatively into the regression equation. These diverging outcomes can only be reconciled with a bequest model of *strategic* exchange. Thus, the Bernheim et al. model predicts, that parents can influence potential beneficiaries' behavior only if there are at least two credible heirs.

We conclude this section by stating that empirical evidence with regard to transfer motives is in large parts inconsistent. If anything, empirical research has established the relative importance of transfers *inter vivos* and confirmed equal division of bequests as a rule. Recall, however, that the latter is neither consistent with altruism and exchange nor a necessary result of accidental bequests.

3. Empirical Facts About Transfers in Germany

As mentioned earlier, data on private intergenerational transfers are scarce – and they are especially scarce for Germany. Nevertheless, this section attempts to provide some empirical evidence on transfer behavior in Germany. Due to data deficiencies the evidence presented is far from being conclusive. In particular, small sample sizes or lack of important explanatory variables rule out econometric testing for alternative transfer motives. The procedure is therefore to produce stylized facts and see if they more or less conform to any of the transfer motives introduced above.

Our data sources are two micro data sets, the Income and Expenditure Survey 1993 (EVS) and the Socio-Economic-Panel (SOEP) (cf. [87] and [88]). The EVS is conducted every 5 years by the Federal Statistical Office and comprises about 40,000 households with more than 100,000 persons. It is a representative cross-section of German households with two exceptions: households with net monthly incomes above DM 35,000 as well as persons living in institutions are excluded. Apart from information on household characteristics such as family status, family size, age of household members etc., the EVS contains detailed data on income by source, wealth by asset category and expenditure by purchased commodity or other objective. Since all figures are carefully computed and reported by means of weekly diaries, at least the data on flows are very precise. Data on stocks are subject to the usual shortcomings. Thus, reported private wealth, when weighted and added up over households, only amounts to a fraction of the aggregate value estimated by the Bundesbank (cf. [89]).

The SOEP is conducted by the *Deutsches Institut für Wirtschaftsforschung* and was started in 1984. Each year about 6,000 households with approximately 12,000 persons are asked about particulars of their social and economic situation. Unfortunately, the SOEP exhibits a much smaller sample size than the EVS, especially when data on wealth and bequests are involved. For one thing only the cross-section of 1988 contained a comprehensive questionnaire on wealth and bequests, for another thing this supplemental questionnaire was not answered by all participants. This disadvantage, however, is made up for by a much broader spectrum of questions including, for example, number of independent children or motives for holding wealth. In addition, the questions on intergenerational transfers are more precise, specifying, for example, whether transfer are made to parents, children, or other relatives. In what follows the two data sets will be discussed in turn.

3.1 The Income and Expenditure Survey 1993

The EVS contains four questions with respect to private transfers. First, respondents are asked, whether they received regular transfers from other households. In case they did, they are requested to indicate the household member receiving the transfer as well as the amount. Second, households are asked to document the sum of all irregular transfers less DM 2,000 received from other households. Third, households are requested to report the amount of irregularly received transfers greater DM 2,000. Finally, households are to indicate the transfer amount given to other households. Apart from the first question, all questions refer to the household level, meaning that the person receiving or making a transfer in the responding household is not specified. Further note, that the questions only refer to cash transfers. In-kind services as well as shared living arrangements are not documented by the figures.

Unfortunately, the data do not allow for a discrimination between transfers across generations and transfers between households of the same generation. Especially, maintenance payments to former spouses and children are likely to account for a significant part of the reported transfers, but constitute no intergenerational transfers.[1] Admittedly, one could correct the sample for single parents and, in this manner, exclude recipients of maintenance. It is, however, impossible to identify and eliminate the payers of maintenance. In order to avoid any asymmetry between recipients and donors in the sample, we therefore refrained from excluding single parents. Despite of their shortcomings the above questions serve as a basis for our investigation, assuming that the lion's share of interhousehold transfers occur across generations. This conjecture is strengthened in the further course of our inquiry.

Table 3.1 gives a description of the sample, including absolute and relative number of cases as well as average transfer amounts. While the first two columns refer to the original sample, the last column as well as all following tables report cases employing case weights. Using the weights provided by the Census makes the sample a representative cross-section of the German population and, at the same time, produces the total number of German households (about 35.6 million). The sample comprises 40,230 households, of which 21 percent receive transfers and 38 percent make transfers to other households. However, in that some households are both recipients and donors, the percentage of net recipients and net donors reduces to 18 and 32 percent, respectively. The discrepancy between the number of recipients and donors

[1] Transfers to dependent children, although across generations, are usually not considered intergenerational transfers.

Table 3.1. Households Giving and Receiving Private Transfers, EVS

	Absolute Number	Relative Number Percent (N=40230)	Average Amount[a] DM (Participants)
Recipients	8331	20.7	7,028
Donors	15171	37.7	4,069
Being Recipient and Donor[b]	3146	7.8	–
Net Recipients	7300	18.1	7,116
Net Donors	13046	32.4	4,248

Source: German Income and Expenditure Survey 1993.

[a] The cases are weighted to produce a representative cross-section of the German population.
[b] For 10 households received and given amounts exactly balance. Consequently: $8331 + 15171 - 3146 - 10 = 7300 + 13046$.

is remarkable and seems to hint at underreporting on the part of the recipients. This conjecture is reinforced, when inspecting the divergence in reported transfer amounts. While donors appear to have documented every little transfer amount, recipients seem to remember only the large ones. In fact, it is a common phenomenon that people "admit more easily that they have given than that they have received" (cf. [90]). A glance at the following Table, however, reveals that there is no underreporting.

Table 3.2 reports the aggregate of specific transfers and the absolute number of involved households, where the sample is blown up to represent a cross section of the German population. Obviously, the aggregates of given and received transfers correspond, suggesting that underreporting is not an issue here. Instead, many donors encounter few recipients, this way producing large receipts relative to donations. Another conclusion can be drawn from the correspondence of reported transfer amounts. Although the EVS questionnaire remains unclear as to whether received transfers shall include inheritances, they were, most likely, left out. Since donor households, as a rule, only report transfers *inter vivos*, the same must hold for recipients. Otherwise the two aggregates would hardly match.

Let us next find out, which share of overall intergenerational transfers is intentional. According to Table 3.2 transfers *inter vivos* amounted to DM 53 billion in 1993. If we want to make sure that maintenance payments to former spouses and children are excluded, we should only take into account irregularly received transfers adding up to DM 26 billion. Let us consider this

Table 3.2. Absolute Transfer Amounts and Number of Households, EVS

Transfer Category	Transferred Amount Billions of DM	Number of Households Millions
Given Transfers	53.2	13.1
Received Transfers	53.0	7.5
Reg. Rec. Transfers	27.3	4.3
Irreg. Rec. Trans.	25.7	4.3
Irreg. Rec. Trans. < DM 2000	2.8	2.4
Irreg. Rec. Trans. ≥ DM 2000	22.9	2.4

Source: German Income and Expenditure Survey 1993.

amount of transfers *inter vivos* as a lower bound estimate for the volume of intentional transfers across generations. Next, the amount of aggregate bequests *per annum* has to be determined, in order to derive the volume of overall transfers across generations. As annual bequest, for reasons that are explicated on page 46, are not obtainable from official statistics, they have to be approximated. This is done by multiplying the 1993 age distribution of aggregate private net wealth with age-specific mortality rates and subsequently summing up over all ages.[2] We obtain bequests that add up to DM 183.1 billion (5.8% of GDP), which is in the same order of magnitude as an estimate by the German Bundesbank for 1999, ranging between DM 200 and 250 billion (cf. [91], page 35). Further taking into account annual transfers *inter vivos* of DM 53 billion yields overall intergenerational transfers of DM 236 billion in 1993 (7.5% of GDP). Intentional transfers, consequently, account for at least 10 percent of total intergenerational transfers in Germany. Compared to Cox and Raines [72] and Gale and Scholz [2], who find corresponding figures of 75 and 31 percent, respectively, this is a rather small proportion.[3] It is sufficient, however, to prove the existence of a transfer motive and, in this way, refute the standard life-cycle model without such a motive.

In order to demonstrate that the majority of transfers covered by the EVS are across generations, we next present an age-profile of recipients and donors. Table 3.3 reports the share of net recipients and donors within a specific age class as well as the average amount they receive or give, respectively. Obviously, the majority of transfers are directed from old to young generations. Thus, the probability of receiving a transfer is highest for the youngest cohorts and decreases with age until about 75. It then increases

[2] How we derive the distribution of private wealth according to age is detailed on page 91 in Section 4.4.2.

[3] Recall that, in contrast to our study, the figures reported by Cox and Raines also include in-kind transfers.

moderately for the very old. In contrast, the probability of making a gift almost monotonously increases with age. A similar pattern is apparent, when

Table 3.3. Age-Profile of Recipients and Donors, EVS

Age	Net Recipients		Net Donors	
	Proportion Percent	Average Amount DM	Proportion Percent	Average Amount DM
19–29	45.0	7,565	12.9	1,797
30–40	24.8	6,768	21.4	2,517
41–51	18.0	7,820	28.2	3,517
52–62	10.1	7,707	38.2	4,886
63–73	9.5	5,984	43.5	5,290
74–84	12.6	5,861	47.0	4,652
85+	16.1	4,975	38.5	5,510

Source: German Income and Expenditure Survey 1993.

looking at the transfer amounts. The receipts are highest when young, while the largest donations are made when old. We will therefore proceed on the presumption that the majority of transfers in consideration are intergenerational transfers.

The next table provides information about the composition of transfer receipts. In particular, it reports for selected groups of recipients the weight of regular versus irregular transfers. Given that maintenance payments are reported as regular transfers, this reveals, where we have to be especially prepared for spurious data. In principle, the weights can be calculated in two different ways. One can either sum up all regular (irregular) transfer amounts within a specific group and divide it by the total transfer amount of this group. Alternatively, one can calculate the quota separately for each group member and successively compute the mean. We follow the first approach, this way producing weighted averages. As indicated by the first row of Table 3.4, overall transfers are received regularly and irregularly, respectively, in almost equal shares. In the following rows, transfer recipients are grouped according to age and disposable income, where disposable income comprises labor and capital income, private and public pensions, other public transfers, less taxes and social insurance contributions. Obviously, age has a significant effect on whether transfers are received regularly or irregularly. While for the very young and very old regular transfers account for approximately 65 percent of received transfers, for the middle-aged the allocation is the other way round. With respect to the young the considerable share of regular transfers can be explained by maintenance payments as well as parents supporting

Table 3.4. The Weight of Regular versus Irregular Transfers, EVS

Selected Group	Share of Received Transfers that is			
	Regularly Received	Irregularly Received	Irreg. Rec. & < DM 2,000	Irreg. Rec. & ≥ DM 2,000
Overall Sample[a]	51.5	48.5	5.2	43.3
aged 20–30[b]	66.4	33.6	5.2	28.4
aged 31–41	48.3	51.7	5.8	45.9
aged 42–52	37.4	62.6	6.3	56.3
aged 53–63	35.5	64.5	5.3	59.2
aged 64–74	55.1	44.9	2.7	42.2
aged 75–85	67.4	32.6	2.5	30.1
Upper Decile[c]	17.9	82.1	5.7	76.4
2nd Decile	28.8	71.2	7.1	64.1
3rd Decile	31.9	68.1	6.6	61.5
4th Decile	48.1	51.9	6.3	45.6
5th Decile	49.6	50.4	5.9	44.5
6th Decile	59.5	40.5	4.5	36.0
7th Decile	63.9	36.1	4.7	31.4
8th Decile	69.9	30.1	4.9	25.2
9th Decile	76.3	23.7	3.9	19.8
Lowest Decile	81.0	19.0	2.9	16.1
Buy/Build House[d]	19.8	80.2	3.5	76.7

Source: German Income and Expenditure Survey 1993.

[a] Only households that received transfers are considered.
[b] Age of the household head.
[c] With respect to disposable income, comprising labor and capital income, private and public pensions, other public transfers, less taxes and social insurance contributions.
[d] Households that had expenditures for buying or building a house in 1993

their children's education. With regard to the old, the driving forces behind regular transfers are less clear. Supposedly, children support their elder parents, as their old age provision – maybe due to severe illnesses – turns out to be insufficient.

Also recipient's income appears to have an effect on the composition of transfers *inter vivos*. Among the affluent regular transfers constitute a mere 18 percent of overall received transfers. In contrast, for those at the lower tail of the income distribution 81 percent of their receipts occur regularly. Consequently, one has to be especially prepared for maintenance payments in the lower segment of the income distribution.

We finally inspect all households, that have reported expenditures for buying or building a house or apartment in 1993. Recall that, according to theory, liquidity constraints on the part of children would induce altruistic parents to make transfers *inter vivos*. In that the above expenditures are a natural indicator for potential liquidity constraints, a significant share of irregular transfers would be evidence in favor of this view. In fact, for the households under consideration 80 percent of all receipts constitute a one-off transfer, a fraction that is in great excess of the sample mean and hard to explain by age and income alone.

In what follows we regress net donors' and recipients' charactersitics on net given and received transfers, respectively. It goes without saying, that this approach, rather than producing any conclusive evidence, constitutes a mere data descriptive analysis of the correlates of intergenerational transfers. In particular, the present OLS regression is not suited for discriminating between transfer motives. Such a procedure would require a database which links donors and recipients of the same transfer, a feature the EVS unfortunately does not provide. In that it is impossible to control for important explanatory variables, the results should be interpreted with utmost caution. The coefficients are reported in Table 3.5. First note, that donor characteristics have a stronger impact on transfer amounts than recipient characteristics, as manifested by a larger number of significant coefficients. At first sight, this evidence seems to challenge the altruistic model, according to which donors take into account all of recipients' circumstances. However, it could as well be a mere statistical artefact, caused by the specific choice of explanatory variables. We further find that transfers increase with donor's economic status, which is in correspondence with all the transfer motives discussed in Section 2. Thus, wealth, capital income, and disposable income all have a highly significant positive effect on transfers given. The negative coefficient of earnings, also highly significant, is not at odds with these findings, but reflects the fact, that retirees make larger transfers (cf. Table 3.3). There are further correlates, which prove the positive relation between economic status and transfers given. For example, transfers by West Germans, who are in general better off, exceed those of East Germans by, on average, DM 620. For obvious reasons also transfer receipts deviate among the two regions, namely by DM 3,250. Moreover, gifts increase with a household's number of earners, although the coefficient is significant only at the 10 percent level. Finally, the receipt of social assistance has a significant negative effect on donations.

While there is no doubt about the positive correlation of donor's resources and transfers, the evidence on the effects of recipient's resources is at best mixed. On the one hand, recipient's wealth and capital income exhibit a highly significant positive coefficient. On the other hand, disposable income

Table 3.5. Correlates of Intergenerational Transfers, EVS

Variables	Estimated Coefficients (OLS)	
	Dependent Variable: Amount Given	Dependent Variable: Amount Received
Constant	501.87	1967.63
	(0.43)[a]	(1.61)
West-German Household	619.78	3249.22
	(2.04)	(6.17)
Number of Household Members	-951.17	578.97
	(-8.08)	(3.15)
Age Household Head	69.56	5.08
	(5.98)	(0.32)
Male Household Head	1004.21	-448.05
	(3.53)	(-0.98)
Married Household Head	-654.28	-348.57
	(-1.99)	(-0.60)
Number of Earners in Household	332.44	-130.47
	(1.65)	(-0.38)
Receiving Social Assistance	-1844.61	1364.12
	(-1.96)	(1.6)
Gross Household Earnings	-0.24×10^{-1}	-0.20×10^{-1}
	(-5.47)	(-1.92)
Household Capital Income	0.48×10^{-1}	0.99×10^{-1}
	(4.18)	(3.65)
Household Wealth	0.18×10^{-2}	0.76×10^{-2}
	(4.16)	(9.05)
Market Value Life Insurance	-0.44×10^{-2}	...
	(-2.40)	
Expenditures Phone/Mail	0.18	1.07
	(1.29)	(4.50)
Exp. for Buying/Building House/Apt.	...	0.62×10^{-1}
		(20.50)
Charitable Donations	-0.34×10^{-1}	...
	(-0.48)	
Received Real Estate as Inher./Gift	110.49	...
	(0.35)	
Disposable Household Income Pre-Transfer	0.65×10^{-1}	-0.31×10^{-1}
	(10.4)	(-2.25)
Household Head Completed No Education[b]	-571.83	-1518.29
	(-0.59)	(-0.80)
Household Head Completed *Hauptschule*	-557.01	-2276.23
	(-1.75)	(-3.79)
Household Head Completed *Realschule*	-656.31	-1028.92
	(-1.92)	(-1.73)
Household Head Completed *Gymnasium*	167.82	693.16
	(0.52)	(1.33)
R^2	0.08	0.11
F-statistic	56.72	50.67
Observations	12781	7102

Source: German Income and Expenditure Survey 1993.

[a] T-values are in parentheses.
[b] The types of schools are listed in ascending order of schooling years.

and earnings enter negatively, if only at a 5 and 10 percent significance level. Other regressors which serve as a proxy for economic status have no impact at all. Thus, it makes no significant difference, whether a household has a female household head, receives social assistance, or includes multiple earners.[4] Transfers *inter vivos* are just as little correlated with education. If at all, those with a high educational level give and receive more. However, most coefficients are not significant or only at the 10 percent level. With respect to age, we find that transfer amounts increase with donor's age, but are not correlated with recipient's age, this being more or less consistent with Table 3.3.

Next, notice that transfer amounts are inversely related to donor's life insurance holdings. Following Ando et al. [84] according to whom life insurance holdings are an indicator for intended bequests, this suggests a substitutive relation between bequests and transfers *inter vivos*. Provided that transfers are motivated by exchange or, more precisely, induced by the attention of children for their elder parents, one would expect a positive relation between transfer amounts and time spent on the phone. While, indeed, for recipients there exists such a correlation at the one percent significance level, it does not hold for donors. In order to find evidence in favor of altruistic parents easing their children's liquidity constraints, we inspect households, that reported expenditures for buying/building a house/apartment. Although these households are especially likely to face binding liquidity constraints, they only receive slightly higher transfers than households without such expenditures. We finally checked, whether households that make charitable donations or have inherited themselves are more likely to make large transfers. Both views are rejected by the data.

We now turn to the size distribution of transfers *inter vivos*. Separately for different transfer categories Table 3.6 reports the share of overall transferred German marks, given or received by households in the 99th, 95th, 90th, and so on percentile, in terms of size of the transfers. Comparing total received to net received German marks as well as total given to net given German marks, we find that the figures do not deviate much. In the further course we can therefore restrict our attention to the first four columns. In accordance with other countries, Germany exhibits a skewed distribution of transfers *inter vivos*, if not as pronounced as, for example, in the United States (cf. [72]). Thus, the one percent highest transfers received account for 14 percent of total received German marks and the top 25 percent comprise 67 percent of received German marks. Even more skewed is the distribution of given transfers. Here the one percent largest transfers given constitute 19 percent and the top 25 percent comprise 75 percent of overall given German marks. Furthermore, irregular transfers exhibit a much greater skewness than regular

[4] The fact, that female household heads, in many cases single parents, do not receive significantly more transfers, once more shows that the data contamination by maintenance payments is not too severe.

Table 3.6. Size Distribution of Transfers, EVS

Percentile	Percent of DM Received			Percent	Percent	Percent
	Total	Regular	Irregular	of DM Given	of Net DM Received	of Net DM Given
Top 1 Percent	14.3	6.7	21.8	18.5	13.9	18.3
Top 5 Percent	31.6	20.6	45.6	39.0	31.3	38.8
Top 10 Percent	44.0	32.8	58.3	52.8	43.9	52.5
Upper Quartile	66.8	57.1	76.6	74.7	66.8	74.5
2nd Quartile	20.4	24.3	15.0	16.3	20.3	16.4
3rd Quartile	10.0	13.6	6.6	6.8	10.0	6.9
Lowest Quartile	2.8	5.0	1.8	2.2	2.9	2.2
Sample Size	8,331	4,462	5,010	15,171	7,300	13,046

Source: German Income and Expenditure Survey 1993.

transfers. In particular, irregular transfers in the 99th percentile account for 22 percent of transferred German marks as compared to only 7 percent in the case of regular transfers. This difference is in part attributable to maintenance payments.

The skewness of intergenerational transfers has been confirmed by several studies and is one of the few facts about intergenerational transfers that has experienced broad acceptance. Any theory on the motives of intergenerational transfers must therefore be reconcilable with this stylized fact. As was outlined in Section 2 the altruistic model as well as the exchange model predict a positive relation between donor's life-cycle income and the transfer amount. Both theories are therefore compatible with observed transfer patterns, in that the concentration of transfers could be attributed to the concentration of income and wealth prevalent in Germany as elsewhere. However, altruism, in addition, establishes an income elasticity of transfers greater unity. It is, thus, particularly suited for producing a skewed distribution of transfers.

We will follow this line of reasoning by scrutinizing the relationship of income and wealth, on the one hand, and transfers *inter vivos*, on the other hand. For this purpose we have, first, sorted and grouped donors according to their level of disposable income. Next, we have ranked and clustered donors with regard to their labor and capital income. Finally, we have arranged donors with respect to their net wealth, where net wealth corresponds to real estate, building-society investments (so-called *Bausparverträge*), bonds, stocks, insurance holdings, money, less liabilities. Successively, we have calculated mean transfer amounts for the corresponding income and wealth groups. Note, however, that cases with zero income or net wealth were excluded.

The results are displayed in Table 3.7. As implied by all transfer motives, transfers *inter vivos* increase with donor's income or wealth, respectively. This is particularly true for disposable income and wealth, where the increase is

Table 3.7. Average Net Donation by Income and Wealth Group, EVS

Decile	Average Net Donation in DM, Grouped According to		
	Dispos. Income[a]	Labor and Capital Income DM	Net Wealth[b]
Upper	8,737	6,927	9,311
2nd	5,719	4,498	6,337
3rd	4,911	3,747	5,062
4th	4,144	3,750	4,248
5th	4,124	3,668	3,328
6th	3,378	4,505	3,936
7th	3,377	5,416	3,248
8th	3,271	4,496	2,662
9th	2,882	3,339	2,523
Lowest	1,938	2,314	2,392
Sample Size[c]	13,046	12,965	12,714

Source: German Income and Expenditure Survey 1993.

[a] Disposable income comprises labor and capital income, private and public pensions, other public transfers, less taxes and social insurance contributions.
[b] Net wealth corresponds to real estate, building-society investments, bonds, stocks, insurance holdings, money, less liabilities.
[c] Only net donors are considered. However, cases with zero income or net wealth are excluded.

almost monotonous. Less clear-cut is the increase relative to labor and capital income. In that the levels of labor and capital income heavily depend on age, income and age-effects obviously intermingle here. Noteworthy as well, where we observe a monotonous increase in average transfer amounts, it is not linear but more than proportional.

Next, we consider relative transfers, where the reference again is donor's disposable income, labor and capital income, and net wealth. After grouping donors according to these characteristics, we have calculated the average ratio for each group. Again, this can be done in two different ways. One can either divide the sum of all transfer amounts within a specific group by the income or wealth aggregate of this group. Alternatively, one can calculate the transfer-wealth-ratio or transfer-income-ratio separately for each case and successively compute the mean. Since, in the present context, we are interested in microeconomic rather than macroeconomic relations we made use of the latter approach, this way weighting all individuals equally. The results are reported in Table 3.8. Independent of the reference we chose, relative trans-

Table 3.8. Share of Net Donation by Income and Wealth, EVS

Decile	Net Given Transfer as Percent of		
	Dispos. Income[a]	Labor and Capital Income	Net Wealth[b]
Upper	6.3	3.7	1.0
2nd	6.3	4.0	1.2
3rd	6.7	4.4	1.3
4th	6.7	5.5	1.5
5th	7.8	7.1	1.7
6th	7.4	14.1	3.9
7th	8.9	34.4	6.1
8th	10.1	56.8	9.2
9th	11.3	166.0	16.7
Lowest	11.4	2287.8	756.9
Sample Size[c]	13,046	12,965	12,714

Source: German Income and Expenditure Survey 1993.

[a] Disposable income comprises labor and capital income, private and public pensions, other public transfers, less taxes and social insurance contributions.
[b] Net wealth corresponds to real estate, building-society investments, bonds, stocks, insurance holdings, money, less liabilities.
[c] Only net donors are considered. However, cases with zero income or net wealth are excluded.

fers seem to decrease as people get richer. Again, this decline across income and wealth groups is almost monotonous. The high ratios for the lower tail of the income and wealth distribution in column two and three should not come as a surprise. Obviously, these groups contain a great deal of people who have neither capital and labor income, nor wealth. Instead, private transfers are financed out of public transfers – supposedly public pensions – and in this manner blow up the ratio under consideration.

The reported ratios hint at an income and wealth elasticity of transfers below unity. In contrast to previous findings on bequests (cf. [92], [58]) transfers *inter vivos* therefore appear to constitute a necessity rather than a luxury. Furthermore, these findings seem to be at odds with the altruistic model, which predicts an elasticity greater unity. We should not, however, jump to conclusions. For several reasons the figures presented should be considered with utmost caution. First, recall that the data is contaminated by the inclusion of maintenance payments. These payments are induced by legal order and in very few cases subject to altruism. Second, recall that the very well-to-do, namely households with a net monthly income of DM 35,000 and more, are not included in the sample. According to Menchik and David [58] this segment of people is especially likely to exhibit an income elasticity of transfers greater unity. Third, while the altruistic model is formulated in terms of life-cycle transfers and income, we only observe transfers and income at a single point in time. This perspective, however, might introduce a significant bias. Imagine, for example, that all people, regardless of their economic status, make transfers of the same magnitude on an annual basis. The affluent, however, make transfers over a longer period of life. The affluent might, for example, continue transferring resources, after their children have completed education, while poor and middle-class households do not. On an annual basis one might then observe an elasticity below unity, while on a life-cycle basis an elasticity greater unity, as suggested by the altruist model, would prevail.

Finally, we do not control for recipient's economic status. If due to genetic or cultural factors or owing to investment in children's human capital, there is a strong correlation of parents' and children's economic status, as suggested, for example, by Becker and Tomes [93, 94], we might not observe an elasticity greater unity, even if transfers were altruistic. For the sake of argument, imagine that parental and filial resources move parallel. Further recall that, according to the altruistic model, parent's consumption depends on family income. Assuming homothetic preferences, an increase in parent's (and children's) resources by one percent then leads to an increase in parent's consumption by the same proportion. In accordance with Equation 2.1 this translates into a corresponding increase in bequests and, ergo, a unitary elasticity of transfers. Due to the preceding qualifications the motives behind transfers *inter vivos* remain unclear.

In what follows, we examine the relationship of transfer amount and recipient's income. As before, this is done by reporting mean transfer receipts by income and wealth group. To begin with, consider the first column of Table 3.9, which sorts recipients according to disposable income. We find a U-shaped relation, meaning that the very rich and the very poor receive most. Of course, one should not draw conclusion from these figures about the underlying transfer motives. While the high transfer amount at the lower tail of the income distribution hints at altruism, this is certainly a statistical artefact induced by maintenance payments.[5] The same is true for the high amounts at the upper end of the income distribution. Instead of pointing to the exchange motive, they are perhaps just picking up the effects of donor income. Indeed, recent studies have found evidence for a rather strong correlation of parent's and children's incomes (cf. [95], [96], [97]). Turning to the next column, which arranges households according to labor and capital

[5] This conjecture is underpinned when making the same analysis, separately for regularly and irregularly received transfers. In the case of regularly received transfers – those which include maintenance payments – the 10 percent poorest receive a higher average amount than the 10 percent richest. However, in the case of irregularly transfers, the richest receive more than the poorest.

Table 3.9. Average Net Receipt by Income and Wealth Group, EVS

Decile	Average Net Receipt in DM, Grouped According to		
	Dispos. Income[a]	Labor and Capital Income DM	Net Wealth[b]
Upper	10,421	10,603	13,761
2nd	8,266	7,864	8,260
3rd	7,307	6,602	8,350
4th	5,711	6,863	6,831
5th	5,335	5,738	6,377
6th	5,784	6,828	6,522
7th	5,466	7,956	5,791
8th	5,253	7,283	5,817
9th	6,212	6,860	5,805
Lowest	10,948	5,629	5,430
Sample Size[c]	7,281	7,129	6,729

Source: German Income and Expenditure Survey 1993.

[a] Disposable income comprises labor and capital income, private and public pensions, other public transfers, less taxes and social insurance contributions.
[b] Net wealth corresponds to real estate, building-society investments, bonds, stocks, insurance holdings, money, less liabilities.
[c] Only net recipients are considered. However, cases with zero income or net wealth are excluded.

income, we can not make out any pattern. Probably, this again hinges on the interaction of income- and age-effects.

Finally, inspect the third column, where transfers are reported according to recipient's net wealth. Instead of the U-shape observed in the first column, we find transfers increasing with recipient's wealth. Furthermore, the average transfer received by the very affluent, is significantly higher than in the first column. This pattern can be explained as follows. For one thing, the very poor do not hold wealth and, for this reason, are not included in the sample any longer. As a consequence, maintenance payments play a minor role and the peak at the lower end of the distribution disappears. For another thing, high wealth on the part of the recipients might be the result of transfers in the past, causing a stronger positive relation between transfers and net wealth than between transfers and disposable income. Table 3.10 reports transfers relative to recipient's income and wealth. In all three columns we clearly perceive an inverse relation between relative transfers and recipient's economic status. This does not come as a surprise, given that the poor already received more

Table 3.10. Share of Net Receipt by Income and Wealth, EVS

Decile	Net Received Transfer as Percent of		
	Dispos. Income[a]	Labor and Capital Income	Net Wealth[b]
Upper	9.4	7.9	1.9
2nd	11.8	9.1	2.3
3rd	13.6	10.3	4.1
4th	13.4	13.9	7.7
5th	15.6	16.3	14.1
6th	21.0	32.3	25.5
7th	24.7	72.5	38.3
8th	30.6	139.5	66.6
9th	48.4	534.8	139.6
Lowest	1605.0	21,474.5	1,994.7
Sample Size[c]	7,281	7,129	6,729

Source: German Income and Expenditure Survey 1993.

[a] Disposable income comprises labor and capital income, private and public pensions, other public transfers, less taxes and social insurance contributions.
[b] Net wealth corresponds to real estate, building-society investments, bonds, stocks, insurance holdings, money, less liabilities.
[c] Only net recipients are considered. However, cases with zero income or net wealth are excluded.

in absolute terms, at least when arranged according to disposable income. Furthermore, compare the first columns of Table 3.10 and Table 3.8 to see, that the inverse relation between relative transfers and economic status is much stronger for recipients than donors. This becomes relevant in what follows.

We finally consider some distributive implications of transfers *inter vivos*. For this purpose, we observe relative inequality of disposable income before and after transfer events. As measure of relative income inequality we employ the variance of the natural logarithm of income (cf. [72]). Table 3.11 reports the degree of relative income inequality for three subsamples, namely net donors, net recipients, and the entire EVS. Note however, that all samples are restricted to households with positive pre- and post-transfer incomes. Among donors transfers *inter vivos* lead to higher relative income inequality. Thus, the degree of inequality increases from 0.35 to 0.41. This is in correspondence with our findings on given transfers relative to disposable income, as reported in Table 3.8. If rich donors transfer relatively less, relative inequality is bound to increase. On the other hand, transfers *inter vivos* alleviate

Table 3.11. Income Inequality before and after Transfers, EVS

Selected Group	Pre-Transfer Disposable Income[a]	Post-Transfer Disposable Income	Sample Size[b]
Net Donors	0.35	0.41	12,986
Net Recipients	0.80	0.43	7,281
Total Sample	0.47[c]	0.39	40,149

Source: German Income and Expenditure Survey 1993.

[a] Disposable income comprises labor and capital income, private and public pensions, other public transfers, less taxes and social insurance contributions.
[b] The sample is restricted to households with positive pre- and post-transfer income.
[c] Income inequality is measured by the variance of the natural logarithm of income.

income inequality among recipients from 0.80 to 0.43. This outcome reflects our findings on received transfers relative to disposable income, as reported in Table 3.10. If the poor receive relatively more, this must translate into a decrease of relative income inequality.

While the effects on the two subpopulations work in opposite direction, the effect on recipients outweighs. This was already indicated above, in that the inverse relation between relative transfers and economic status is much more pronounced for recipients than donors. The combined effect of transfers *inter vivos*, thus, reduces the degree of relative income inequality from 0.47 to 0.39.

So far, our findings can be summarized as follows. Due to the deficiencies of the EVS data, our understanding of transfer motives remains unclear. Admittedly, transfers are positively correlated with donors income, which is in correspondence with our theory. However, due to the lack of important explanatory variables, the identification of a predominant motive is impossible. Despite these shortcomings, we provided some rather robust evidence on transfer patterns. First, the majority of transfers *inter vivos* is directed from old to young. Second, the distribution of *inter vivos* transfers is fairly skewed. Finally, a considerable share of intergenerational transfers seem to be intentional, this way challenging the standard life-cycle model without a transfer motive. We try to complement our understanding of transfer patterns by further inspecting the German Socio-Economic Panel.

3.2 The Socio-Economic Panel

The SOEP includes three sets of questions that are relevant to our problem. Respondents are asked about transfers *inter vivos* given to children, parents, and so forth. Furthermore, respondents are inquired about bequests received between 1960 and 1988. Finally, participants are requested to report particulars about their wealth holdings, including why they hold wealth in old age. We will turn to these issues one by one.

3.2.1 Transfers *Inter Vivos*

First, consider the SOEP data on transfers *inter vivos*, to see whether the results conform to those of the EVS. Each year respondents report the amount transferred to persons outside the household. In addition, the recipients are specified as children, parents, separately living or divorced spouses, other relatives, or other non-relatives.[6] Our figures refer to the most recent cross-section, namely 1997. Note, however, that the results are quite robust to alternative periods of investigation. Table 3.12 documents the number of

Table 3.12. Households making Transfers *Inter Vivos*, SOEP

Transfer Recipients	Absolute Number of Donors	Relative Number of Donors N=6305	Average Transfer Amount DM
Total	920[a]	14.6	5,864
Children	519	8.2	6,694
Parents	214	3.4	3,270
Wife/Husband	59	0.9	8,422
Other Relatives	177	2.8	3,417
Non-Relatives	82	1.3	1,747

Source: Socio-Economic Panel, Wave 14, 1997.

[a] In that some households make transfers to several recipients, not necessarily belonging to the same category, the following rows do not sum up to 920.

households making transfers *inter vivos*, classified by destination of transfer. Among 6,305 sample households 920 make donations, which amounts to a share of 14.6 percent. The corresponding share for the EVS is 37.7 percent

[6] Children include daughters- and sons-in-law, parents include mothers- and fathers-in-law.

(cf. Table 3.1), suggesting severe underreporting in the SOEP. While the aggregate is not reliable, the composition of transfers most likely conforms to reality. As a consequence, the detailed information on transfer recipients contained in the SOEP allows us to cross-check the reliability of our former findings. Recall, that, lacking detailed data, we proceeded on the assumption, that the majority of interhousehold transfers in the EVS were across generations. This assumption seems to be confirmed by Table 3.12. Transfers to children and parents, those sensibly subsumed under intergenerational transfers, constitute 70 percent of all reported transfers.[7] Taking into account that transfers to other relatives and non-relatives probably include further intergenerational transfers, our initial working hypothesis seems warranted.

We also find reinforced our earlier conclusion that the majority of transfers are directed from old to young. For one thing, more than half of the donor households make transfers to their children. For another thing, the resources transferred to offspring are significant. To see this, consider the last column of Table 3.12. This column shows the average transfer amount, where cases – as in the previous and following tables – are weighted to produce a representative cross-section of the German population in 1997. Transfers to children exhibit the second-highest transfer amount, surmounted only by payments to former wives and husbands.

The size distribution of SOEP transfers *inter vivos* is reported in Table 3.13, again separated by destination of transfer. Remarkably, interhousehold transfers widely differ in their degree of skewness, with transfers towards children and parents being much less concentrated than the rest. While for children and parents the top 1 percent transfers constitute about 12 percent of overall received resources, this share increases to 22, 26, or even 35 percent in the case of spouses, other non-relatives, or other relatives, respectively. An obvious explanation for this finding would be that transfers towards children and parents exhibit a smaller elasticity with respect to donor's income or wealth. In accordance with intuition, those transfers could then be considered a necessity, whereas especially transfers towards distant relatives or non-relatives appear to be more of a luxury. Next, compare the present concentration of transfers *inter vivos* to the corresponding EVS figures. As documented by the last columns of Table 3.6 and 3.13, transfers are more skewed in the EVS as compared to the SOEP. This is puzzling, given that the EVS is the database, which explicitly excludes the very well-to-do, that is

[7] Admittedly, the question with respect to children is ambiguous. In particular, it is not clear, whether transfers to children also include maintenance payments, which conventionally are not counted as intergenerational transfers. Among households, that have transferred resources to their children, 19 percent are divorced or live separated from their spouse. Given that this is an upper-bound estimate for the proportion of maintenance payments, the data contamination is likely to be small. If we exclude donors, that are divorced or live separated from their spouse, transfers to children and parents still constitute 66 percent of all reported transfers.

Table 3.13. Size Distribution of Transfers *Inter Vivos*, SOEP

Percentile	Percent of Total Amount Transferred to					
	Children	Parents	Wife/ Husb.	Other Relatives	Non-Relatives	Total
Top 1 Percent	12.4	12.6	21.9	35.4	25.8	13.0
Top 5 Percent	27.0	22.3	28.7	39.3	40.6	30.1
Top 10 Percent	42.0	34.8	47.6	53.4	52.5	43.2
Upper Quartile	64.5	60.6	71.6	73.9	69.6	66.8
2nd Quartile	21.7	23.5	17.3	16.0	20.5	20.8
3rd Quartile	10.6	11.9	8.9	7.5	6.8	9.7
Lowest Quartile	3.2	4.0	2.2	2.6	3.1	2.8
Sample Size	519	214	59	177	82	920

Source: Socio-Economic Panel, Wave 14, 1997.

households with net monthly incomes above DM 35,000. It was pointed out, however, that there is severe underreporting of transfers *inter vivos* in the SOEP (cf. page 42). Obviously, this underreporting is especially pronounced among the affluent. In what follows, we restrict our analysis to intergenerational transfers directed from parents to children. In order to correct the data for maintenance payments, 98 households that make transfers to their children and, at the same time, are divorced or live separated from their spouse are excluded from the sample. While transfers to parents just as much constitute intergenerational transfers, they are subject to different economic rationales, making a joint analysis inappropriate.

Moreover, the restriction to downward transfers seems warranted on the basis of their relative importance. Table 3.14 gives the share of household heads within a specific age bracket that have reported transfers to their children. In addition, it shows the average transfer amount as well as the number of cases. The probability of transfer events is hump-shaped with hardly any transfers before age 40, a peak between age 50 and 70, and a slightly falling trend thereafter. Note that this transfer pattern is better reconcilable with altruism than with exchange. If the predominant motive of transfers *inter vivos* were exchange, one would expect most transfers to occur later in life, when donors, due to illness or loneliness, are especially dependent on their children. In contrast, we observe most transfers during a time, when recipients have particular needs. Thus, assuming a generation gap of about 30 years, transfers are especially likely, when recipients are in their twenties and thirties - a period that is characterized by education expenditures, starting a family, or building a house. Altruism is especially suited to account for this

Table 3.14. Transfers to Children by Age of Donor, SOEP

Age	Proportion of Donors Percent	Average Amount DM	Number of Cases[a]
19–29	0.8	272	2
30–40	1.9	4,060	32
41–51	6.2	5,518	93
52–62	11.4	8,111	151
63–73	11.7	7,442	96
74–84	8.4	9,562	40
85+	7.1	2,009	7

Source: Socio-Economic Panel, Wave 14, 1997.

[a] A number of 98 households that make transfers to their children and, at the same time, are divorced or live separated from their spouse were excluded from the sample.

positive relation between recipients' needs and transfer events. With respect to transfer amounts no particular pattern can be identified. This is to a large extent attributable to the small sample size within the single age classes.

The following table reports some mean characteristics for selected groups, namely for the entire sample, for households transferring resources to their children and for households reporting no such gifts. Of course, it would be more desirable to regress donor characteristics on transfer amounts, this way isolating single variables by controlling for the rest. In contrast to the earlier regression using EVS data, however, the sample size in the present case is very small. On the basis of 421 observations no significant coefficients were obtained. We therefore resort to reporting mean characteristics. To begin with, donors are older than the rest of the population and educated above average. In correspondence with earlier findings the SOEP data further confirms, that donors of transfers are in general better off. In particular, donors are less likely to be unemployed, single parent or recipient of social assistance. Furthermore, donor households receive significantly higher net incomes. The extremely low proportion of unmarried donors reflects the fact, that children are the chief recipients of intergenerational transfers, whereas never being married, in most cases, implies being childless.

Next, consider some variables, possibly correlated with exchange motivated transfers. Specifically, we have checked, whether donors exhibit characteristics, which make them particularly dependent on services by the extended family. Indeed, some figures could be interpreted as evidence in favor of the exchange motive. Donors, for example, are more likely to be in bad

Table 3.15. Mean Characteristics of Parents Making Gifts, SOEP

Variable	Sample[a]	Donors	Non-Donors
Age	50	60	49
% Unmarried	19.6	3.6	20.7
% Unemployed	7.5	5.3	7.6
% With Female Head	42.9	29.9	43.8
% with Bad Health	19.6	25.2	19.2
% Handicapped Due To Bad Health	42.5	61.2	41.2
% Bad Provision for Illness	16.1	11.1	16.4
% Bad Provision for Old Age in General	41.3	29.0	42.2
% Bad Provision for Old Age Care	48.3	39.4	48.9
% Few Social Life	23.8	24.9	23.7
% Households Rec. Social Assistance	2.9	0.8	3.0
Net Household Income	44,888	54,650	44,227
% Rec. Old Age Care from Relatives	0.8	1.5	0.7
% Having Completed[b]			
No Education	3.3	1.5	3.4
Hauptschule	46.9	46.3	47.0
Realschule	26.3	25.4	26.4
Gymnasium	14.8	17.0	14.7
Number of Cases	6,207	421	5,786

Source: Socio-Economic Panel, Wave 14, 1997.

[a] A number of 98 households that make transfers to their children and, at the same time, are divorced or live separated from their spouse were excluded from the sample.

[b] The types of schooling are listed in ascending order of schooling years.

health, handicapped, lacking social life, or receiving old age care from relatives outside the household. On the other hand, we also find evidence against the exchange motive. Thus, the share of donors reporting bad provision for illness, old age care, or old age in general, is below average. It is needless to say, that this issue can not be settled without econometrics. Formal tests, however, are precluded due to the lack of data on recipient's characteristics. We conclude the investigation of transfers *inter vivos* by inspecting the relation of parental income and transfers given. Although a comparison with earlier results is intended, our findings are presented in a slightly different way. While, earlier, donor households were divided into ten income groups, small sample size restricts the current analysis to merely four income groups.

Table 3.16. Transfers to Children by Income Group of Parents, SOEP

Percentile	Average Amount DM	As Percent of Net Household Income	Number of Cases[a]
Upper Quartile[b]	9,479	10.7	109
2nd Quartile	7,514	14.0	96
3rd Quartile	5,610	14.1	119
Lower Quartile	5,468	23.5	97

Source: Socio-Economic Panel, Wave 14, 1997.

[a] A number of 98 households that make transfers to their children and, at the same time, are divorced or live separated from their spouse were excluded from the sample.
[b] With respect to net household income.

Nevertheless, a quantitative comparison remains practical. As indicated by Table 3.16, transfer amounts seem to increase with donor's income. At the same time, the share of income, spent on transfers, seems to decline with income. This is in correspondence with our findings based on the EVS (cf. Tables 3.7 and 3.8) and once more suggests, that transfers from parents to children constitute a large share of the transfers recorded by the EVS.

3.2.2 Bequests Between 1960 and 1988

As mentioned earlier, the SOEP includes few data on bequests. For one thing, only the panel's 1988 wave includes questions on bequests. For another thing, these questions were answered only by a fraction of total participants generating a mere 4,187 valid cases instead of the usual 6,000.[8] In that we primarily focus on households receiving bequests, sample size decreases further to some hundred observations. Still this data set is among the best available for Germany, not least because inheritance tax records are of little use. It is true that until 1978 the Federal Statistical Office published the amount of inheritances subject to inheritance taxation, but all figures were highly aggregated. From 1979 onward, the Office even confined itself to reporting mere tax revenues. Owing to generous tax-free amounts a significant share of inheritances are not included in these figures. Moreover, tax statistics assign real estates and unincorporated enterprises a value, which is a legal construct and far below

[8] Strictly speaking, 4,564 participating households answered the supplemental questionnaire on wealth and bequest. However, apart from wealth and bequests, we are interested in a variety of other socio-economic household characteristics. Consequently, only households making valid statements for all of the relevant variables were included.

the true economic value (the so-called *Einheitswert*). This introduces a further bias, making the data useless altogether (cf. [9]). Despite its deficiencies, we, thus, resort to the SOEP data on bequests.

Households are asked, whether they received one or more inheritances between 1960 and 1988. In case they did, they can report for up to three inheritances the year of the receipt as well as its value at that time. In addition, households are requested to classify the inheritance according to the following asset categories: real estate, securities, money, or other items. Note that in order to be considered recipient of an inheritance households had to give an affirmative answer to the first question as well as answer all follow-up questions. Among 4,187 households, 432 reported the receipt of at least one inheritance in the respective period. Without doubt, a share of 10 percent is much to low to conform with reality. This is reinforced, when inspecting the aggregated value of reported bequests. Employing sample weights, the aggregate comes to DM 213 billion in the period 1960 through 1988. Given that for a single year, namely 1993, bequests already sum up to DM 183.1 billion – as has been shown in Section 3.1 – the former figure is way to low, suggesting severe underreporting in the SOEP. Notwithstanding, we proceed with Table 3.17,

Table 3.17. Bequests between 1960 and 1988, SOEP

	Absolute Number	Relative Number Percent (N=481)	Average Amount[a] in 1000 DM (Participants)
All Bequests	481	100.0	138.0
Real Estate	208	43.2	221.3
Securities	7	1.5	41.6
Money	216	44.9	37.7
Other	50	10.4	285.6

Source: Socio-Economic Panel, Wave 5, 1988.

[a] In prices of 1988. Bequests that occurred before 1988 are adjusted for inflation and productivity growth.

showing the number and average amount of received inheritances, classified by asset category. Since some of the 432 households, reporting the receipt of an inheritance, made multiple inheritances, their total number amounts to 481. The majority of these inheritances occur in the form of real estate and money, accounting for about 200 cases each. Securities constitute only a small fraction of overall bequests, that is 1.5 percent, while about 10 percent are categorized as other items. Next, consider the third column of Table 3.17.

It reports the average value of inheritances, where all receipts before 1988 are adjusted for inflation and productivity growth.[9] Inheritances classified as other items have the highest value, namely DM 280,000 on average, suggesting a high proportion of family businesses in this category. They are followed by real estate with an average value of DM 220,000. Inheritances in form of money and securities, finally, are worth much less with average values in the neighborhood of DM 40,000. Thus, taking into account both frequency and aggregate value, real estate seems to be the predominant form of bequest in Germany. We next turn to the age distribution of heirs. Knowing the year in which an inheritance was received as well as respondent's year of birth, one can easily calculate the age at the time of the receipt. One should, however, refrain from just documenting the absolute frequency of inheritances by age. In that people who can state the receipt of an inheritance in young age are over-represented, this would introduce a significant bias. An inheritance at age 30, for example, can be reported by people being 30 years and older in

Table 3.18. Bequest by Age of Heir, SOEP

Age[a]	All Heirs		Heirs Not Widowed	
	Per Thousand	Amount[b] in 1000 DM	Per Thousand	Amount in 1000 DM
0–9	0.3	(110.2)[c]	0.3	(110.2)
10–19	4.2	413.3	4.2	413.3
20–29	13.8	109.9	13.7	110.0
30–39	24.4	138.3	24.1	139.1
40–49	47.5	108.3	43.0	96.5
50–59	34.9	113.3	25.7	121.8
60–69	37.3	152.7	21.9	93.5
70–79	11.0	(54.5)	8.7	(60.9)
80+	19.0	(7.8)	0.0	0.0

Source: Socio-Economic Panel, Wave 5, 1988.

[a] Age of household head at the time, when the inheritance occurred. If the household received several inheritances within the period under consideration, the mean age and amount are taken.
[b] In prices of 1988. Bequests that occurred before 1988 are adjusted for inflation and productivity growth.
[c] Parentheses indicate less than 15 observations.

[9] Productivity defined as GDP divided by labor force.

1988, whereas an inheritance at age 50 can only be declared by people being 50 and older. We correct for this bias by expressing the age-distribution in terms of probability. Specifically, we divide the number of people reporting a bequest at a specific age by the number of people being of this age and older in 1988. The results are displayed in Table 3.18, which apart from relative

Table 3.19. Mean Characteristics of Heirs, SOEP

Variable	Non-Heirs	All Heirs	Heirs of Real Estate	Heirs of Money
% Unemployed	4.5	2.8	2.5	2.4
% With Social Commitment	38.8	42.8	41.2	42.6
% Making Transfers to Parents	2.5	1.8	1.4	1.5
Amount Transferred to Parents (DM)	62	36	38	29
% Without Assets in Old Age	53.8	31.6	29.9	36.3
% With Financial Worries	16.5	12.5	17.9	9.0
Net Household Income (DM)	32,658	41,188	40,031	37,667
% Receiving Social Assistance	3.0	0.5	0.5	0.6
% Household Head Having Completed[a]				
No Education	2.6	0.6	1.5	0.0
Hauptschule	59.7	49.5	55.5	47.0
Realschule	18.5	16.1	21.2	30.1
Gymnasium	11.8	18.8	10.9	18.2
Number of Cases	3755	432	186	180

Source: Socio-Economic Panel, Wave 5, 1988.

[a] The types of schools are listed in ascending order of schooling years.

frequencies also gives the average amount of inheritances. Furthermore, we distinguish two distributions, one comprising all heirs and another excluding 48 heirs, which report being widowed in 1988. By the latter, we hope to isolate bequests across generations, which might be of particular interest in the present context. Up to age 40 the probabilities of receiving a bequest do not deviate much between the two samples. They also peak within the same age-class, namely 40 through 50, if at different levels. Hereafter, however, the decline in relative frequency is much steeper for intergenerational bequests, turning zero for those being 80 and older.

With respect to the amount inherited the following patterns can be identified. Those inheriting in early years, on average receive high amounts. This is in correspondence with the life-cycle hypothesis according to which parents who die unexpectedly early, have not yet run down their assets. Another possible interpretation is that the affluent more often bequeath to their grandchildren. Those inheriting at old ages, receive relatively little. This as well can be interpreted in light of the life-cycle hypothesis. Thus, long-lived parents may use up their bequeathable wealth (cf. [98]). Finally, we find that, where inheritances are relatively numerous, between 40 and 50, they are, at the same time, relatively small on average. This phenomenon already hints at a skewed size distribution of bequests, which will be confirmed in due course.

For the moment, however, we will briefly review some mean characteristics of selected groups. Table 3.19 presents characteristics for heirs in general, non-heirs, heirs of real estate, and heirs of money. The main findings can be summarized as follows. Heirs are on average better off and better educated than the rest of the sample. While they exhibit a relatively high degree of social commitment, which is in correspondence with bequests-as-exchange, they make fewer transfers to their parents, at least, weakening the idea of reciprocity. Finally, we could not find any systematic deviations between heirs of real estate and heirs of money. We now investigate the size distribution

Table 3.20. Size Distribution of Bequests, SOEP

Percentile	Percent of Overall Inherited Value[a]				
	All Bequests	Real Estate	Securities	Money	Other
Top 1 Percent	28.5	24.0	(22.8)[b]	12.5	44.3
Top 5 Percent	41.8	36.1	(29.1)	29.1	48.2
Top 10 Percent	56.5	47.1	(36.9)	44.5	58.7
Upper Quartile	78.0	70.1	(72.2)	68.8	75.4
2nd Quartile	15.2	19.1	(9.9)	21.2	15.1
3rd Quartile	5.6	8.3	(16.2)	7.7	7.0
Lowest Quartile	1.2	2.5	(1.7)	2.3	2.5
Sample Size	481	208	7	216	50

Source: Socio-Economic Panel, Wave 5, 1988.

[a] In 1988 prices. Bequests that occurred before 1988 are adjusted for inflation and productivity growth.
[b] Parentheses indicate less than 5 observations.

of received bequests as displayed in Table 3.20. First, bequests are highly concentrated, with a share of almost 57 percent in bequeathed wealth for the top 10 percent. This figure matches quite closely the share of 60 percent reported by Davies [99] on the basis of a simulation that was benchmarked to Canadian data for 1970. Moreover, we observe that bequests are much more skewed than transfers *inter vivos*. While the 99th percentile accounts for 14 percent of all received transfers *inter vivos* (cf. Table 3.6), this share doubles when turning to bequests. Table 3.20 further reveals that bequests of real es-

Table 3.21. Average Inheritance by Income Group of Heir, SOEP

Percentile[a]	Average Receipt[b] (in 1000 DM)	As Percent of Net Household Income	Number of Cases
Overall Bequests			
Upper Quartile	139.6	203.9	114
2nd Quartile	135.2	297.1	111
3rd Quartile	138.7	425.8	114
Lowest Quartile	107.2	778.7	93
Real Estate			
Upper Quartile	186.0	263.2	48
2nd Quartile	273.9	604.7	50
3rd Quartile	198.3	592.3	53
Lowest Quartile	202.4	1341.8	35
Money			
Upper Quartile	35.5	59.5	47
2nd Quartile	39.9	91.2	45
3rd Quartile	38.9	137.2	46
Lowest Quartile	25.0	148.0	42

Source: Socio-Economic Panel, Wave 5, 1988.

[a] With respect to net household income.
[b] In 1988 prices. Bequests that occurred before 1988 are adjusted for inflation and productivity growth.

tate are more concentrated than bequests of money, while the highest degree of concentration is found for bequests classified as other items, supposedly family businesses. The discrepancies in the degree of concentration to a great extent reflect differences in concentration to be found among testators. One reason, however, might also be the divergent degree of divisibility exhibited by the different assets.

We conclude this subsection with Table 3.21, illustrating the relation between heir's income and the value of received inheritance. Again, total inheritances, inheritances of real estate, and inherited money are considered separately. By and large, the figures display the same pattern as for transfers *inter vivos* – at least qualitatively (cf. Tables 3.9 and 3.10). Thus, for neither of the three cases one can make out any correlation of recipient's income and absolute receipt. As a consequence, relative receipts are bound to decline as heir's income increases.

3.2.3 Particulars about Wealth Holdings

In 1988 the Socio-Economic Panel included in its fifth wave the question, whether people had, or believed they would have in the future, wealth apart from pension wealth and, if this were the case, what were the motives for holding additional wealth. The respondents could chose among four answers, namely (1) I need additional wealth to live on, (2) to live comfortably and enjoy old age, (3) to provide for hardship and severe illnesses, (4) to make a bequest to my offspring/family. In terms of economic theory the first two answers translate into pure life-cycle saving, where the former and latter only differ in the respondent's economic status. If any, bequests are likely to be small. The third answer points to precautionary saving and implies accidental bequests, whereas the last option identifies intentional bequests, be they motivated by altruism or exchange.

The fifth wave includes 3,905 households that answered the first question as well as further questions on their economic and social particulars, such as household income, education or age of the household head. Among these households 1,383 indicated to hold wealth apart from pension wealth and, thus, answered the follow-up question about their motives. Of course, there might be a considerable discrepancy between what people say, they save for – due, for example, to social norms – and what they actually do save for. However, as Jürges [85] has convincingly shown, people's answers to the above questions conform quite well with their actual behavior. In particular, respondents who declare to hold wealth for bequests dissave significantly less than those without a bequest motive. We, thus, proceed on the assumption, that there is no systematic bias in what people answer. Table 3.22 presents for different samples the proportion of respondents naming a specific savings motive. Note, that multiple motives were admitted. To begin with, consider the first row of Table 3.22, which reports results for the entire sample. While life-cycle saving and wealth accumulation for bequests is cited by approximately 50 percent of all respondents holding wealth in old age, the majority, namely 63 percent, save out of precaution.[10] In proportion to the entire German population the latter corresponds to a share of more than 20 percent. While this already is a fairly strong case in favor of accidental bequests, the proportion increases further, when restricting the sample to older respondents. These, of course, are particularly relevant when it comes to bequests. Among wealth holders aged 60 and above more than 70 percent, for those

[10] The shares slightly deviate from those reported by Jürges [85], who finds that 54.7 percent name saving for subsistence, 55.3 saving for comfort, 68.1 saving out of precaution, and 57.0 saving for bequests. There are two possible explanation for this deviation. As will become obvious by the following table, we are interested in a variety of wealth holders' characteristics. As a consequence we had to restrict our sample to only those households which made valid statements for all of the relevant variables. In that our samples might differ, also the composition can slightly deviate. Second, Jürges might simply have refrained from weighting the cases.

Table 3.22. Motives for Holding Wealth by Age, SOEP

Age of Household Head	Subsistence	Comfort	Precaution	Bequest	Number of Cases[b]
		Percent[a]			
20 and above[c]	49.0	50.8	63.0	48.6	1,383
30 and above	49.7	48.8	63.4	50.3	1,260
40 and above	49.1	45.4	64.7	55.0	951
50 and above	47.3	42.7	69.2	57.9	586
60 and above	43.9	44.1	72.7	59.5	314
70 and above	39.3	38.3	78.9	61.3	117

Source: Socio-Economic Panel, Wave 5, 1988.

[a] Respondents could name multiple motives. Therefore column 2 through 5 do not add up to 100 percent.
[b] Only households that hold wealth apart from pension wealth.
[c] These cases comprise the whole sample.

aged 70 and above even 80 percent save out of precaution. Also the incidence of saving for bequests increases with age peaking at a level of 60 percent for the very old. In contrast, ever fewer people name life-cycle saving as they age, falling to a share of merely 40 percent for the oldest cohorts. Evidence based on direct questions, thus, suggests, that accidental bequests are the predominant form of transfers *post mortem*. Whether they also constitute the major share in terms of money value, however, remains an open question.

Next, we investigate whether people with distinct bequest motives also differ in other respects. For this reason, we report mean characteristics of wealth holders, grouped according to declared savings motive. Respondents who named multiple motives will, of course, show up in more than one group. The results are given in Table 3.23. We, first, find reconfirmed the results of Table 3.22, namely that the incidence of saving for precaution or bequests increases with age. It further turns out, that children, while not being the best proxy for a bequest motive, nevertheless are one major cause for planned bequests. Thus, household heads, who never were married and therefore exhibit a higher probability of being childless, are less likely to report a bequest motive. Net household incomes vary only slightly across subgroups, with savers for comfort earning most and precautionary savers earning the least. Correspondingly, savers for comfort also exhibit the highest educational level, whereas people with a bequest motive, on average, completed the fewest years of schooling. The latter fact is puzzling and might in part depend on a cohort effect. In particular, the incidence of naming the bequest motive is positively and the number of schooling years negatively correlated with age. Respondents indicating a bequest motive make significantly more

Table 3.23. Mean Characteristics of Potential Testators, SOEP

Variable	Whole Sample	Subsi-stence	Com-fort	Pre-caution	Be-quest
Age	51	50	48	52	54
% Unmarried	15.4	15.0	21.2	16.1	7.9
Net Household Income (DM)	41,070	41,052	44,172	40,785	42,801
% Having Completed[a]					
No Education	1.1	1.5	1.1	1.2	1.7
Hauptschule	51.8	51.6	44.0	54.1	58.3
Realschule	23.6	22.6	27.0	22.7	19.0
Gymnasium	15.5	16.0	18.5	14.7	13.9
% Making Transfers *i.v.*	7.5	6.4	8.2	7.1	10.4
Amount of Transfers *i.v.* (DM)	399	380	308	377	484
% Living in Own Apt./House	58.6	59.8	53.2	59.6	72.2
% Owning other Apt./Houses	24.6	28.4	24.1	23.5	30.8
% Owning Company	15.7	23.1	13.1	13.3	14.6
% Having a Savings Account	91.2	89.1	92.5	93.2	93.3
% Saving with Building Society	45.0	45.8	47.5	44.0	48.6
% Holding Securities	34.0	31.6	38.4	34.2	31.8
% Holding Live Insurance	64.0	66.8	67.8	60.9	58.2
% Rec. Inheritance (1966 – 1988)	23.4	24.7	23.9	25.9	28.5
% Amount of Inher. Rec. (DM)	18,917	18,247	20,352	20,579	28,355
Number of Cases	1,383	712	704	859	715

Source: Socio-Economic Panel, Wave 5, 1988.

[a] The types of schools are listed in ascending order of schooling years.

transfers *inter vivos* than the rest, this way obviously anticipating part of the bequest. Note, that this challenges the strategic bequest model according to which parents would not dissipate their bargaining power by making transfers *inter vivos* (cf. [39]). If at all, it suggests altruistic parents, who anticipate bequests either to save taxes or to ease their children's borrowing constraints. In the further course, we investigated whether wealth holders' portfolios differ across bequest motives. We could not identify any meaningful pattern with the following exceptions. People, who own houses or apartments are more likely to plan for a bequest, which is in correspondence to earlier findings on the relative importance of real estate in overall inheritances (cf. Table 3.17). Moreover, owners of companies are particularly likely to be subsistence savers. Since in Germany the public pension program is not mandatory for the self-employed, many rely on private wealth after retirement. A high rate of subsistence savers among self-employed is therefore not surprising. Finally, respondents who plan to leave a bequest are more likely to have inherited themselves, a fact being at odds with complete intergenerational mobility.

Following Bernheim [83] and Ando et al. [84] we conclude this section by investigating the age-pattern of life insurance holdings. Provided that independent children are the accessories, life insurances can be regarded as further evidence in favor of intended intergenerational transfers. The procedure is to separate households with living children from those without, to see, whether the probability of holding life insurance at a specific age varies across the two subsamples. This approach serves several purposes. First, in that transfers towards dependent children are not subsumed under intergenerational transfers, our foremost interest lies on life insurances, which name independent children as accessories. While we have no information on who the accessory is, the life-cycle perspective allows us to identify policyholders with independent children, in general those being older 60. Just as little, we are interested in life insurances which name the spouse or partner as accessory. If, however both samples include about the same proportion of such policies, they will not introduce any bias.[11]

Another problem might arise from the use of cross-section data, since age-profiles can not be interpreted as individual life-cycle profiles. In particular, for old cohorts the profiles might be upward biased, owing to a negative correlation of economic status and mortality risk, or downward bias due to productivity growth (cf. [100]). However, the same argument applies as before. Unless mortality risk and cohort effects are correlated with the existence of living children, both subsamples are affected in the same manner and their relation will not be biased (cf. [85]). Finally, the data do not allow for a distinction between capital sum and term life insurance. While the latter is a valid indicator for a bequest motive, the former is a mere investment instrument – especially in Germany where, due to generous tax exemptions, capital sum life insurances compete with ordinary bonds. If, however, life insurances are purchased only because they bear more interest this applies to both households with and without children and one would not expect any difference in profiles. Consequently, deviations across profiles must be attributed to term insurances or equivalently to the desire of leaving a bequest to ones offspring.

For every year the SOEP reports the existence of life insurance holdings as well as children within the household. However, only two waves of the SOEP, namely the 1991 and 1996 cross-sections, contain an additional question on the existence of children living outside the household. These two waves were pooled in order to increase sample size. As a result the overall sample comprises 13,265 households, of which 9,634 have dependent or independent children, and 3,631 are childless. The outcome is displayed in Table 3.24, which, separately for households with and without children, gives the proportion of

[11] A small bias could arise in that singles are both less likely to have children and less likely to buy an insurance, which names a spouse or partner as accessory. The profiles would then be biased in favor of the bequest motive. We believe this bias to be small, however.

policyholders within a specific age class. Inspecting first the entire sample

Table 3.24. Life Insurance Holdings by Age, SOEP

Age[a]	Overall Sample	Households with Children[b]	Households without Children
		Percent[c]	
0–29	54.9	64.0	50.0
30–39	66.9	70.9	58.7
40–49	67.2	68.8	63.2
50–59	60.5	61.8	56.7
60–64	45.9	48.3	37.3
65–69	32.6	34.4	26.1
70–74	20.7	23.7	10.8
75–79	15.4	17.6	8.1
80+	10.5	10.2	11.0

Source: Socio-Economic Panel, Wave 8, 1991 and Wave 13, 1996.

[a] Age of household head.
[b] Dependent and independent children.
[c] The proportion of households with life insurance in the specified age bracket.

we find that the probability of holding life insurance, conditional on age, increases initially and peaks between age 40 and 49 to decreases monotonously thereafter. This hump-shaped pattern confirms what Fischer [101] has predicted. In particular, the need for life insurance is most pronounced in middle ages, when the loss of human capital would leave dependent family members without an income. Furthermore, German households appear to be very well endowed with life insurance by international standard. Among German households aged 40 to 49 the share of policyholders amounts to 67 percent, while, for example, in Italy only 20 percent hold life insurance in the corresponding age bracket (cf. [84]). This fact is certainly attributable to the specific role of life insurances in Germany. Thus, tax exemptions, as stated earlier, make the capital sum component of the insurance a profitable investment tool. Apart from the level, however, the German and Italian profiles exhibit a striking resemblance, with the peak occurring within the same age bracket.

Turning to the next two columns, we find that households with dependent children, commonly those aged 20 to 60, are more likely to hold life insurance than childless households of corresponding age. This does not come as a surprise, given that the loss of human capital is the worse the more dependents are affected. More relevant for the present context, however, is a comparison of the age-profiles after age 60, revealing the correlation between independent children and life insurance holdings. In fact, households with independent children are much more likely to hold life insurance than their childless counterparts. With the exception of the oldest old, we find a gap in the neighborhood of 10 percentage points for each of the considered age classes, indicating a significant concern for independent children. Whether this concern is driven by altruism or exchange, however, remains an unsolved issue.

Let us conclude this section by summarizing the main results. Where transfers *inter vivos* are concerned the SOEP confirms earlier findings on the basis of the EVS. In particular, the SOEP reinforces, that transfers *inter vivos* are fairly concentrated, positively related with donor's economic status, and in the majority of cases directed from old to young. In addition, by separately reporting transfers towards children, the SOEP reveals, that these transfers are especially frequent at periods, when children face particular needs. This can be interpreted as weak evidence in favor of altruism.

The SOEP provides further evidence on bequest patterns. Thus, we find that bequests are much more concentrated than transfers *inter vivos*, that real estate is the predominant form of bequests in Germany, and that, according to respondents' statements, precaution is the primary motive for holding wealth in old age. Finally, we find additional evidence for intended bequests, in that life insurance holdings vary considerably between households with and without independent children. Note, that these findings are subject to an important qualification, namely that the data sources consulted either explicitly or implicitly underreport transfers by the very well-to-do. Their share in overall bequeathed wealth, however, may be considerable. On the whole, we do not find any clear-cut evidence in favor of a specific transfer motive. Given the crude data sources and as varied a phenomenon as intergenerational transfers, this does not come as a surprise. For the following exposition this implies, that all outcomes have to be tested with respect to different transfer motives.

4. Private versus Public Transfers During a Demographic Transition

Intergenerational transfers, be they mediated by the government or the family, are to a great extent contingent on the age structure of the underlying population. In most western countries this age structure, owing to a decline in fertility and mortality, will change dramatically in the coming decades, and so will both public and private intergenerational transfers. It thus follows from pure logic that the size of flows will be affected as the relative number of transfer recipients and donors changes. For example, in face of population aging a pay-as-you-go pension system can guarantee constant pensions or constant contributions, but the constancy of both magnitudes is impractical. In the same manner it is possible that the overall resources bequeathed by parents to all of their children stay constant, or that the inheritance *per capita* received by each offspring remains unchanged. But it is not possible for both of these magnitudes to remain constant (cf. [102]). In the case of public intergenerational transfers the specific design of fiscal policy determines in which way transfers adjust and, as a consequence, benefits or burdens are spread among recipients and donors. In the case of private intergenerational transfers adjustment and distributive consequences hinge on the underlying transfer motives.

For quite a time, considerable research has been dedicated to the impact of population aging on public intergenerational transfers (cf. [103], [104], [105], [13]). In the early nineties this research was further boosted by the development of generational accounting, a tool to assess the long-run stance of fiscal policy and its implications for intergenerational distribution (cf. [106], [5], [107]). By assigning the government's overall budget to specific generations and taking into account the demographic development, generational accounting allows to quantify the fiscal burden left to future generations. Recent generational accounting studies for Germany find an overwhelming imbalance to the detriment of future generations. In fact, the most recent calculations by Besendorfer et al. [108] indicate that future generations will face a lifetime net tax burden that amounts to about 290 percent of what currently living generations pay into the public coffers. While part of this imbalance can be attributed to public debt, which has sharply risen in the aftermath of German unification, the lion's share is due to a pay-as-you-go social insurance system that has to cope with pronounced population aging.

Much less attention has been paid to the effects of population aging on private intergenerational transfers, probably due to the scarcity and poor quality of data related to these transfers.[1] What makes them so hard to observe is their variety of appearance. Thus, private intergenerational transfers can assume the form of bequests, in-kind services, interest-free loans, shared living arrangements or investment in the children's human capital. Notwithstanding these difficulties, the following chapter tries to complement our understanding of private intergenerational transfers in the course of demographic transition. In particular, we ask whether private intergenerational transfers might compensate future generations for the fiscal burden incurred on them. Given that private and public transfers run in opposite direction and provided that both are affected in the same manner by population aging, this is what we would expect.

The proceeding of the investigation is as follows. In the next section we will present facts and forecasts on population aging. In Section 4.2, we will by means of two demographic indicators illustrate, to which extent private and public intergenerational transfers are affected by population aging. As already mentioned, the distributive effects of private intergenerational transfers crucially depend on the underlying transfer motives. Section 4.3 will therefore discuss the implications of various transfer motives for the adjustment of private transfers during a demographic transition. Finally, in Section 4.4 we will extend the methodology of generational accounting to private intergenerational transfers. This method, apart from being especially suited for monitoring otherwise hard to observe transfers *inter vivos*, allows a direct comparison of the magnitude of public and private intergenerational transfers.

4.1 The Demographic Transition

In the not so far future Germany, like most other industrialized countries, will undergo a demographic change which is unprecedented in history and will dramatically increase the median age of the population. At the same time, the fraction of the population that is elderly will increase, the share of children will decline, and the population as a whole will shrink. The driving forces of population aging, as of any change in the structure or level of a population, are fertility, mortality, and net migration. These determinants will be considered in turn in order to identify past trends and make adequate assumption as to their future development, the latter being a prerequisite for projecting populations into the future.

Figure 4.1 presents the total fertility rate for West and East Germany from 1950 through 1997. The total fertility rate is defined as the average number of

[1] Noteworthy exceptions are Weil [109] and Ablett [12], with our exposition in Section 4.4.2 owing considerably to the latter.

children per woman, or, technically speaking, the sum of age-specific fertility rates summed up over all childbearing years (age 15 to 44). Until 1965 we

Fig. 4.1. Birth Rates for East and West Germany 1950 – 1997

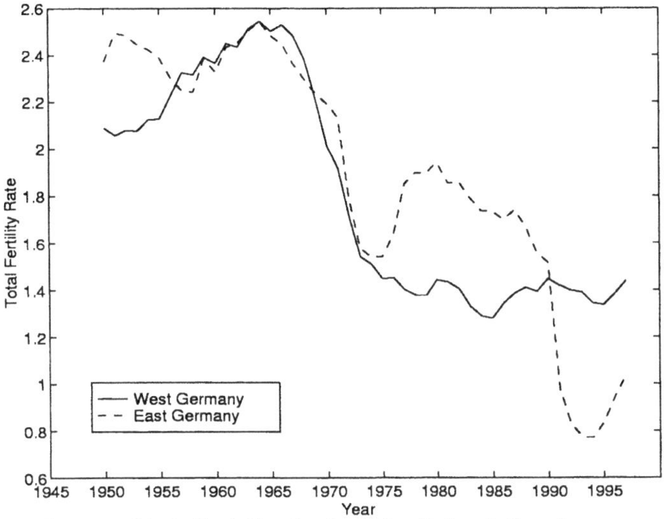

Source: Statistical Yearbook of the Federal Republic of Germany, Statistical Yearbook of the German Democratic Republic, several years. Notes: East German figures from 1950 through 1954 do not take into account East Berlin.

observe in both East and West Germany fertility rates well above the level necessary to sustains a constant population level, that is approximately 2.1. This baby-boom is followed by a sharp decline in the total fertility rate from about 2.5 in 1965 to 1.5 in 1975. While up to 1975 fertility rates in East and West Germany develop quite parallel, they diverge thereafter. In West Germany fertility remains on its all-time low until the present, with rates closely oscillating somewhere around 1.4. In contrast, in East Germany the baby-bust is followed by a renewed increase in fertility, if not to a level consistent with a constant population. Supposedly, the divergence in fertility across east and west to some extent owes to the fact that in the east from 1972 onward housing facilities were allocated according to family status and number of children. Eastern fertility, already since the 1980ies slightly falling, drops dramatically as the Wall comes down. By 1991 it falls below the western figure, reaching the bottom in 1994 at a value less than 0.8. Since then its trend is again increasing, though the level is still considerably below the western rate.[2]

The observed baby-boom is a large temporary rebound in a long-run trend of falling fertility. While falling fertility, by increasing the share of elderly, already requires considerable adjustments, the baby-boom renders the demographic transition particularly complicated. In that it produced cohorts which are larger than those both preceding and following, the share of elderly will, during a period of 20 years, be higher than ever experienced before and to be expected in the future.

In contrast to macroeconomic forecasts, there is no quantifiable theory to base our fertility projections upon. However, given that there has been no trend in western fertility during the last 25 years, it is most straightforward to assume that western fertility will remain at its post-1975 level. With respect to eastern fertility it seems most probable that there will be an adjustment to western levels as living conditions converge. Next, consider Figure 4.2, which

Fig. 4.2. Life Expectancy at Birth 1970 – 1995, FRG

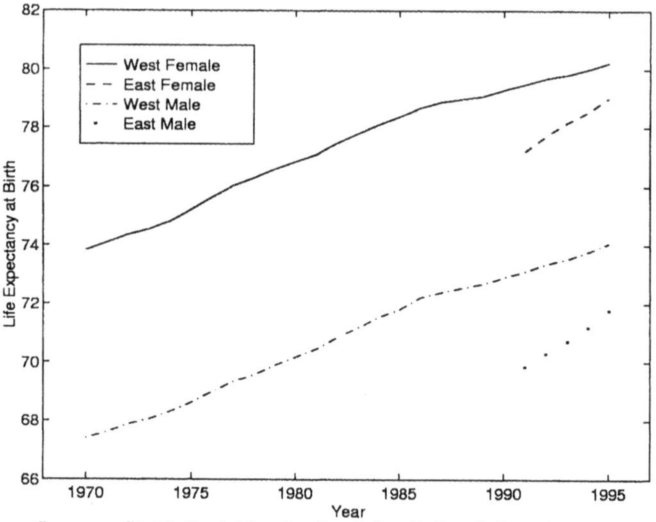

Source: Statistical Yearbook of the Federal Republic of Germany (FRG), several years.

shows the development of life expectancy at birth from 1970 to 1995. The gender-specific figures refer to the Federal Republic of Germany and are since

[2] To some extend this movement can be explained by an increase in the eastern proliferation age to western levels. Such a shift, although in the long-run compatible with identical birth rates, will in the short-run lead to a drop below the western fertility level.

1992 reported separately for old and new German *Länder*. First note, that life expectancy was considerably lower in the German Democratic Republic than in the Federal Republic of Germany. Thus, in 1992 female (male) life expectancy in the eastern part of Germany still amounted to mere 77.2 (69.9) years as compared to 79.5 (73.1) years in the west. As indicated by Figure 4.2, however, life expectancy will converge, as those people spending most of their life under the unfavorable conditions of the eastern state will pass away.

We next observe a pronounced upward trend, with both male and female life expectancy increasing by more than 6 years within the last 25 years. The beginning of this increase in life expectancy can be dated back to the 19. Century and is attributable to an improvement in hygienic circumstances and medical care. Thus, female (male) life expectancy amounted to 38.5 (35.6) years in 1875, 48.3 (44.8) years in 1905, and 62.8 (59.9) years in 1933 (cf. [110], [111], [112]). While the early improvements in life expectancy are due to a reduction in infant mortality, the recent development is increasingly the result of a rise in old-age life expectancy (cf. [102]). In addition to falling fertility, which results in a declining number of children, this increase in longevity, raises the number of elderly. It is for this reason that some authors have referred to the demographic transition as a "double aging process" (cf. [113]).

It is almost impossible to make sensible forecasts as to the development of future life expectancy. In particular, it is far from clear, whether life expectancy will due to advances in medical technology continue to rise or will soon have reached its intrinsic biological limit. Notwithstanding these problems, one may proceed by international comparison. In particular, the figures of countries with higher life expectancy could serve as target figures for Germany, assuming that those countries' favorable conditions are attainable in the not so distant future (cf. [114]). To give an example, in Japan, the country with the most favorable figures worldwide, female (male) life expectancy amounts to 83.0 (76.6) years in 1994 as compared to 79.7 (73.3) years in unified Germany (cf. [115]).

Immigration is the third and final determinant of a population's size and structure. Figure 4.3 plots total net immigration as well as net immigration of Germans, both by law and ethnic origin, for the period 1952 through 1998. Obviously, net migration varies considerably, ranging from net emigration of more than 200,000 in 1975 to net immigration of almost 800,000 in 1992. These rather erratic movements of the migration flow make it hard to project. Roughly speaking, two main factors seem to be decisive for migration: Germany's economic status relative to the rest of the world and migration policy. Since Germany is likely to remain one of the world's richest countries in the foreseeable future, immigration pressure will not cease to exist. Policy, by limiting the number of incomers, will therefore most likely become the principal determinant of prospective immigration. In contrast to fertility and mortality, migration works against an aging of the German population. To see this,

Fig. 4.3. Net Immigration 1952 – 1998, FRG

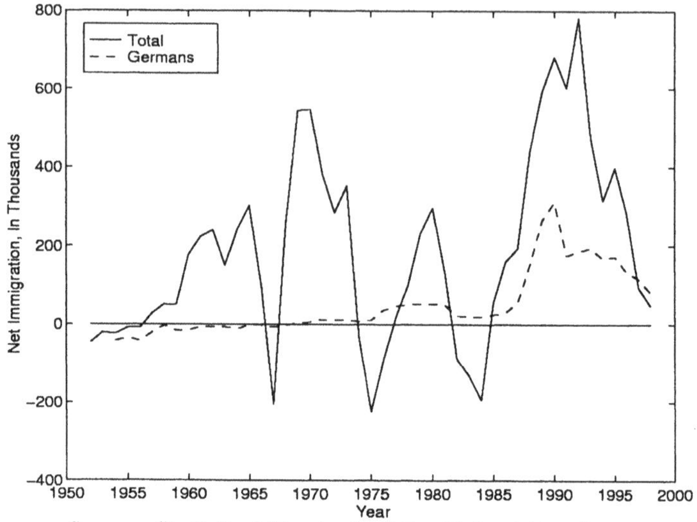

Source: Statistical Yearbook of the Federal Republic of Germany (FRG), several years. Notes: Until 1957 the Federal Republic of Germany does not include the Saarland. Separate figures for foreigners and Germans are only available since 1954.

take a look at Figure 4.4, which shows the age structure of immigrants as well as of the German population – inclusive of foreigners permanently residing in Germany – in 1995. We find that relative to the German population immigrants are overrepresented until age 26 and underrepresented thereafter, owing to a higher mobility in early stages of the life-cycle. A liberal immigration policy, aiming at young and qualified individuals, might therefore help to ease the problems related to population aging (cf. [116]). Unfortunately, the median age of the population can only be reduced at the cost of greatly increasing the size of the population and, as a consequence, the difficulties associated with integration and congestion (cf. [102]). This trade-off is illustrated in Table 4.1, which reports the population's size and age structure in 2040 under alternative immigration scenarios. In particular, we vary the level of immigrating non-Germans while holding constant their 1995 age and gender composition.[3] Non-Germans' net immigration is assumed to start from 277,000 in 1995, reach the value reported in the first column of Table 4.1 by 2000, and stay constant thereafter. Furthermore, immigrant's fertility equals

[3] Since ethnic Germans from eastern Europe are, by order of the constitution, guaranteed German citizenship, they are not subject to any immigration policy. The number of immigrating ethnic Germans is therefore unaffected by the experiment.

Fig. 4.4. Age Structure of Population and Immigration Flow 1995

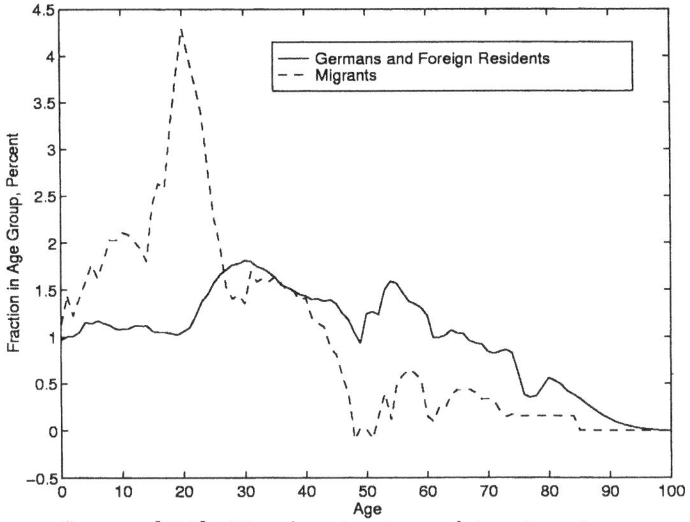

Source: [119]. The Age-structure of immigrants was provided by the Federal Statistical Office.

that of foreigners permanently residing in Germany (1.6), while mortality does not vary across immigrants, Germans and permanent residents. The remaining assumptions underlying the population projection will be discussed in due course. Turning to the results, one finds that increasing the number

Table 4.1. The Trade-Off Between Population Size and Structure

Annual Net Immigration In Thousands	Population in 2040 In Millions	Fraction of People Aged 0–19 in 2040 Percent	Fraction of People Aged 65+ in 2040 Percent
0	62.9	15.4	30.8
200	73.7	16.9	27.5
400	84.4	18.1	25.0
600	95.2	19.0	23.1
800	105.9	19.7	21.6

Source: Author's Calculations.

of foreign immigrants from 0 to 200,000, raises the size of the population by more than 17 percent, while the fraction of people being 65 and older is only reduced from 30.8 to 27.5 percent. Next, consider an increase in immigration from 200,000 to 800,000, the former being the average amount of immigrants between 1950 and 1998 and the latter amounting to 1 percent of the current German population, that is an immigration quota experienced by the classical immigration country USA during its peak decade of 1901-1910. While this policy leads to an increase in population by almost 44 percent, the share of elderly is only reduced from 27.5 to 21.6 percent. Given that the share of elderly at present amounts to approximately 15 percent, it becomes clear that even drastic measures such as quotas of 1 percent are not capable of significantly alleviating the demographic transition.

We can summarize that immigration is not a particularly efficient instrument for tackling the problem of population aging. Taking into account the cost of greatly increasing a population's size, it therefore seems most improbable, that immigration policy will have a significant impact on population dynamics. Nevertheless, in what follows we will at times test the sensitivity of outcomes with respect to alternative migration assumptions. So far we have

Table 4.2. Mortality and Fertility for Six OECD Countries

	Female Life Expectancy[a]		Total Fertility Rate[b]	
	1950	1995	1950	1995
France	68.5	81.6	2.9	1.7
Germany	68.5	78.7	2.1	1.4
Italy	67.2	80.4	2.6	1.3
Japan	67.8[c]	83.0[d]	2.4	1.5[e]
UK	71.2	79.3	3.0	1.7
USA	71.3	79.3	2.2	2.1[f]

Sources: Federal Statistical Office [117], OECD [105], Raffelhüschen [118].

[a] Female Life Expectancy at birth in years.
[b] The sum of age-specific fertility rates over child-bearing years.
[c] 1955
[d] 1994
[e] 1990/95 average
[f] 1990/95 average

discussed the determinants of population aging in Germany. Before turning to the assumptions underlying the German population projection, however, we will briefly review evidence for other countries. It is important to recognize – especially when contemplating, whether to model the demographic transition in a partial or general equilibrium setting – that population aging is a phenomenon experienced around the world, and especially pronounced in the industrialized countries. To see this consider Table 4.2, which reports for six OECD countries life expectancy and total fertility for the years 1950 and 1995. Obviously, all of the countries under inspection experience a decline in mortality and fertility, if at different degrees. While the changes are most dramatic for Italy and Japan, population aging is less pronounced in the United Kingdom and the United States. Germany, with an absolute increase in life expectancy of about 10 years and an absolute decline in fertility of 0.7 lies somewhere in the middle. We next turn to the age and gender structure

Fig. 4.5. Age Composition of the German Population in 1995

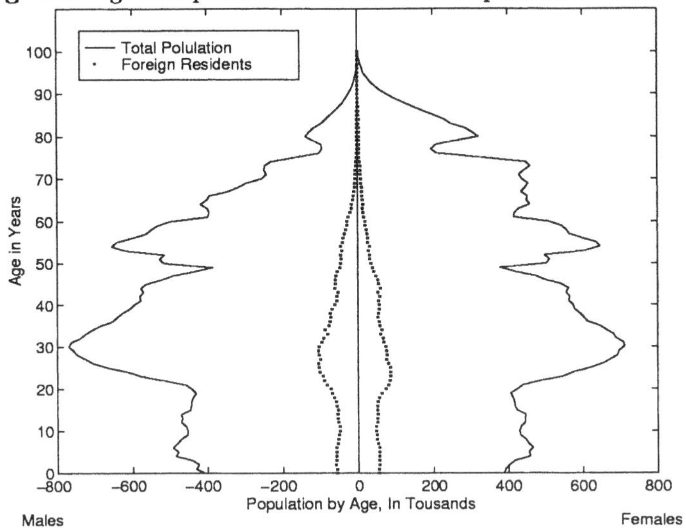

Source: [119].

of the German population in 1995, which serves as a starting point for our population projection. Figure 4.5 reports female cohort size to the right and male cohort size to the left of the zero axis, where the share of foreign permanent residents is marked by the doted line. First, females are more numerous in old age, owing to both higher life expectancy and World War II. One can further make out the consequences of the baby-boom and baby-bust as manifested in relatively strong working-age cohorts and relatively weak cohorts of age 20 and below. With respect to foreign residents, we observe a peak between age 20 and 30. Note, that due to immigration patterns and higher fertility the median age of foreign residents is considerably lower than that of Germans.

Although our knowledge as to the prospective development of future flows, namely fertility, mortality, and migration, is very limited, rather reliable population forecast are possible solely on the basis of the present population structure. We can, for example, anticipate quite well the number of retirees over the next 65 years, given that they are already born and therefore unaffected by future fertility. In the same manner, we can foresee the size of working-year cohorts over the next 20 years. While mortality and migration will also affect those cohorts' size, their order of magnitude is not sufficient to cover the traces left by baby-boom and baby-bust in the present population structure.

In projecting future fertility, mortality, and net migration we closely follow the assumptions of the Federal Statistical Office (cf. [120]).[4] Specifically, male (female) life expectancy at birth is assumed to increases from 72.2 (78.7) years in 1995 to 74.7 (81.1) years in 2005 and to remain constant thereafter.[5] Fertility varies across the three distinct subpopulations of West Germans, East Germans, and foreigners. Thus, western gross fertility stays constant at 1.36, while eastern fertility reaches that level in 2005 having started at 0.78 in 1995. Resident and immigrating foreigners' fertility is assumed to remain at its 1995 level of 1.6. Finally, net migration of non-Germans decreases from 420,000 in 1995 to a constant 200,000 *p.a.* from the year 2000 onward. Immigration of ethnic Germans from eastern Europe is supposed to phase out by 2010. The aging process implied by this baseline projection is illustrated

Table 4.3. Demographic Indicators for Germany 1995 – 2060

	1995	2020	2030	2040	2050	2060
Median Age	38	45	46	47	48	47
Percent Aged 0-19	21.6	18.4	17.5	17.1	16.9	17.0
Percent Aged 65+	15.3	19.8	22.5	27.2	26.9	26.7
Pop. Aged 85+ (million)	1.4	1.9	2.4	2.2	2.7	3.1

Source: Author's Calculations.

[4] We further had access to the population projection program underlying Bonin et al. [141].

[5] As 1995 value we employ the life expectancy calculated from the complete life table 1986/88 (cf. [122]). It therefore deviates from the figure calculated on the basis of the 1994/96 abridged life table, that is 79.7 years for females and 73.3 years for males (cf. [115]). However, in that life expectancy is assumed to increase until 2005 anyway, the deviation is negligible. Further note, that the Statistical Office's forecast of life expectancy is rather conservative. In its subsequent population projection, which is not yet published, the Federal Statistical Office assumes that female (male) life expectancy at birth increases to 84 (77) years by 2035 and to 85 (78) years by 2050 (cf. [123]).

in Table 4.3 by means of some common demographic indicators. First, consider the evolution of the population's median age. Amounting to 38 years in 1995 this indicator increases steadily reaching its peak in 2050 at 48 years. During the same period the fraction of the population aged 0 to 19 drops to its all-time low of 16.9 percent, having started at 21.6 percent in 1995. In contrast, the share of elderly, those aged 65 and older, peaks in 2040. By that time it will have increased from 15.3 to 27.2 percent. Finally, the absolute number of people being 85 years and older more than doubles, raising from 1.4 million in 1995 to 3.1 million by 2060. As should have become clear by now, the extent of the demographic transition is dramatic and will have profound consequences for intergenerational relations. We will turn to these consequences in what follows.

4.2 What Demographics Reveal About Public and Private Transfers

Demographics have a great influence on both public and private intergenerational transfers. Thus, for a pay-as-you-go Social Security scheme, an aging population implies increasing contribution rates for the young, unless the entire burden is passed on to pensioners. On the other hand, it is likely that young generations benefit from the demographic transition in the form of increased inheritances, as a bequest is shared by fewer offspring. Of course, the latter only holds if an adjustment in the overall bequest does not offset the increase in *per capita* inheritances. For the major bequest motives, however, this is not the case, as will be shown in Section 4.3.

A common indicator to illustrate the increase in contribution rates or, generally speaking, the financial strain of the Social Security system, is the old-age dependency ratio. This is defined as the number of people in a population above age 64 divided by the number of people aged 20 to 64. Accordingly, it depicts the number of public transfer recipients relative to the number of public transfer payers. In the same manner, one can calculate the ratio of private transfer payers to private transfer recipients. This ratio, when observed over time, could serve as an indicator for the increase in private intergenerational transfers.

Due to German data limitations on transfers *inter vivos*, the paper, for the moment, focuses on bequests. The number of prospective testators is calculated by multiplying the population structure of future years with age-gender-specific mortality rates. In order to derive the number of prospective heirs we can make use of our findings on bequest patterns as presented in Section 3.2.2. Recall that respondents of the Socio-Economic Panel (SOEP) were asked, whether they had received an inheritance between 1960 and 1988 and, in case they had, when the inheritance occurred. From this we were able to calculate the probability of receiving an inheritance contingent on a specific age. Furthermore, the SOEP provided information on the respondent's

Fig. 4.6. Age-Specific Fertility Rates 1950 – 1995, FRG

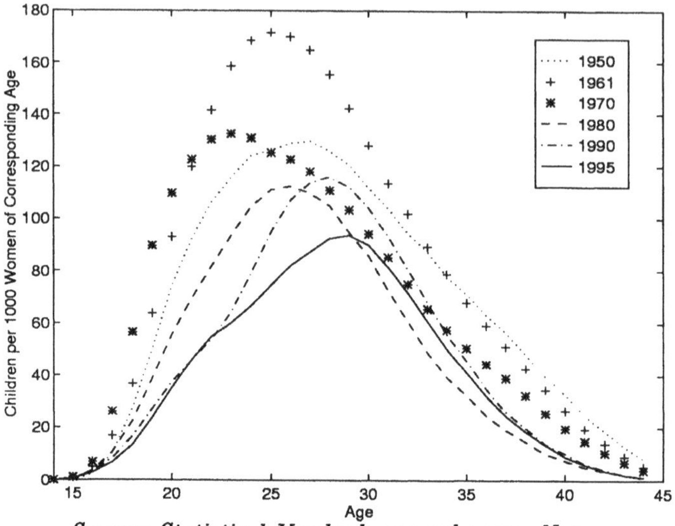

Source: Statistical Yearbook, several years. Notes: In 1950 without Berlin West and the Saarland. In 1995 for Unified Germany.

marital status, allowing us to separate interspousal from intergenerational bequests (cf. Table 3.18). We can, thus, obtain the number of prospective heirs by multiplying the age-specific probability of receiving an inter-generational inheritance with the population structure of future years.

By proceeding in this manner we, of course, abstract from the fact that population aging, in addition to changing the size of inheritances, also changes the timing of the receipt. In particular, the average age at which an inheritance is received will raise as longevity increases. Thus, Wolf [124] has shown on the basis of a simulation that a 5 percent increase in life expectancy increases the fraction of the population aged 55-59 that has a living mother from 32 to 44 percent. Applying probabilities which correspond to the period 1960 to 1988 will therefore introduce a bias. We believe this bias to be small, however, especially when taking into account that also the proliferation age has increased. This can be seen in Figure 4.6, which shows age-specific fertility rates for selected years between 1950 and 1995. While there is no pattern identifiable in the immediate post-war period, the age at which proliferation peaks increases steadily since 1970. Although there certainly is a biological limit to this development, it might continue into the future. A parallel movement of life expectancy and proliferation age would leave unaffected the average age, at which inheritances are received. One is now in the position to calculate what could be called an inheritance index, the ratio of testators to heirs. In Figure 4.7 the development of this index is contrasted to the prospec-

Fig. 4.7. Old-Age Dependency Ratio and Inheritance Index

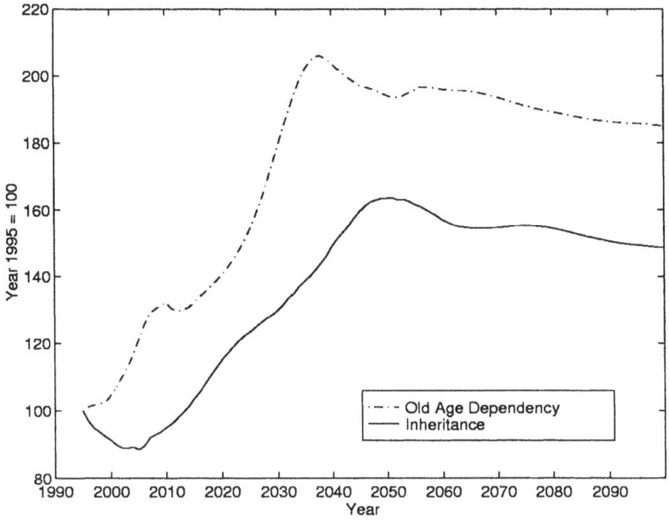

tive evolution of the old-age dependency ratio over the next century. In order to make the indices comparable, they were expressed relative to their base year values. First, consider the old-age dependency ratio which, from 1995 onward, increases steadily until it reaches a maximum around 2035. At that time, the ratio will have doubled, which means that the number of workers supporting a pensioner will have been cut half. A great deal of this pattern can be understood in light of past fluctuations in fertility, namely the baby-boom which lasted from 1945 to 1965 and was followed by a pronounced baby-bust. As the baby-boomers reach retirement age and the baby-busters enter the work force, the dependency ratio is bound to increase. Moreover, the ratio will peak when the last baby-boomer has reached retirement age, which will be in the thirties of the next century.

Now consider the inheritance index. Apparently, the ratio of testators to heirs is subject to the same driving forces as the ratio of pensioners to workers. In contrast to the dependency ratio, however, the inheritance index decreases initially. Furthermore, it lags behind the dependency ratio and peaks at a somewhat lower level. The observed pattern can be interpreted as follows. The initial decrease in the index is due to the mentioned increase in life expectancy which causes fewer deaths and bequests up to year 2005. The rightward shift of the inheritance index hinges on the fact that bequests on average occur 15 years after retirement. Note, that this time span corresponds to the vertical distance between dependency ratio and inheritance index.

Finally, inspect the indices' nominator and denominator to understand, why their maxima fall apart. While workers and pensioners belong to different generations, the cohorts of heirs and testators overlap. In particular, about 30 percent of all deceased are 75 and younger and, hence, belong to the same cohort as potential heirs. Consequently, the variation of the inheritance index must be smaller relative to the dependency ratio as baby-boomers work their way through the age distribution.

The findings up to now can be summed up as follows. While young generations might be compensated for rising contribution rates by increased inheritances, this does not occur until the year 2010. It should further be kept in mind that the compensation lags behind significantly, which could be a severe problem in view of liquidity constraints. At last, one should take into account that the compensation is only partial, since burdened and compensated generations are not necessary congruent.

4.3 The Impact of the Transfer Motive

Up to now, we have implicitly assumed that young generations are to bear the fiscal burden in form of increased contribution rates, but at the same time, also profit from the declining number of heirs via higher inheritances *per capita*. The first assumption seems warranted given that the German pay-as-you-go pension system is a defined benefit scheme with a guaranteed pension level and contribution rates determined endogenously in order to meet the system's annual budget constraint. In fact, the German Supreme Court has declared pension entitlements as equivalent to property rights (cf. [125]). Furthermore, an unanticipated loss in resources will more severely hit the elderly than the young, given that they have a shorter remaining lifespan over which to spread the drop in consumption. This, of course, makes it more probable that the young will have to shoulder the major burden of the fiscal adjustment.

The assumption that young generations will profit from the decline in the number of heirs is less straightforward. In particular, it is also imaginable that testator generations will appropriate the windfall gain by increasing own lifetime consumption and holding constant their offspring' inheritances *per capita*. A priori this question can only be answered in the light of the common transfer models. In what follows, we will therefore investigate what a declining number of offspring implies for the size of the inheritance *per capita* according to the transfer motives introduced in Chapter 2.[6] Subsequently, some empirical evidence will be discussed.

Altruistic transfers

In analyzing the impact of the number of children on the inheritance received by each child, we have to decide in which way children's utility enters parent's

[6] For a formal treatment please refer to Appendix A.3.

utility. Thus, parent's utility can depend on the *per capita* utility of their children or on the sum of their children's utility. These cases will be discussed in turn. First imagine, that the parent derives utility from the *per capita* utility of his offspring, implicitly assuming that all offspring are identical. If, furthermore, n denotes the population growth rate and I the inheritance *per capita*, the parent's maximization problem can be stated as follows:

$$\max_{c_t, c_{t+1}} \; u_t(c_t, u_{t+1}(c_{t+1}))$$

$$\text{s.t.} \quad c_t = w_t - (1+n)\,I \tag{4.1}$$

$$c_{t+1} = (1+r)\,I \tag{4.2}$$

$$I \geq 0\,. \tag{4.3}$$

Let us further assume, that the non-negativity constraint is not binding and u_t additive separable in its arguments with $\partial u_t / \partial u_{t+1} = \psi > 0$. The problem's first order condition then reads:

$$(1+n)\frac{\partial u_t}{\partial c_t}(c_t) = \psi(1+r)\frac{\partial u_{t+1}}{\partial c_{t+1}}(c_{t+1})\,. \tag{4.4}$$

The left hand side of Equation (4.4) stands for the marginal cost of making a bequest in form of forgone own consumption. The right hand side denotes the marginal benefit resulting from an increase in children's consumption. While the right hand side of Equation (4.4) is unaffected by a decline in the population growth rate n, the left hand side is affected in two ways. For one thing, parents need give up less consumption in order to provide a marginal unit of inheritance per child, when the number of children decreases. This is reflected in a decline of the first term. For another thing, the utility loss per unit of inheritance becomes smaller, given that parents consume more and marginal utility decreases in consumption. This can be seen, when Equation (4.1) is inserted into the left hand side of Equation (4.4). A shrinking number of children therefore reduces the marginal cost of bequeathing, and as a consequence, induces parents to increase their children's inheritances, $\partial I / \partial n < 0$.

Next, consider the case where the sum of children's utility enters the parent's utility function, as proposed, for example, by Blinder [50] and Drazen [21]. In this variant the parent's utility function reads $u_t(c_t, (1+n)u_{t+1}(c_{t+1}))$ and the first order condition reduces to

$$\frac{\partial u_t}{\partial c_t}(c_t) = \psi(1+r)\frac{\partial u_{t+1}}{\partial c_{t+1}}(c_{t+1})\,. \tag{4.5}$$

As before, a decline in the population growth rate will increase parental consumption according to Equation (4.1) and, as a consequence, reduce the marginal loss associated with an increase in I. We therefore get $\partial I / \partial n < 0$, leaving our previous results unchanged. Thus, assuming altruistic parents, population aging will result in higher inheritances per child, this way compensating young generations – at least partly – for the fiscal burdens associated with population aging.

An even stronger case can be made in favor of altruistic parents compensating their children when resorting to Ricardian Neutrality. Recall from Section 2.1 and Appendix A.1 that any government redistribution across generations is offset one-by-one via private transfers in the opposite direction, provided altruism is operational. According to this line of reasoning, population aging would have no impact whatsoever on intergenerational distribution. However, in light of the empirical findings by Altonji et al. [69, 70] it seems highly questionable, whether the extended family, let alone a whole country, can be modeled as a single representative individual with an infinite horizon. We therefore content ourselves with the fact that altruistic individuals increase inheritances per child as the number of children declines.

Transfers for Joy-of-Giving

In investigating the impact of family size on the size of inheritances under the joy-of-giving hypothesis, we have to make a similar distinction as earlier, namely whether the inheritance *per capita* or the overall bequest enter the parent's utility function. Let us begin with the first option. Assuming, as usual, a well-behaved utility function, the parent's maximization problem can be expressed as

$$\max_{c_t, I} \; u_t(c_t, I)$$
$$\text{s.t.} \quad c_t = w_t - (1+n)I \; . \tag{4.6}$$

Obviously, a decline in the number of children corresponds to a reduction in the price of inheritances, with both income and substitution effect working towards an increase in the inheritances *per capita*, $\partial I/\partial n < 0$.

Let us next consider, whether the result carries over to a situation, where parents are only concerned about the overall bequest left to their children, b. In this case the parent's maximization problem reads

$$\max_{c_t, b} \; u_t(c_t, b)$$
$$\text{s.t.} \quad c_t = w_t - b \; . \tag{4.7}$$

and is obviously independent of the number of children, as is the Marshall demand function for bequests, $\partial b/\partial n = 0$. Further taking into account that $b = (1+n)I$ yields $\partial I/\partial n = -b/(1+n)^2 < 0$ and, thus, corresponds to the previous finding on joy-of-giving transfers. Also note the analogy between altruism and joy-of-giving with respect to their qualitative implications. This analogy was already mentioned in Section 2.4 and will be exploited in the further course of this investigation.

Transfers-as-Exchange

In order to examine, how parents making exchange motivated transfers react to a decline in fertility, we add a further assumption to the model introduced in Section 2.3. In particular, we assume that parents consider the services provided by each of their (identical) children, a, as perfect substitutes. As a consequence, they are only interested in the overall amount of services $(1+n)a$ and not, who provides them. The parent's maximization problem can then be stated as

$$\max_{c_t,a} \; u_t(c_t,(1+n)\,a)$$

$$\text{s.t.} \quad c_t = w_t - (1+n)I \tag{4.8}$$

$$u_{t+1}((1-a)w_{t+1} + I) \geq u_{t+1}(w_{t+1}) \tag{4.9}$$

$$0 \leq a \leq 1\,. \tag{4.10}$$

As before we assume that the non-negativity constraint (4.10) is not binding and Equation (4.9) holds with strict equality. We have seen earlier that, in this case, Equation (4.9) can be replaced by $I = w_{t+1}a$ (cf. page 13). Substituting this relation into Equation (4.8), the maximization problem reduces to

$$\max_{c_t,a} \; u_t(c_t,(1+n)\,a)$$

$$\text{s.t.} \quad c_t + w_{t+1}(1+n)\,a = w_t \tag{4.11}$$

$$0 \leq a \leq 1\,. \tag{4.12}$$

Finally, denoting the amount of overall attention $(1+n)a$ by A, it becomes clear that the parent's choice of overall attention does not depend on the number of children. It, thus, follows from $\partial A/\partial n = 0$ and $A = (1+n)a$ that $\partial a/\partial n = -A/(1+n)^2 < 0$. According to $I = w_{t+1}a(n)$ inheritances *per capita* therefore depend inversely on the number of offspring. The intuition is that parents, wishing a specific level of attention, have to 'purchase' more attention per child, as the number of children decreases. Consequently, they have to increase inheritances *per capita*. Finally, note the correspondence between the exchange model and the joy-of-giving model with overall bequests entering the parent's utility function. In accordance with the latter model overall bequests in the exchange model, $b = I(1+n) = w_{t+1}a(1+n)$, are not affected by a variation in the number of children.

While the pure exchange model yields rather strong implications as to the impact of fertility on the size of inheritances, the model of strategic exchange remains vague in this respect. Bernheim et al. [39] conclude that declining population growth, by increasing the number of single-child families, will deprive parents of the opportunity to play children off against each other and, thus, depress strategic bequests. On the other hand, Weil [126] and Disney [127], chapter 8 stress that a reduction in the number of children, by weakening the threat to disinherit any one heir, will increase the price for attention.

Given an inelastic demand for attention this would lead to an increase in inheritances. In our opinion, the strategic bequest model does not permit vigorous conclusions as regards the effect of family size. The author's verdicts therefore remain *ad hoc* and inconclusive.

Accidental Bequests

Accidental bequests, by definition, are not affected by the number of heirs. Consequently, inheritances *per capita* are bound to increase as the number of heirs decreases.

We can summarize the results as follows. All of the discussed transfer models suggest that children will – at least partly – profit from a decline in the population growth rate throught higher inheritances *per capita*. In addition, three models, namely the joy-of-giving model (with respect to overall bequests), the exchange model, and the accidental bequest model predict that parents do not even adjust overall bequests as the number of children decreases. This implies that the decline in heirs translates one-by-one into increased inheritances *per capita*. In our analysis, we have not taken into account the cost of raising children and, consequently, have abstracted from the fact that parental saving will increase as the number of children decreases (cf. [128]). However, since this effect, if anything, reinforces our initial point, it can be safely ignored.

Our theoretical findings on the relation between fertility and inheritance are confirmed by empirical evidence. To our knowledge, all studies on the subject find concurrently that the transfer received by each child decreases with

Table 4.4. Overall Transfers by Donor's Number of Children, SOEP

Number of Independent Children	Average Transfer Amount[a] DM	Average Transfer Amount per Recipient DM	Number of Cases
1	5,871	5,871	290
2	6,047	3,024	291
3	6,753	2,251	104
4	3,889	972	38
5	5,095	1,019	9

Source: Socio-Economic Panel, Wave 8, 1991 and Wave 13, 1996.

[a] In 1996 prices and adjusted for productivity growth, if transfers occurred in 1991.

the number of siblings (cf. [129], [56], [128], [62], [58], [65]). This is further strengthened, when consulting data from the German Socio-Economic Panel (SOEP). In the Panel's 1991 and 1996 waves respondents were questioned about the number of independent children. In addition, those waves included the common question about the amount of money transferred to children living outside the household. Thus, it was possible to calculate average transfer amounts, contingent on the number of independent children. In order to increase sample size the observations of the two waves were pooled and transfer amounts from 1991 adjusted for productivity growth and expressed in 1996 prices. Consequently, the sample included 13,047 households, of which 738 reported transfers to their children. The results are displayed in Table 4.4. Considering first the overall transfer amount given by parents to all of their children, we can not identify any meaningful pattern regarding the number of children. Next, assume that parents on average give equal amounts to all of their children, which permits us to calculate the average amount received by each child. This amount, as is shown in column two, clearly decreases with the number of children. Of course, equal sharing is a strong assumption, openly at odds with the altruistic model. We therefore review further evidence based directly on the amount received and the number of siblings. Recall that respondents were asked in the Panel's 1988 wave, whether they had received at least one inheritance in the period 1966 through 1988 and, if this was the case, what the amount was. Moreover, in 1991 and 1996 respondents were questioned about the number of siblings. We identified all individuals that

Table 4.5. Received Inheritance by Number of Siblings, SOEP

Number of Siblings[a]	Average Inheritance Received[b] DM	Number of Cases
0	132,552	136
1	102,722	122
2	109,609	68
3	88,944	37
4	71,721	21

Source: Socio-Economic Panel, Wave 5, 1988, Wave 8, 1991, and Wave 13, 1996.

[a] The household head is the unit of reference.
[b] If the household received several inheritances within the period under consideration, the mean amount and year of receipt are taken. Furthermore, bequests that occurred before 1988 are adjusted for inflation and productivity growth.

both reported having received an inheritance and gave the number of siblings, amounting to a sample of 407 households.[7] If the household received several inheritances within the period under consideration, the mean amount and year of receipt were taken. Furthermore, bequests that occurred before 1988 were adjusted for inflation and productivity growth. Table 4.5 reports the average inheritance grouped according to the heir's number of siblings.

Apart from a slight outlier in the case of two-child families, we observe an monotonous decline in received inheritances as the number of siblings increases. In view of the empirical evidence as well as the theoretical considerations, we can therefore proceed on the conjecture that young generations will profit from an increase in inheritances as population ages.

4.4 A Generational Accounting Approach

In the following section we will investigate private transfers by means of generational accounting. This tool allows us to answer two questions of mayor interest. First, what is the volume of private intergenerational transfers relative to the magnitude of public intergenerational transfers. Second, might private transfers to young generations make up for the fiscal burdens imposed on them. In addressing these questions one has to define young and old generations. In principle, this definition is arbitrary in generational accounting. One could, for example, define all individuals of age 65 and beyond as old and all individuals of age 64 and less, inclusive all individuals yet unborn, as young. Generational accounting then reveals the distribution between those two groups of generations. In conventional generational accounting, however, the age separating young and old is much lower. In effect, it has become standard to compare all generations presently alive to generations born in the future. We will stick to this definition in what follows. It should further be stressed that generational accounting in addressing the question of intergenerational distribution starts from the assumptions specified above. In particular, future generations are assumed to bear the entire burden of today's fiscal policy but, at the same time, also reap off the complete windfall gain induced by a declining number of heirs.

4.4.1 Conventional Generational Accounting

Generational accounting was introduced by Auerbach et al. [5] in 1991 and since then, with slight modifications, has been applied to a wide array of problems and countries (e.g. [130], [131], [118]). In the following methodological exposition we draw on Auerbach et al. [5], Boll [132], and Raffelhüschen [133].

---

[7] With respect to the latter question we first checked the 1991 wave. In case the individual did not answer the question in this wave, we checked the 1996 wave.

Methodology

The starting point of generational accounting is the government's intertemporal budget constraint as stated in Equation (4.13):

$$\sum_{s=t}^{\infty} G_s(1+r)^{t-s} = W_t^{g} + \sum_{s=0}^{D} N_{t,t-s} + \sum_{s=1}^{\infty} N_{t,t+s} \,. \tag{4.13}$$

The term on the left-hand side discounts and adds up projected government spending for every future period s, G_s. The streams are discounted to the base year t at a pre-tax real interest rate, r. This present value of government spending is financed out of three sources: 1) public net wealth, 2) net taxes projected to be paid by living generations, and 3) net taxes paid by future generations, where a generation is defined as all people born in the same year. In Equation (4.13), W_t^{g} represents government net wealth in the base period, t. $N_{t,k}$ stands for the present value of net taxes, that is taxes minus transfers, to be paid by all individuals born in year k. Furthermore, D denotes the maximum age of an individual. The second term on the right-hand side of Equation (4.13) then depicts the present value of net taxes to be paid by all generations alive in base year t. Analogously, the third term on the right-hand side represents the net taxes paid by all generations born after the base year.[8]

The intertemporal budget constraint communicates a hard message: a policy change that alters one of these components must be accompanied by a corresponding change in one or more of the other terms to finance the initial change. For example, a reduction in living generation's projected net tax payments must be accompanied either by a reduction in the present value of government spending, or an increase in the present value of net taxes paid by future generations, or both. Government net worth is given in the base period t and usually cannot be altered through a change in policy.

The principle idea of generational accounting is as follows. The term on the left-hand side and the first two terms on the right-hand side of Equation (4.13) can be numerically specified, as will be outlined in detail below. As a consequence, Equation (4.13) can be solved for the last term on the right-hand side. This term represents the total payment in time t present

[8] At times, annual flows of government spending G_s have been treated as in-cash transfers towards the private sector (cf. [134] and [133]). As a consequence, the first term in Equation (4.13) is dropped and government spending, instead, included in the net taxes of living and future generations. This approach considers net taxes (or generational accounts) as welfare indicator. In that individuals derive utility from public goods, their monetary equivalent should, consequently, be included in net taxes. In the present study, however, we stick to the traditional approach, which restricts net taxes to purely monetary transfers between the public and private sector (the boundaries are somewhat blurred in the case of health care expenditure). In the context at hand net taxes serve to infer the volume of private intergenerational transfers. As public goods, by definition, are not transferred privately, they are not included in net taxes.

value that future generations have to make if the intertemporal budget constraint is to hold. Stated differently, this term represents the part of public burden, that is not covered by government wealth or payed for by living generations. It thus has to be financed by future generations.

In what follows, we will describe in more detail, how each term in Equation (4.13) is numerically specified. Government spending, as already mentioned, comprises all expenditures for the provision of public goods. Correspondingly, we also include education expenditure for the provision of schools or universities, in contrast to, e.g. Franco et al. [135], who consider it a part of net taxes. Government spending of future periods is inferred from spending in the base year by assuming that spending *per capita* grows according to productivity with a constant rate g. This assumption is not considered to describe actual fiscal policy in the future, rather it is a thought-experiment: What we are interested in, is the distribution of the public burden, if prevailing policies are not altered. Due to discounting, government spending 200 years from now is negligible. The first term therefore becomes a finite sum. As already noted W_t^g depicts net wealth of the public sector, which is typically negative.

We now turn to the specification of the third term. $N_{t,k}$ depicts the period t present value of rest-of-life net taxes paid by a living generation born in year k (prior or coincident to t). It can be decomposed as follows:

$$N_{t,k} = N_{t,k}^{\mathrm{m}} + N_{t,k}^{\mathrm{f}}$$

$$= \sum_{s=t}^{k+D} T_{s,k}^{\mathrm{m}} P_{s,k}^{\mathrm{m}} (1+r)^{t-s} + \sum_{s=t}^{k+D} T_{s,k}^{\mathrm{f}} P_{s,k}^{\mathrm{f}} (1+r)^{t-s} . \tag{4.14}$$

In Equation (4.14) $T_{s,k}^{\mathrm{f}}$ ($T_{s,k}^{\mathrm{m}}$) stands for the average net payment made in year s by a representative female (male) member of the generation born in year k. Moreover, $P_{s,k}^{\mathrm{f}}$ ($P_{s,k}^{\mathrm{m}}$) stands for the number of female (male) members of the generation born in k who survive until year s. Hence, $T_{s,k}^{\mathrm{f}} P_{s,k}^{\mathrm{f}}$ represents the net taxes paid by female members of generation k in year s. All annual amounts are discounted to year t with the help of r, the exogenous interest rate, and summed up for the years t to $k+D$, the remaining lifetime of generation k. The same holds for male agents. The division in payments of male and female members is done, because age profiles of net taxes differs considerably according to gender.

We first need to specify demographics ($P_{t,k}^{\mathrm{m}}, P_{t,k}^{\mathrm{f}}$). This is done by the population projection discussed in Section 4.1. As a second step we have to compute the net payments $T_{s,k}$ for all male and female agents of generation $k \leq t$. Indicating the type of payment, that is a particular tax or transfer, by i we can specify

$$T_{s,k}^{\mathrm{m}} = \sum_i h_{s-k,i,s}^{\mathrm{m}} , \tag{4.15}$$

with $h^{\mathrm{m}}_{s-k,i,s}$ referring to the average transfer received or tax paid by a representative male agent of age $s-k$ in year s. The same holds for female agents, so we confine our analysis to male agents without loss of generality. In the following, we index the age by a. Both, average payments and receipts grow in correspondence with productivity at the constant rate g. Again, this is not believed to occur, it is just a thought-experiment. Thus, the average tax or transfer for males in year $s > t$ can be calculated from Equation (4.16):

$$h^{\mathrm{m}}_{a,i,s} = h^{\mathrm{m}}_{a,i,t}\ (1+g)^{s-t}\ . \tag{4.16}$$

With an almost perfect data base, this would already be the end of it. In the base year we would observe average tax payments or transfer receipts contingent on age. These age-profiles could be extrapolated into the future according to Equation (4.16), summed up in line with Equation (4.15), and multiplied with the population structure of future years as stated by Equation (4.14). This would give us all information necessary to specify the third term in Equation (4.13).

Unfortunately, the data are far from perfect. In particular, the summation of transfers and taxes, which we derive from micro data, would never reproduce the aggregate values of government receipts and transfers we find in the official statistics for the base year. As a consequence, the average payments and receipts by age and gender that refer to our base year have to be modified in a meaningful way in order to fit aggregate values found in statistics. Stated technically, the deficient micro-profiles have to be *calibrated* to observable macro data. This is done as follows. The average base year payments and receipts by age and gender are expressed relative to the average payments and receipts of a 40-year-old male individual. The levels of those relative age profiles are then adjusted to the aggregate values by varying the 40-year-old male's tax or transfer levels, respectively. Let $H_{i,t}$ denote the aggregate value of a specific type of tax or transfer i in the base year t. It can be expressed as follows:

$$H_{i,t} = \sum_{a=0}^{D} (h^{\mathrm{m}}_{a,i,t} P^{\mathrm{m}}_{t,t-a} + h^{\mathrm{f}}_{a,i,t} P^{\mathrm{f}}_{t,t-a}) \qquad \forall i\ . \tag{4.17}$$

From micro data we compute the relative age-payment profiles according to Equations

$$R^{\mathrm{m}}_{a,i} \equiv \frac{h^{\mathrm{m}}_{a,i,t}}{h^{\mathrm{m}}_{40,i,t}} \qquad \forall a, i \qquad \text{and} \tag{4.18}$$

$$R^{\mathrm{f}}_{a,i} \equiv \frac{h^{\mathrm{f}}_{a,i,t}}{h^{\mathrm{m}}_{40,i,t}} \qquad \forall a, i\ , \tag{4.19}$$

where $R^{\mathrm{m}}_{a,i}$ ($R^{\mathrm{f}}_{a,i}$) stands for the relative payment of an a-year-old male (female) agent in the payment category i with reference to a 40-year old male.

If we solve Equations (4.18) and (4.19) for $h^{\mathrm{m}}_{a,i,t}$ and $h^{\mathrm{f}}_{a,i,t}$ and substitute into Equation (4.17), we obtain

$$H_{i,t} = \sum_{a=0}^{D} (h^{\mathrm{m}}_{40,i,t} R^{\mathrm{m}}_{a,i} P^{\mathrm{m}}_{t,t-a} + h^{\mathrm{m}}_{40,i,t} R^{\mathrm{f}}_{a,i} P^{\mathrm{f}}_{t,t-a}) \qquad \forall i \,. \tag{4.20}$$

This can easily be transformed into

$$h^{\mathrm{m}}_{40,i,t} = \frac{H_{i,t}}{\sum_{a=0}^{D} (R^{\mathrm{m}}_{a,i} P^{\mathrm{m}}_{t,t-a} + R^{\mathrm{f}}_{a,i} P^{\mathrm{f}}_{t,t-a})} \qquad \forall i \,. \tag{4.21}$$

By means of Equation (4.21) we derive the values of all $h^{\mathrm{m}}_{40,i,t}$ and, thus, the levels of micro-profiles which make them reproduce the aggregate values to be found in official statistics. Note, that the values of all variables on the right hand side of Equation (4.21) are observable. The value of the numerator is found in the government budget statistics, the values of $R^{\mathrm{m}}_{a,i}$ ($R^{\mathrm{f}}_{a,i}$) were computed above, and the values of $P^{\mathrm{m}}_{t,t-a}$ ($P^{\mathrm{f}}_{t,t-a}$) can be obtained from our demographic projection. We are, thus, in a position to specify the third term in Equation (4.13). Equations (4.18) and (4.19), solved for $h^{\mathrm{m}}_{a,i,t}$ and $h^{\mathrm{f}}_{a,i,t}$, give us the calibrated age-payment profiles by gender and category of payment. On the basis of these profiles and Equations (4.16) through (4.14) we determine the burden of living generations.

Let us next turn to the fiscal burden imposed on future generations, as represented by the last term in Equation (4.13). In determining net taxes of generations born in $k > t$, our procedure is in principle identical to the calculation of current generations' burdens. In particular, we use the same calibrated micro-profiles of the base year to infer future generations' *per capita* payments by age and gender. In the case of future generations, however, Equation (4.15) is modified to include a scaling constant θ_i:

$$T^{\mathrm{m}}_{s,k} = \sum_{i} \theta_i h^{\mathrm{m}}_{s-k,i,s} \,. \tag{4.22}$$

This scaling constant is determined endogenously and ensures that the government's intertemporal budget constraint is satisfied. In principal, the vector θ_i can mimic a wide range of fiscal policies aimed at securing fiscal sustainability. In order to guarantee comparability across studies and countries, however, one specific policy experiment has become standard. This is an increase (reduction) in all taxes paid by future generations necessary to meet the intertemporal budget constraint, implying $\theta_i = \theta_{\mathrm{tax}} > 1$ ($\theta_i = \theta_{\mathrm{tax}} < 1$) for all i associated with taxes and $\theta_i = 1$ for all i associated with transfers.

The scaling constant θ_{tax} is a common indicator to illustrate the degree of fiscal imbalance. Another indicator is the amount of true public debt. It is calculated by bringing the terms in Equation (4.13) on the left-hand side and setting all θ_i at unity:

$$TPD_t = \sum_{s=t}^{\infty} G_s(1+r)^{t-s} - W_t^{g} - \sum_{k=t-D}^{\infty} N_{t,k} \,. \tag{4.23}$$

If true public debt amounts to a value greater zero, this implies uncovered demands on future budgets. Note, that in contrast to officially reported public debt, true public debt includes implicit liabilities such as, e.g., worker's pension entitlements, which from an economic point of view do not differ from printed bonds. While the indicators so far have illustrated fiscal imbalance in terms of macroeconomic aggregates or quotas, it can also be expressed by comparing individual net tax burdens across generations. This is done by means of generational accounts. The generational account in base year present value for a generation born in k is defined as

$$GA_{t,k}^{\text{pub}} = \frac{N_{t,k}}{P_{s,k}}, \qquad \text{with} \qquad s = max(t,k) \;,^{9} \tag{4.24}$$

where the superscript *pub* denotes public as opposed to private generational accounts, $N_{t,k}$, as already noted, depicts the base year present value of this generation's rest-of-life net tax payments, and $P_{s,k}$ stands for the number of members of generation k that are still alive in period s.[10] A generational account simply represents the *per capita* wealth or debt vis-à-vis the government for each cohort born in point of time k. In order to illustrate the degree of fiscal imbalance, the generational account of a representative living individual is compared to the account of a representative future individual, where future generations' taxes are adjusted via θ_{tax} to meet the government's intertemporal budget constraint. Although any individual born in the future could serve as a representative, given that all future generations are treated alike, it has become common practice to refer to an individual born in $t+1$, the year succeeding the base year. In contrast, only a base year newborn can represent generations currently alive, since owing to the account's rest-of-life perspective only a newborn is recorded over his entire lifetime. The accounts of current and future newborns, respectively, are stated as follows:

$$GA_{t,t}^{\text{pub}} = \frac{N_{t,t}}{P_{t,t}} \tag{4.25}$$

$$GA_{t+1,t+1}^{\text{pub}} = \frac{N_{t,t+1}}{P_{t+1,t+1}} \frac{(1+r)}{(1+g)} \,. \tag{4.26}$$

Note, that in order to permit a meaningful comparison the future newborn's generational account has to be expressed in present value of his time of birth

[9] To keep the exposition simple, we abstract from immigration in the present context. Anyone interested in the formulation of generational accounts in the presence of immigration is referred to [116].

[10] Of course, generational accounts can also be expressed separately for males and females: $GA_{t,k}^{\text{pub,m}} = N_{t,k}^{\text{m}}/P_{s,k}^{\text{m}}$, $GA_{t,k}^{\text{pub,f}} = N_{t,k}^{\text{f}}/P_{s,k}^{\text{f}}$ with $s = max(t,k)$.

and adjusted for productivity growth. Usual generational accounting studies, in addition, report the accounts of other generations currently alive. It should be stressed, however, that these accounts, diverging in the covered lifespan, are not comparable among each other.

Data

Before presenting the German generational accounting results for the base year 1995, let us briefly outline the underlying data. The aggregate revenues of specific taxes are obtained from the Federal Statistical Office [136, 119] and the Ministry of Finance [137]. Aggregate receipts or expenditures of particular social insurance contributions or benefits, respectively, are available from the Ministry of Work and Social Affairs [138], the statistical yearbook [119], and the national product and income accounts [139]. The latter also provide the data on government spending G. One of the advantages of generational accounting over traditional budgeting is that it takes into account the entire public sector including all federal levels and off-budget authorities. This made it necessary to adjust inconsistencies in data stemming from different sources and netting out intergovernmental grants.

The calculation of government wealth W_t^g starts with the sum of the net debt figures of federal, state, and local budgets. The net debt of five additional funds – among them the German Unity Fund and the Redemption Fund for Inherited Liabilities, which are both directly related to the transformation process following German unification – are then added. All debt figures are reported in the monthly bulletin of the German Bundesbank [140]. For every single aggregate we need a corresponding age-gender-profile. These were either derived from the Socio-Economic Panel DIW [88] or provided by the Federal Statistical Office on the basis of the Income and Expenditure Survey 1988. Future flows are discounted at a constant interest rate of 5 percent *per annum*. This estimate is midway between the average yield on government bonds and the real rate of return on private capital. The productivity growth rate g is set to 1.5 percent.

Due to the still very divergent economic and social circumstances, distinct calculations are carried through for East and West Germany, which are subsequently aggregated. Specifically, in the early years, fertility rates as well as micro-profiles differ across the two regions. By the year 2005 eastern fertility will have reached the western level, while the economic catch-up process is terminated by the year 2010. During the catch-up process eastern micro-profiles will converge against their western counterparts, which implies that *per capita* figures have to grow by more than the usual 1.5 percent.

Results

The generational accounting results for the German public sector are presented in Table 4.6.[11] The top part gives the accounts for generations presently alive – irrespective of gender in the first column and separately for males and females in the following columns. The bottom part of Table 4.6 presents the generational accounts of a future newborn as well as two further indicators of fiscal imbalance, the percentage increase in future generations' taxes necessary to balance the intertemporal budget constraint and true public debt as percent of GDP. To begin with, consider the resources that living generations on average transfer to the public sector. While a base year newborn faces a lifetime net tax burden of DM 222,000, this tax burden increases steadily as one approaches the working year cohorts. After peaking at age 20, the generational accounts decline steadily, turning negative between the ages of 45 and 50 and reaching the minimum at age 65. Thereafter, they increase again, though they stay negative for the remaining lifespan.

This age profile can be explained by the conjunction of two factors. First, generational accounting is a prospective method, which, by definition, only takes into account rest-of-life tax and transfer payments. Hence, the public account of an elderly is negative as his tax-intensive working years lie behind him and for the rest of his life he benefits from pension payments. Moreover, after age 65, the net transfer declines as the remaining lifetime shortens. Secondly, due to discounting, payments that occur in the future are of lesser importance than current payments. Accordingly, young agents display relatively low accounts, as their tax-intensive working years still lie in the distant future.

In the same manner it can be explained that the generational account becomes zero between the ages of 45 and 50. It is at this age that the present value of future pension entitlement exactly balances the present value of remaining working year taxes. Recall that the prospective nature of generational accounting does not allow for a comparison of different cohorts' accounts. The divergence in the covered lifespan renders any such comparison meaningless. While gender-specific accounts exhibit the same general pattern, the net tax burdens of males and females deviate significantly. In particular, we observe that women pay substantially less taxes during working years, but, on the other hand, receive only insignificantly less transfers after retirement. These findings can be explained by a lower female participation in the labor force, lower wages on the part of women, and a social insurance scheme that greatly redistributes in favor of women.

Let us next inspect the degree of fiscal imbalance. Obviously, fiscal policy as of 1995 is not sustainable, leading to a true government debt of 135.8 percent of GDP when maintained into the indeterminate future. In contrast

[11] I was kindly permitted access to the generational accounting program used by Bonin et al. [141]. With slight modifications, concerning for example the treatment of government spending, this program underlies the following results.

Table 4.6. Public Generational Accounts in Germany

Age in 1995	Average	Male	Female
0	222.3	291.3	149.6
5	270.0	353.1	182.8
10	321.1	420.3	216.5
15	375.3	493.9	250.6
20	415.7	553.6	272.1
25	414.2	564.4	253.3
30	373.4	520.9	214.1
35	309.6	439.2	171.8
40	222.5	325.3	115.6
45	115.2	189.5	38.2
50	-17.1	23.1	-58.1
55	-150.2	-150.4	-150.0
60	-267.8	-305.7	-231.0
65	-302.1	-353.2	-256.7
70	-270.7	-315.3	-244.8
75	-229.8	-262.8	-213.2
80	-182.5	-208.9	-171.2
85	-140.2	-164.0	-131.8
90	-103.8	-127.6	-96.4
95	-71.8	-93.7	-66.5
100	-25.1	-33.4	-21.6
True Public Debt (Percent of GDP)	135.8	–	–
Increase in Future Taxes (Percent)	58.7	–	–
Future Generat. Account	443.8	557.4	324.1

Note: In thousands of German Marks; $r = 0.05$, $g = 0.015$. *Any significant deviations from the figures presented by Besendorfer et al. [108] and Bonin et al. [141] are due to the different treatment of government spending G.*

to the 57.7 percent explicit debt, this figure includes uncovered demands on future budgets, such as current workers' entitlement to social insurance. In order to serve this true government debt and, thus, satisfy the government's intertemporal budget constraint, future generations' net taxes would have to be increased by 58.7 percent. This implies a future newborn's generational account of DM 443, 800 and, consequently, a net tax burden that is twice as high as that of a representative living individual.

It remains to be shown, that the cause of this pronounced fiscal imbalance is population aging. This is done by a counterfactual experiment, namely the calculation of true public debt in absence of a demographic transition. In fact, assuming that the favorable population structure of the base year remains unchanged turns true public debt into government wealth, adding up to 11.5 percent of GDP. The results of this section can, thus, be summarized as follows. Population aging necessitates an immense adjustment in fiscal policy. Given the inertia of public policy as well as the protected claims of elder generations, young and future generations will most likely bear the major burden of this adjustment.

4.4.2 The Extension to Private Transfers

In the following section we follow Ablett [12] in extending generational accounting to include private intergenerational transfers.[12] While this is a natural extension as regards content – after all it complements our understanding of intergenerational transfers – it is open to methodological criticism. One might object that private intergenerational transfers being determined by maximizing agents are intrinsically different from public intergenerational transfers that are governed by fiscal policy. In particular, one might argue, the extrapolation of base-year circumstances, while being warranted in the case of public transfers, would neglect important adjustments in the case of private transfers. We will address this objection in Chapter 5 by imbedding the methodological approach into a general equilibrium model. For the time being, however, we present the methodology and German results.

Methodology

The starting point of this broader concept of generational accounting is the intertemporal budget constraint of the private sector. In analogy to the government's intertemporal budget constraint it states that the present value of resources must equal the present value of consumption. Rearranged it can be formulated as follows:

[12] Related in methodology is also the seminal article by Kotlikoff and Summers [1]. Instead of calculating what living generations bequeath to future generations, however, they infer what current generations have inherited from preceding generations.

$$W_t^{\mathrm{p}} + \sum_{s=0}^{D} L_{t,t-s} - \sum_{s=0}^{D} N_{t,t-s} - \sum_{s=0}^{D} C_{t,t-s} +$$
$$\sum_{s=1}^{\infty} L_{t,t+s} - \sum_{s=1}^{\infty} N_{t,t+s} - \sum_{s=1}^{\infty} C_{t,t+s} = 0 \,. \tag{4.27}$$

W_t^{p} depicts private net wealth in the base year t. Furthermore, let D denote the maximum age, and let $L_{t,k}$, $N_{t,k}$, and $C_{t,k}$ stand for the present value of future labor income, net taxes, and consumption attributed to all members of the generation born in year k. The first line of Equation (4.27) then represents the private resources of all generations alive in the base year left to future generations or, stated differently, the aggregate of their net private transfers. Accordingly, the second line equals the net private transfers of future generations, an amount which is opposite in sign and equal in magnitude to that of living generations.

Next, it is assumed that the government's intertemporal budget constraint, as stated by Equation (4.13) is satisfied. In correspondence with conventional generational accounting, this implies that base year fiscal policy remains unchanged for currently living generations, while future generations bear the incurred fiscal burden of this policy. Taking into account this budget constraint and denoting public debt as B_t^g, Equation (4.27) can be reformulated as follows:

$$W_t^{\mathrm{p}} + \sum_{s=0}^{D} L_{t,t-s} - \sum_{s=0}^{D} C_{t,t-s} + \sum_{s=1}^{\infty} L_{t,t+s} - \sum_{s=1}^{\infty} C_{t,t+s} = \sum_{s=t}^{\infty} G_s(1+r)^{t-s} + B_t^{\mathrm{g}} \,. \tag{4.28}$$

The first three terms on the left-hand side of Equation (4.28) now stand for the overall assets – both private and public – which living generations leave behind. If adjusted for government spending and public debt they, at the same time, represent the overall resources future generations will inherit. Accordingly, Equation (4.28) illustrates the broader context of intergenerational distribution, of which conventional generational accounting captures only a fraction, namely public intergenerational transfers.

In what follows let us briefly review, how the terms of Equation (4.28) are numerically specified. The quantification of the terms on the right-hand side was already detailed in the previous section. The aggregate value of private net wealth can be found in official statistics. The specification of the present value of future earnings and consumption flows, finally, is identical to the specification of net taxes in conventional generational accounting. To see this, note that the difference in the present value of living generations' earnings and consumption can be reformulated in the following way:

$$\sum_{s=0}^{D} L_{t,t-s} - \sum_{s=0}^{D} C_{t,t-s} = \sum_{s=0}^{D} (L_{t,t-s} - C_{t,t-s}) \tag{4.29}$$

with

$$L_{t,t-s} - C_{t,t-s} = \sum_{s=t}^{k+D} l_{s,k} P_{s,k} (1+r)^{t-s} - \sum_{s=t}^{k+D} c_{s,k} P_{s,k} (1+r)^{t-s} \quad (4.30)$$

$$= \sum_{s=t}^{k+D} (l_{s,k} - c_{s,k}) P_{s,k} (1+r)^{t-s} , \quad (4.31)$$

where $l_{s,k}$ and $c_{s,k}$ denote earnings and consumption in year s referring to a representative individual born in year k. Technically speaking, Equation (4.31) is identical to Equation (4.14), with $(l_{s,k} - c_{s,k})$ corresponding to $T_{s,k}$.[13] According to Equation (4.15) $l_{s,k}$ and $-c_{s,k}$ are therefore analogous to individual tax and transfer payments in conventional generational accounting, $h_{s-k,i,s}$. To find these age-specific earnings and consumption figures *per capita*, $l_{s,k}$ and $c_{s,k}$, we proceed in the same way as before. In particular, *per capita* age-profiles for earnings and consumption are derived from cross-section micro data. Subsequently, these micro-profiles are calibrated to 1995 aggregate data with the help of Equations (4.17) to (4.21). Assuming, that *per capita* age-profiles stay constant over time, except for an annual productivity growth of 1.5 percent, the calibrated base year profiles can, finally, be projected into the future by means of Equation (4.16).

In the same way, we specify the difference in the present value of future generations' earnings and consumption. As earlier, however, this magnitude has to be determined endogenously in order to satisfy the private intertemporal budget constraint. In correspondence with Equation (4.22) we therefore adjust future generations' consumption through a scaling constant θ_{con}.

We are now in a position to answer the central question of this chapter, whether private intergenerational transfers compensate future generations for the fiscal burden imposed on them. This is done by bringing all terms in Equation (4.28) on the left-hand side and inserting their numerical values, while at first θ_{con} is set at unity. If the left-hand side adds up to a value greater zero, it is assumed, in analogy to conventional generational accounting, that this surplus will accrue to future generations. As a consequence, future generations' consumption is increased by raising θ_{con} above unity. On the other hand, if this summand is lesser zero, this seems to indicate, that currently living generations live at the expense of their children. In that case private transfers obviously do not suffice to ease the demographic burden.

It is worthwhile to express the imbalance in *per capita* terms to get a better idea of its magnitude. Again, this is done with the help of generational accounts. If $W^{\text{p}}_{t,k}$ denotes the private net wealth held by generation k in the base year, the overall or total generational account of generation k in base year present value is defined as

[13] To keep the exposition simple, we have not in the present equations distinguished according to gender.

$$GA_{t,k}^{\text{tot}} = \frac{(W_{t,k}^{\text{p}} + L_{t,k} - C_{t,k})}{P_{s,k}} \qquad \text{with} \qquad s = max(t,k) \,. \tag{4.32}$$

The magnitude of the imbalance can be illustrated by comparing the overall generational account of a base year newborn with the overall generational account of a future newborn, given that future generations' consumption is adjusted as to satisfy the intertemporal budget constraint (cf. Equation (4.28)). These accounts are expressed as follows:

$$GA_{t,t}^{\text{tot}} = \frac{(L_{t,t} - C_{t,t})}{P_{t,t}} \tag{4.33}$$

$$GA_{t+1,t+1}^{\text{tot}} = \frac{(L_{t,t+1} - C_{t,t+1})}{P_{t+1,t+1}} \frac{(1+r)}{(1+g)} \,. \tag{4.34}$$

Recall, that through the second term, the future newborn's overall transfers are growth adjusted and expressed in present value of their year of birth. Furthermore, as earnings, consumption, and transfers are assumed to occur at the end of each period, the wealth of any newborn – whether current or future – equals zero.

Before future generations' consumption is adjusted in order to meet the private intertemporal budget constraint, $GA_{t,t}^{\text{tot}}$ usually equals $GA_{t+1,t+1}^{\text{tot}}$.[14] The constraint then indicates whether future generations' consumption has to be scaled up or down, that is whether future generations receive more or less net transfers over their life-cycle than current newborns.

Up to this point we have exclusively dealt with the calculation of overall transfers between living and future generations. It might be of greater interest, however, to know the magnitude of private as compared to public transfers between these generations. This question can be answered on the basis of the following relation:

$$GA_{t,k}^{\text{pri}} = \frac{(W_{t,k}^{\text{p}} + L_{t,k} - C_{t,k})}{P_{t,k}} - \frac{N_{t,k}}{P_{t,k}} = GA_{t,k}^{\text{tot}} - GA_{t,k}^{\text{pub}} \,, \tag{4.35}$$

where $GA_{t,k}^{\text{pri}}$ and $GA_{t,k}^{\text{pub}}$ depict private and conventional generational accounts of generation k in base year present value. Thus, in order to derive the private transfer a member of a specific cohort leaves to others, one only has to subtract that individual's conventional or public generational account from his overall account.

Finally, Equation (4.35) illustrates quite well, why for the question we want to address one should stick to the traditional approach, which in calculating public generational accounts only takes into account monetary trans-

[14] The current newborn's account $GA_{t,t}^{\text{tot}}$ can slightly deviate from the future newborn's account $GA_{t+1,t+1}^{\text{tot}}$, if life expectancy varies over time or if, during a period of time, the aggregates grow at a rate distinct from g as is the case in East Germany during the catch-up process.

fers. Instead, attributing government spending to the public generational accounts, as suggested, for example, by ter Rele [134] and Raffelhüschen [133], would reduce public accounts and, as a consequence, increase private accounts by the monetary equivalent of public goods. In that public goods are not part of private intergenerational transfers this procedure would not yield meaningful results.

Data

The additional data requirements of this extended version of generational accounting comprise aggregates and age-profiles for private net wealth, consumption and earnings. Aggregate private net wealth is derived from the German Bundesbank [91] and Bach [142], and in 1995 amounted to DM 12,852 billion. It comprehends unincorporated firms, real estate, durables, securities, and money, less private liabilities. In that the value of unincorporated firms was only available for 1993, it was assumed that from 1993 to 1995 their value increased in correspondence with incorporated firms. The aggregate of consumption amounts to DM 1,974 billion and is available from the national product and income accounts [143]. Aggregate earnings sum up to DM 2,197 and contain gross income out of dependent employment and wages of entrepreneurship (cf. [144]).

The corresponding age-profiles *per capita* are derived from the Income and Expenditure Survey 1993 [87] and are subsequently calibrated to 1995 aggregates. As data on wealth and consumption were collected on a household level, the figures had to be attributed to specific household members. Household members were assumed to consume in equal shares, while household wealth was distributed uniformly among members with the exception of children, who were assumed to hold no wealth at all. Furthermore, having too few observations, we dropped the values of respondents older 87, and instead, extrapolated the trend. Finally, profiles were subjected to a five year moving average. In order to calculate total or private generational accounts one needs the age distribution of aggregate private wealth (cf. Equations (4.32) and (4.35)). This can be derived by multiplying the 1995 age composition of the population with the age-wealth profile *per capita*.

As earlier, we run distinct calculations for East and West Germany, which are subsequently aggregated, permitting us to take into account the East German catch-up process. We also carry through distinct calculations for males and females, this way considering diverging earnings histories. Later the results need to be aggregated in order to preclude the problem of interspousal transfers.

Results

This section presents and compares the findings on private and public intergenerational transfers in Germany for the base year 1995. The baseline simulations were conducted employing an interest rate of 5 percent and a productivity growth rate of 1.5 percent. Since there are no data available as to the wealth, specific cohorts of immigrants bring into the country, in the baseline calculations it is presumed that they bring no wealth at all. Subsequently, the results will be tested with respect to their sensitivity by varying the exogenous variables within a realistic range. Moreover, it will be outlined to what extent alternative population projections and alternative assumptions with respect to immigrant's wealth will modify the outcomes.

Table 4.7 displays the baseline findings with columns 1 to 3 containing public, private, and overall generational accounts, respectively. Recall that according to Equation (4.35), the last column is the sum of the previous two columns. The last row reports the transfers a future newborn will make over his lifetime, while the *per capita* transfers made by living cohorts over the remaining lifespan can be found in the previous rows. Public generational accounts have already been discussed in Section 4.4.1 and are only restated for completeness. Let us therefore begin with considering private generational accounts.

A current newborn receives, in present value, a net private transfer of DM 323,400 over his life-cycle. These received transfers decrease with age until individuals become net donors between age 20 and 25 and stay donors for the rest of their lives. Net private transfers to other generations peak at age 45 and again on a somewhat lower level at 65. While they remain on a relatively high level thereafter, the trend is slightly falling. As with conventional generational accounts, one should, of course, refrain from comparing different generations' net transfers. In fact, for older generations, many transfers *inter vivos* might have occurred before the base year and, thus, are not included in the figures reported.

At first sight, it is remarkable that individuals are net recipients only until age 25. Recall that the age distribution of heirs which we derived from the Socio-Economic Panel indicates that most inheritances occur between age 40 and 50 (cf. Table 3.18). In addition, the Income and Expenditure Survey reveals that until age 40 it is more likely to receive than to give an *inter vivos* transfer (cf. Table 3.3). In view of this evidence, it is surprising that net transfers do not remain negative until later in life. However, in the calculations at hand, children's consumption is not allocated to the parents, which produces large intergenerational transfers within a household. Consequently, transfers to generations which would be expected to receive high transfers, are offset by transfers to their children leaving them with a positive net transfer. With respect to the relation of private and public transfers it is remarkable that, apart from the cohorts between the age of 25 and 45, they are directed in opposite direction, in most cases reducing overall transfers to a 5-digit number.

Now consider private intergenerational transfers between living and future generations by inspecting the private generational account of a representative current and future newborn. As explained in the methodological paragraph,

Table 4.7. Public and Private Transfers in Germany

Age in 1995	Public GA	Private GA	Overall GA
0	222.3	-323.4	-101.1
5	270.0	-291.0	-21.0
10	321.1	-248.5	72.6
15	375.3	-189.3	186.0
20	415.7	-105.7	310.0
25	414.2	10.4	424.6
30	373.4	129.5	502.9
35	309.6	190.7	500.3
40	222.5	211.9	434.4
45	115.2	234.8	350.0
50	-17.1	232.3	215.2
55	-150.2	196.8	46.6
60	-267.8	206.0	-61.8
65	-302.1	244.8	-57.3
70	-270.7	242.1	-28.6
75	-229.8	239.0	9.2
80	-182.5	215.5	33.0
85	-140.2	223.9	83.7
90	-103.8	190.9	87.1
95	-71.8	168.2	96.4
100	-25.1	148.0	122.9
-1	443.8	-327.8	116.0

In thousands of German Marks;$r = 0.05$, $g = 0.015$.

the latter is calculated by adjusting future generations' consumption in order to meet the intertemporal resource constraint specified by Equation (4.28). Future generations 'inherit' only slightly more than currently living generations. Thus, a future newborn receives private intergenerational transfers which sum up to DM 327,800 as compared to the DM 323,400 DM a present newborn receives. At first sight this result might be counterintuitive, given that the existing capital stock is bequeathed to cohorts that are substantially smaller than today's. One should keep in mind however, that living cohorts can consume part of the capital stock before it is bequeathed to successive generations. Obviously, living generations' savings as reflected in the base year age-profiles is not high enough to let future generations profit from the declining number of heirs.

The inheritance received by future generations is not sufficient to make up for the fiscal burden imposed on them by population aging. Making allowances for both public and private transfers, one finds that a future newborn is still left with an overall burden of DM 116,000. In contrast, a current newborn, when netting out his liabilities to the public sector, is still left with a positive 'inheritance' of DM 101,100. In what follows, the robustness of the

Table 4.8. Sensitivity Analysis, OverallTransfers ($GA^{tot}_{t,t}$; $GA^{tot}_{t+1,t+1}$)

		Growth Rate		
		0.01	0.015	0.02
	0.03	-50.6 ; 386.7	-31.8 ; 478.4	-16.1 ; 559.8
Interest Rate	0.05	-114.4 ; 26.5	-101.1 ; 116.0	-85.5 ; 207.7
	0.07	-144.3 ; -291.9	-139.3 ; -211.8	-132.5 ; -130.1
		Migration		
		Low	Baseline	High
Relative Imm.	0	-101.1 ; 120.6	-101.1 ; 116.0	-101.1 ; 119.4
Wealth	1	-101.1 ; 103.5	-101.1 ; 91.8	-101.1 ; 89.6

In thousands of German Marks.

findings with respect to the underlying parameters and migration assumptions will be investigated. Table 4.8 reports in the top section the current and future newborns' overall accounts for varying interest and growth rates. In the bottom section the results for alternative migration scenarios are displayed, coupled with a variation in the wealth that immigrants bring into the country. In particular, we consider the two polar cases that immigrant wealth amounts to 0 and 100 percent, respectively, of the wealth a native German holds at corresponding age, uprated for growth in future years.[15]

Unfortunately, the results vary considerably under different interest and growth rate assumptions. Indeed, the baseline's qualitative outcome that future generations will not be compensated for fiscal burdens ceases to hold if one assumes a real interest rate of 7 percent. Coupled with productivity growth rates of 1 or 1.5 percent an interest rate of 7 percent even leads to an

[15] A sensitivity analysis separately for public and private generational accounts is given in Appendix A.4.

inheritance that more than compensates future generations for the net taxes imposed on them.

Alternative migration assumptions only have a minor effects on the outcomes. The migration scenarios we consider are suggested by the Federal Statistical Office cf. [120]. While in the baseline scenario immigration decreases from 277,000 in the base year to 200,000 in year 2000 and remains constant thereafter, in the low and high migration scenario it amounts to 100,000 and 300,000, respectively, by year 2000. Not even the quantitative results are much altered by these modifications. Note that the results for current newborns do not change with varying migration. This reflects the fact that the figures presented only refer to native residents. Any increase in the liabilities or surplus of both the government's and private sector's intertemporal budget constraint that is caused by migration is allocated solely to future generations (cf. Bonin et al. [116]).

Finally, compare the baseline results to the last line in Table 4.8. Bear in mind that the former scenario assumes that immigrants hold no wealth at all, while the latter scenario suggests immigrant wealth that, adjusted for growth, equals natives' endowments in the base year. Hence, the two scenarios seem to be the lower and upper bound of any realistic range of parameters. Obviously, the wealth endowment of migrants has very little impact on the outcomes and can, thus, be safely ignored.

4.4.3 Caveats and Conclusion

Before turning to the conclusion, some qualifying remarks seem adequate. It goes without saying that the calculation at hand is a mere accounting framework, necessarily abstracting from any adjustments induced by population aging and bequests. Especially when taking into account that population aging is a phenomenon experienced throughout the western world, it is likely that prices will adjust to a shrinking population, suggesting a general equilibrium model as the adequate setting for analysis. While we assume a constant discount rate, the real interest rate is likely to fall as the population shrinks and the capital-labor ratio increases. For example, de Nardi et al. [145] show that in a general equilibrium model interest rates fall from almost 6 to below 4 percent during a demographic transition. On the other hand, one can state in our defense that we have conducted a sensitivity analysis, which covers the range in interest rates that de Nardi et al. suggest. We have therefore, at least, reported the spectrum of likely outcomes, given an endogenous interest rate.

Furthermore, by projecting cross-section earnings and consumption age-profiles into the future, we neglect that the savings age-profile will probably change, as relative prices adjust to a declining labor force. This certainly is a severe shortcoming of our approach and can only be justified by the immense computational costs associated with the implementation of a generational accounting framework into a general equilibrium model of 50 or more generations. Also note that the procedure of weighting base year savings-profiles with future cohort sizes, while not totally satisfying, has been used by a couple of other authors to project aggregate saving, notably Bosworth et al. [146], Auerbach and Kotlikoff [147], and Wachtel [148].

We further abstract from the fact that the transfer or bequest left by parents to their children might be adjusted as the number of children decreases. As shown in Section 4.3, however, no such adjustment will occur in the case of accidental, exchange-motivated, or joy-of-giving (with respect to overall bequests) transfers. For the remaining motives, the adjustment is likely to be small, given that declining fertility reduces the cost of raising children and, in this way, enables parents to save more.

Apart from the objections to the disregard of general equilibrium effects, some additional caveats are in order. The first refers to the adjustment of future generations' consumption in order to satisfy the private sector's intertemporal budget constraint (cf. Equation (4.28)). Note that the impact of this adjustment in consumption on future tax revenues is neglected. This is to ensure the comparability to traditional generational accounting calculations. Second, lacking adequate data, expenditures for durable goods are included in consumption. Ideally, such goods have to be treated as investment, including only current year depreciation in consumption. Accordingly, our procedure tends to underestimate the assets accumulated by living generations and bequeathed to future generations. The figures on private intergenerational transfers should therefore be considered a lower bound estimate.

Finally, it can be argued that by not attributing children's consumption to their parents, and thus treating it as intergenerational transfer the approach breaks with the conventional definition of intergenerational transfers according to which they must occur between households (cf. Modigliani [75], page 27). While, in fact, the allocation of children's consumption has an impact on the age-profile of living generations' private transfers as displayed in Table 4.7, it does not affect the aggregate left to future generations. It therefore has no influence on the central questions of this chapter, namely the volume of private versus public intergenerational transfers and the overall distribution between living and future generations. The latter fact together with the desirable compatibility with conventional generational accounting were decisive for the approach chosen.

The main findings of this section can be summarized as follows. In the baseline scenario we find that a current and future newborn inherit about the same amount over their lifetime. As a consequence, private intergenerational transfers can not make up for the pronounced fiscal imbalance between living and future generations. On the other hand, we find that this result to a great extent depends on the underlying discount rate. For low interest rates no compensation takes place, while interest rates in the neighborhood of 7 percent can even reverse the intergenerational distribution in favor of future generations.[16] In order to achieve a better understanding of the working of the interest rate and to counter the above objections to the neglect of micro- and macroeconomic adjustments the problem will be incorporated into a general equilibrium model in Section 5.3.

Despite the uncertainty as to the distributive implications of private intergenerational transfers, we find that their volume is significant relative to the financial needs of social insurance. Thus, the lifetime inheritance of a current newborn in the baseline amounts to almost 150 percent of his net taxes. For a future newborn the private generational account in absolute terms still comes to 75 percent of his public generational account.[17] Hence, further research should focus on the question if and how, when possible, these private resources could be exploited to ease the financial strain of the social insurance system during a demographic transition. In line with this argument, we will in the following chapter investigate the taxation of private intergenerational transfers.

[16] It should be stressed, that from the equality of private and public accounts in absolute terms, one should not, of course, conclude that a longtime overdue reform of the German social insurance system has become unnecessary. For one thing, social insurance contributions are payable long before a large fraction of private transfers, namely inheritances, occur. Therefore, in the presence of liquidity constraints private transfers can hardly alleviate the welfare loss due to increasing contribution rates. For another thing the preceding investigation only aims at the average individual and thus neglects an important aspect. While almost everybody within a specific cohort bears the burden of social protection programs, inheritances are concentrated among few members of this cohort. Consequently, the conjunction of private and public transfers is not valid on an individual basis. Finally – and this argument carries more weight – if the government renders an unsustainable fiscal policy sustainable through the levy of distortionary taxes, excess burden will result. Given that the excess burden increases more than proportional with tax rates and taking into account that tax rates are already on a relatively high level in Germany, a further increase due to population aging would entail substantial welfare losses, not included in the preceding calculations. This issue will be explored in Section 5.4.

[17] The result that the volume of private transfers is significant relative to the magnitude of public transfers also holds for alternative parameter specifications. This is illustrated by Tables A.1 and A.2 in Appendix A.4, which give public and private generational accounts for alternative interest rates, growth rates and migration scenarios.

5. Intergenerational Transfers in a General Equilibrium Setting

The following chapter aims at answering three central questions. First, how do private intergenerational transfers affect generations' welfare during a demographic transition? While the joint welfare effect of public intergenerational transfers and population aging has extensively been investigated (e.g. [103], [149]), so far relatively little has been said on the welfare implications of private intergenerational transfers. Where private transfers have been taken into account, the authors usually confine their analysis to a single transfer motive (cf. [13], [14], [109]). Lacking empirical evidence in favor of a predominant transfer motive, this approach seems little satisfactory. Section 5.2 therefore investigates the welfare implications of private transfers during a demographic transition by making allowances for different bequest motives.

Second, this chapter explores, whether overall generational accounts, recording both public and private intergenerational transfers, serve as a valid indicator for generations' welfare. As pointed out earlier, the extended generational accounting exercise of Chapter 4 necessarily abstracts from substitution effects induced by population aging and bequests. It therefore remains to be shown, whether a mere accounting framework can shed light on the incidence of the demographic burden. This issue will be addressed in Section 5.3.

Finally, Section 5.4 examines, how private resources can be taxed efficiently to ease the government's financial strain during a demographic transition. In the preceding chapter we tacitly assumed that the government had lump-sum taxes at its disposal and, as a consequence, could extract resources from the private sector at no cost. It was exactly for this reason that we could derive the overall burden of a representative individual by netting out taxes paid and bequests received. However, if the government renders an unsustainable fiscal policy sustainable through the levy of distortionary taxes, the welfare loss of taxation exceeds the pure income effect. Section 5.4 inquires into how this excess burden can be minimized.

All of the above questions will be addressed by means of an overlapping generations model in the tradition of Samuelson [3] and Diamond [4]. This unified framework allows to change the representative agent's transfer motive and labor supply decision simply by modifying some parameters in his utility function. Accordingly, the effects of specific transfer motives or distortionary taxes can be isolated by way of comparative static analysis.

5.1 The Model

Consider an economy that is made up of individuals with identical preferences and a maximum life expectancy of two periods. While everybody lives through the first period of live, the probability of surviving to the end of the second period is π. After the first period of life each individual has $(1+n_t)$ children, where t is the parent's generation index. Consequently, at any given point in time, the economy comprises two overlapping generations.

It is assumed that the preferences of a representative agent born in t can be described by the following expected utility function with constant elasticities of substitution:

$$u_t = \left[\left((c_t^1)^{1-1/\rho} + \nu(l_t)^{1-1/\rho}\right)^{\frac{1-1/\gamma}{1-1/\rho}} + \frac{\pi}{1+\delta}(c_{t+1}^2)^{1-1/\gamma} + \right.$$
$$\left. \frac{\pi\mu}{1+\delta}(I_{t+1}^{\mathrm{j}})^{1-1/\gamma} + \frac{\pi\phi}{1+\delta}(A_{t+1})^{1-1/\gamma}\right]^{\frac{1}{1-1/\gamma}} . \quad (5.1)$$

According to this formulation the individual derives utility from first and second period consumption c_t^1 and c_{t+1}^2, leisure l_t, the *per capita* inheritance left to his children I_{t+1}^{j}, and overall attention provided by his children A_{t+1}. Consumption and inheritances are measured in units of a single commodity, leisure and attention as the fraction of his or, respectively, his children's overall disposable time not dedicated to work. Agents value future less than present consumption for two reasons. Not knowing whether they will still be alive, they weight future consumption with the probability of survival π. In addition, they discount future consumption at the rate of time preference δ illustrating the general uncertainty associated with events in the future. The parameters ν, μ, and ϕ determine the intensity of the desire for leisure, bequeathing, and attention, respectively. While γ stands for the general elasticity of substitution, ρ denotes the elasticity of substitution between first period consumption and leisure whenever the labor supply is endogenous. Lacking empirical evidence on the substitutability between consumption, bequests, and attention, there is little reason to resort to a more general and, thus, more complicated functional form.[1]

The agent works in the first period of life. With overall disposable time set to unity, a fraction l_t dedicated to leisure and a fraction a_t of the remainder dedicated to his parents, the agent's labor supply equals $(1-l_t)(1-a_t)$. He

[1] Note that with the omission of labor supply in the second period of life, we abstract from any intertemporal distortions of the labor supply.

earns a wage w_t per unit of time, which is taxed at a rate τ_t. In addition to his earnings, the representative agent receives an inheritance I_t^{a}, where the superscript a stands for 'accidental'. This inheritance is left behind by short-lived parents who, in the absence of corresponding markets, were unable to annuitizes the wealth provided for the possibility of longevity. With savings denoted s_t, the agent's first period budget constraint can be stated as

$$c_t^1 = I_t^{\mathrm{a}} + (1 - a_t)(1 - l_t)(1 - \tau_t)w_t - s_t \,. \tag{5.2}$$

If the agent survives to the end of the second period, he gains interest on his savings at a rate r_{t+1}. Furthermore, he receives an inheritance I_t^{j} his parents left behind for joy-of-giving as well as an inheritance I_t^{x} in exchange for filial attention. Since both inheritances constitute wealth accumulated in the previous period they too yield interest at the market interest rate. These earnings together with an old-age benefit tr_{t+1} are spent on second period consumption and bequests. The latter, be they motivated by exchange or joy-of giving, are taxed at a uniform rate τ_t^{i} and shared equally among the agent's $(1+n_t)$ offsprings.[2] The second period budget constraint is therefore given by

$$c_{t+1}^2 = (s_t + I_t^{\mathrm{j}} + I_t^{\mathrm{x}})(1 + r_{t+1}) + tr_{t+1} - (1 + \tau_{t+1}^{\mathrm{i}})(1 + n_t)(I_{t+1}^{\mathrm{j}} + I_{t+1}^{\mathrm{x}}) \,. \tag{5.3}$$

With respect to exchange-motivated bequests we assumed in Section 2.3 that parents reap off all gains from the exchange. This implies that the agent bequeaths to his children an amount just enough to compensate them for the earnings forgone while spending time with him, that is

$$I_{t+1}^{\mathrm{x}} = (1 - \tau_{t+1})w_{t+1}a_{t+1} \,.^3 \tag{5.4}$$

We further assumed, that the representative agent derives utility from all of his children's attention. In view of the model's symmetry this overall attention can be stated as

---

[2] While in most countries' inheritance taxation is progressive in design, the present model considers a proportional tax. We will later return to this matter.

[3] To be precise, this inheritance corresponds to the cost of providing attention only in the case, where the labor supply is exogenous. To see this derive the life-cycle budget constraint by solving Equation (5.3) for s_t and substituting into Equation (5.2): $c_t^1 + (1-a_t)(1-\tau_t)w_t l_t + \frac{c_{t+1}^2}{1+r_{t+1}} + \frac{(1+n_t)(1+\tau_{t+1}^{\mathrm{i}})(I_{t+1}^{\mathrm{j}}+I_{t+1}^{\mathrm{x}})}{1+r_{t+1}} = I_t^{\mathrm{a}} + I_t^{\mathrm{j}} + I_t^{\mathrm{x}} + (1-\tau_t)(1-a_t)w_t + \frac{tr_{t+1}}{1+r_{t+1}}$. Obviously, attention a_t enters the constraint in two ways. For one thing it reduces the endowment of labor income, for another thing it reduces the price of leisure. However, only the first effect is neutralized by the inheritance I_t^{x} as formulated in Equation (5.4). Therefore, unless the labor supply is exogenous and, thus, $l_t = 0$, parents more than compensate children for providing attention. The use of Equation (5.4) instead of an explicit expenditure function seems justifiable, given that the assumption of parents appropriating all gains from exchange is quite extreme anyway.

$$A_{t+1} = (1 + n_t)a_{t+1} \; . \tag{5.5}$$

Finally, the accidental bequest received by the agent when young equals

$$I_t^{\mathrm{a}} = \frac{(1-\pi)s_{t-1}(1+r_t)}{(1+n_{t-1})(1+\tau_t^{\mathrm{i}})} \; , \tag{5.6}$$

where s_{t-1} denotes *per capita* saving of his parent's cohort, $(1 + r_t)$ accrued gross interest, and $(1 - \pi)$ the fraction of predecessors dying prematurely. The accidental bequest will be divided equally among the agent and his n_{t-1} siblings and taxed at the uniform rate τ_t^{i}.

Next, consider the specification of the government sector. In the present model the government is confined to providing a pay-as-you-go social insurance scheme. In order to finance old-age benefits, the government can resort to a proportional labor tax, a proportional inheritance tax, or both. The government is therefore constrained by the following equations:

$$(1-\beta_t)\frac{\pi tr_t}{1+n_{t-1}} = (1-l_t)(1-a_t)w_t\tau_t \tag{5.7}$$

$$\beta_t \frac{\pi tr_t}{1+n_{t-1}} = \pi I_t^{\mathrm{j}}\tau_t^{\mathrm{i}} + \pi I_t^{\mathrm{x}}\tau_t^{\mathrm{i}} + \frac{(1-\pi)s_{t-1}(1+r_t)\tau_t^{\mathrm{i}}}{(1+n_{t-1})(1+\tau_t^{\mathrm{i}})} \; . \tag{5.8}$$

The left hand side of Equations (5.7) and (5.8) denotes government expenditure *per capita* of the period t working population to be financed out of labor and inheritance taxation, respectively. Specifically, tr_t is the benefit per pensioner, π the fraction of surviving individuals, $(1+n_t)$ the pensioner's number of children, and β_t the (exogenously set) proportion of overall government expenditure to be financed by inheritance taxation. Correspondingly, the equations' right hand side gives the respective tax revenue *per capita* of the period t working population. In what follows we restrict our analysis to a benefit-defined pay-as-you-go program. Consequently, tr_t is exogenous and, with all other variables determined outside the government sector, τ_t and τ_t^{i} governed by the above equations. Note, that the social insurance scheme includes an actuary element. Thus, while private annuity markets are non-existent in the model, public annuitization is assumed to work. The rationale is that a statutory insurance program might overcome the problem of adverse selection, which impedes the formation of private annuity markets (cf. [150]).

The economy's technology is expressed by means of a Cobb-Douglas production function. Expressed *per* efficiency unit it reads $y_t = k_t^{\alpha}$, where y_t stands for output per unit of labor, k_t for capital intensity, and α for the capital income share. Technical progress is not explicitly modelled, however, labor-augmenting progress is implicitly taken into account in the population growth rate. Furthermore, factor markets are assumed perfectly competitive so that factors earn their marginal product:

$$w_t = (1-\alpha)k_t^{\alpha} \tag{5.9}$$

$$r_t = \alpha k_t^{(\alpha-1)} \; . \tag{5.10}$$

Finally, the capital market equilibrium condition

$$k_{t+1} = \frac{s_t + \pi I_t^{\mathrm{j}} + \pi I_t^{\mathrm{x}}}{(1+n_t)(1-l_{t+1})} \tag{5.11}$$

states that the capital stock is formed by gross saving of the preceding period.[4]

In order to solve the model, the representative individual's utility is maximized subject to his life-cycle budget constraint. The latter is obtained by means of Equations (5.2) through (5.6). This way we derive Marshallian demand functions for all arguments included in the utility function. Subsequently, by substituting for the tax rates and factor incomes according to Equations (5.7) through (5.10), we make the microeconomic decision conditional on the economy's capital intensity. Finally, the corresponding demand functions are substituted into the capital market equilibrium condition and we end up with the equation of motion $k_{t+1} = f(k_t)$. On the basis of this equation we could solve for the steady-state values of all variables. Furthermore, we could determine the trajectories for all variables following an exogenous shock. Unfortunately, this non-linear difference equation is too complex to be solved analytically. For this reason we will specify the model numerically and analyze the shocks in questions by way of simulation.

The model's parameterization requires numerical values for the preference parameters γ, ρ, δ, ν, μ, ϕ, the probability of survival π, the capital income share α, the old-age benefit tr, and the population growth rate n_t. Of these parameters only α and n_t are relatively straightforward. The population growth rate is initially set to 1 percent *per annum* falling to 0.5 percent in $t = 0$, which may be considered the present point in time. Remember that this figure reflects both reproduction of the population and labor-augmenting progress. Likewise clear-cut is the share of capital income in GDP, which is commonly estimated at around 25 percent (e.g. Auerbach and Kotlikoff [103], page 52). While the parameters γ and ρ have at least been estimated, albeit under slightly different assumptions – e.g., non of the studies included a desire for bequests and attention in the utility function – the remaining parameters are arbitrary, altogether.

In view of these difficulties we proceed in the following manner. Our point of reference is the most basic model including as few preference parameters as possible. With most preference parameters set to zero and a relatively reliable estimate for γ – since now the utility function does not include a desire for bequests and attention – the rate of time preference δ and the pension tr can be chosen so as to generate realistic values for the real interest rate, the capital-output ratio, and the contribution rate to social insurance. Subsequently, the parameters initially set to zero will be increased marginally, one at a time, to see how the inclusion of a specific bequest motive or an endogenous labor supply changes the outcomes. This is, what in the context

[4] The general equilibrium model is summarized in Appendix A.5.

of an intertemporal general equilibrium model was meant by comparative static analysis.

5.2 Private Transfers, Demographic Transition, and Generational Welfare

5.2.1 No Private Transfers

To begin with, let us investigate the implications of an aging population in the most basic model, featuring a pay-as-you-go social insurance scheme but ignoring private intergenerational transfers. This model serves as a reference for subsequent analysis and is generated by setting ν, μ, ϕ, β to zero and π to unity. Accordingly, the representative agent maximizes the utility function

$$u_t = \left[\left(c_t^1\right)^{1-1/\gamma} + \frac{1}{1+\delta}\left(c_{t+1}^2\right)^{1-1/\gamma} \right]^{\frac{1}{1-1/\gamma}}, \tag{5.12}$$

subject to the life-cycle budget constraint

$$c_t^1 + \frac{c_{t+1}^2}{(1+r_{t+1})} = w_t - \frac{(r_{t+1} - n_{t-1})tr}{(1+n_{t-1})(1+r_{t+1})}, \tag{5.13}$$

based on Equations (5.2), (5.3), and (5.7). The factor market equilibrium continues to be characterized by Equations (5.9) and (5.10), while equilibrium in the capital market requires $k_{t+1} = s_t/(1+n_t)$. Before simulating the fall of fertility in general equilibrium, it is helpful to briefly contemplate the partial equilibrium effect. In this case, wage and interest rate are unaffected by the demographic shock and merely the pay-as-you-go social insurance scheme induces a negative income effect. Thus, from Equation (5.13) it follows that a permanent drop in fertility starting with generation t, that is $...n_{t-2} = n_{t-1} > n_t = n_{t+1} = ...$, will depress social insurance wealth and welfare of all subsequent generations.

Of course, the partial equilibrium assumption is only adequate for a small open economy. Given that Germany is the world's third biggest economy and that, moreover, all Western economies undergo a similar demographic transition, this assumption is certainly inappropriate. We therefore move on to the general equilibrium analysis and parameterize the model. As to the intertemporal elasticity of substitution γ, Auerbach and Kotlikoff [103], page 50 report several estimates most of which lying within in the range 0.3 to 1.0. In the light of this evidence, we chose a value of 0.8. The rate of time preference is set to 1.5 percent *per annum*, ensuring somewhat realistic values for capital coefficient and real interest rate on an annual basis, namely 3.4 and 0.04, respectively. Finally, our choice of the old-age transfer tr brings about a contribution rate τ_t of 25 percent in the initial steady-state. In Germany the joint contribution rate to Social Security, health insurance, and old-age care ('Pflegeversicherung') amounts to 35 percent (cf. [144], table 93). Taking into account that all of these programs entail, albeit not exclusively, public intergenerational transfers from young to old, our estimate compares fairly well with reality.

Now consider the solid line in Figure 5.1 which, for the specified parameter values, depicts generations' welfare during a demographic transition. Welfare is measured as relative equivalent variations in life-cycle earnings. Owing to the linear-homogeneity of the utility function it can be expressed as

$$REV_t = \frac{u_t}{\bar{u}} - 1 , \tag{5.14}$$

with $\bar{u}$ indicating the initial utility level. Period $t = 0$ may be associated with the present point in time and generation 0, the one born and working in period $t = 0$, is the first to have fewer children. For convenience, generation 0 is sometimes referred to as baby-boomer, although in the present analysis this generation does not differ from previous ones. Accordingly, generation 1 is at times referred to a baby-buster.

Strikingly, and contrary to the partial equilibrium analysis, already generation 0 is adversely affected by the fertility shock. This welfare effect, how-

Fig. 5.1. Welfare Without Private Transfers

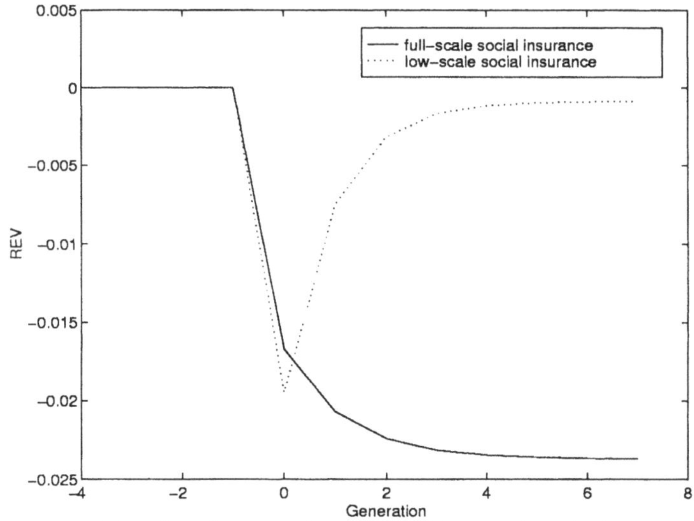

Note: For the complete simulation results of the full-scale and low-scale social insurance scenario, please refer to Appendix A.12, Tables A.3 and A.4, respectively.

ever, does not work through the pay-as-you-go scheme, but is attributable to the transition's direct effect on factor incomes. In particular, the decline in labor relative to capital will lead to a lower interest rate in period $t = 1$, thereby increasing that generation's price of old-age-consumption.[5] Generation 1 will, on top of this price effect, be burdened by higher social insurance contributions but also profit from a higher wage. The latter effect, however, is not sufficient to offset the adverse effect of higher net taxes, making future generations worse off than presently living.

In the light of Figure 5.1 one might argue, that the welfare loss of generation 1 relative to generation 0 is of secondary order compared to the relative welfare loss of generation 0. This amounts to saying, that the real thing to be concerned about, faced with a demographic transition, is its effect on factor incomes rather than its effect on the pay-as-you-go social insurance scheme. However, in the present model the adverse welfare effect of increasing contribution rates is highly understated by abstracting from an endogenous labor supply. Making allowances for distortionary taxes will reverse the relative importance of factor price and tax effects, as will be shown in Section 5.4.

For the present, we contend ourself with the model's simpler version and focus on the welfare of generation 0 as compared to the welfare of all subsequent generations. In this context it is important to note, that the qualitative outcome, according to which future generations are worse off as compared to presently living, hinges on the extent of the pay-as-you-go scheme. Employing the same model and parameterization but assuming a somewhat lower degree of public intergenerational redistribution, Raffelhüschen and Risa [149] demonstrate that the time-path of generations's welfare can perfectly behave as depicted by the dotted line in Figure 5.1. In this case, the wage increase induced by the relative scarcity of labor is sufficient to compensate future generations for the fiscal burden imposed on them, making them better of than their parents.

While the authors' example is highly illustrative of the need for general equilibrium considerations, they stress that the parameters were chosen in order to generate the desired result. The assumed contribution rate totalling 15 percent of the payroll does not adequately reflect the true extent of intergenerational redistribution in Germany. Furthermore, their qualitative result would probably not carry over to a model incorporating distortionary taxation. In view of these objections, the first scenario seems to be the relevant one for our purpose. Let us therefore summarize this section's finding by stating that in the absence of private intergenerational transfers future generations are adversely affected by population aging.

[5] Admittedly, the decline in interest rates will also have an effect on the social insurance wealth of generation 0. This effect, however, is welfare-enhancing and negligible anyhow.

5.2.2 Joy-of-Giving

In this section we investigate, how the inclusion of bequests for joy-of-giving might change the outcome. For this purpose we set ν, ϕ, β to zero, π to unity, and μ greater zero. The general model's utility function then boils down to:

$$u_t = \left[\left(c_t^1\right)^{1-1/\gamma} + \frac{1}{1+\delta}\left(c_{t+1}^2\right)^{1-1/\gamma} + \frac{\mu}{1+\delta}\left(I_{t+1}\right)^{1-1\gamma} \right]^{\frac{1}{1-1/\gamma}} . \quad (5.15)$$

On the basis of Equations (5.2), (5.3), and (5.7) the household budget constraint becomes:

$$c_t^1 + \frac{c_{t+1}^2}{(1+r_{t+1})} + \frac{(1+n_t)I_{t+1}}{1+r_{t+1}} = I_t + w_t - \frac{(r_{t+1} - n_{t-1})tr}{(1+n_{t-1})(1+r_{t+1})} . \quad (5.16)$$

While factor markets are unaffected by bequests, the capital market equilibrium condition is altered to $k_{t+1} = (s_t + I_t)/(1 + n_t)$. As before, let us first inquire into the partial equilibrium effects of a fertility shock starting with generation t, i.e. $...n_{t-2} = n_{t-1} > n_t = n_{t+1} = ...$ As is obvious from Equation (5.16), life-cycle resources of generation t are unchanged by the fertility shock. However, with their number of children decreasing, the 'price' of inheritances is reduced. Consequently, baby-boomers are better off as compared to previous generations and inheritances *per capita* of recipients unambiguously increase.

In correspondence with Section 5.2.1, baby-busters are adversely hit by the increase in social insurance contributions. In the present scenario, however, this adverse effect will be cushioned through the receipt of higher inheritances. Whether the increase in private intergenerational transfers is sufficient to offset the increase in public intergenerational transfers is an empirical question which can not be answered on merely analytical grounds. We therefore proceed by simulating the fertility shock in the general equilibrium context. Figure 5.2 gives generations' welfare for different specifications of μ or, stated differently, for a varying degree of private intergenerational transfers. The dotted line depicts the case previously discussed where generations are merely linked by public transfers. As one moves to higher trajectories the volume of bequests relative to GDP increases, with the corresponding ratio given in the legend.

In each of the cases under inspection the baby-boomers lose as a consequence of the fertility shock. This is due to the adverse price-effect caused by a declining interest rate. The loss is smaller, however, the stronger the private linkages between generations, in that the first price effect is increasingly counterbalanced by a declining price of bequests. Of course, the larger the share of resources devoted to bequests, the larger the gain induced by a declining price of bequests. Generation 1, as we have seen above, experiences an increase in gross wages, though not sufficient to make up for the rising fiscal burden. In the present scenario, however, the declining net wage

Fig. 5.2. Welfare With Bequests for Joy-of-Giving

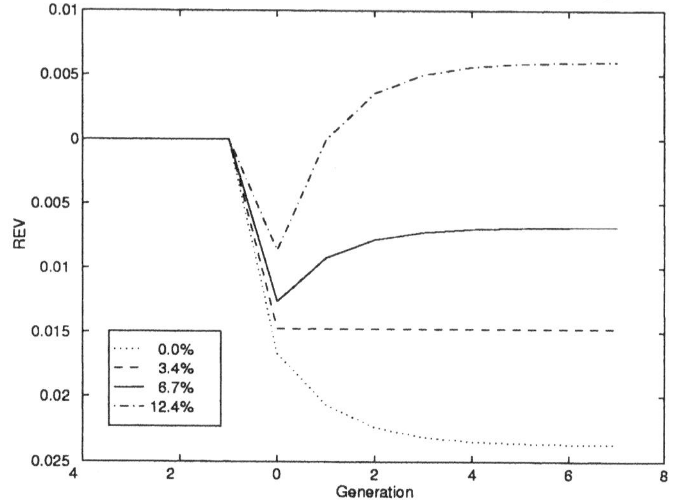

Note: The scenarios differ by the extent of private intergenerational transfers. The figures given in the legend refer to the ratio of bequests to GDP. The solid line depicts the baseline case. The complete simulations underlying the dotted, broken, solid, and broken-dotted line are reported in Appendix A.12, Tables A.3, A.6, A.5, and A.7, respectively.

goes with higher receipts of inheritances. In order to derive the extent of private compensation, Figure 5.2 distinguishes three polar cases. With bequests relative to GDP lying within the range of 0 and 3.4 percent, private transfers cushion, if not offset, the decline in net wages. Future generations are still worse off than the baby-boomer generation and the outcome is not qualitatively different from the one analyzed in Section 5.2.1. With bequests to GDP ranging from 3.4 through 12.4 percent, future generations are more than compensated for the decline in net wages. As a consequence, they are better off than the baby-boomers. Finally, with bequest exceeding 12.4 percent of GDP, future generations are compensated for the decline in both net wages and interest rates, making them even better of than pre-baby-boomer generations. To figure out which scenario conforms best to the circumstances in Germany, recall our findings of Section 3.1. With bequests, transfers *inter vivos*, and GDP amounting to DM 183 billion, 53 billion, and 3,169 billion, respectively, in 1993, overall private transfers to GDP come to approximately 7.5 percent. Hence, the intermediate scenario seems to be the relevant here. For the further course of the analysis we have defined a joy-of-giving baseline case, depicted as the solid line in Figure 5.2. In this case μ is set so as to generate a bequest to GDP ratio of 6.8 percent as well as reasonably realistic values for the capital coefficient, the real rate of return, and the contribution rate to social insurance.[6]

5.2.3 Accidental Bequests

Next, we investigate a demographic shock in a setting, where bequests are accidental. Accordingly, ν, μ, ϕ, β are set to zero and π lower unity. The representative agent's utility function then amounts to:

$$u_t = \left[\left(c_t^1\right)^{1-1/\gamma} + \frac{\pi}{1+\delta} \left(c_{t+1}^2\right)^{1-1/\gamma} \right]^{\frac{1}{1-1/\gamma}} . \tag{5.17}$$

Based on Equations (5.2), (5.3), (5.6), and (5.7) the life-cycle budget constraint changes into:

$$c_t^1 + \frac{c_{t+1}^2}{(1+r_{t+1})} = I_t + w_t - \frac{[(1+r_{t+1})\pi - (1+n_{t-1})]tr}{(1+n_{t-1})(1+r_{t+1})} . \tag{5.18}$$

Factor incomes continue to be determined by Equations (5.9) and (5.10), while the capital stock evolves according to $k_{t+1} = s_t/(1+n_t)$. Once more, we begin with a partial equilibrium analysis. For this purpose we replace I_t in Equation (5.18) by means of Equation (5.6) to obtain

$$c_t^1 + \frac{c_{t+1}^2}{(1+r)} = w + \frac{tr}{(1+r)} - \frac{\pi tr - (1-\pi)s_{t-1}(1+r)}{(1+n_{t-1})} . \tag{5.19}$$

Now, the last term depicts *per capita* net transfers between the current and preceding generation, i.e. contributions to the pay-as-you-go scheme less received bequests. From Equation (5.19) it follows that generation t, the first to have fewer children, is unaffected by the fertility shock, implying that $\partial s_t/\partial n_t = 0$. This in mind, we can easily derive, whether baby-busters will be compensated through higher inheritances for the fiscal burden imposed on them by population aging. Transpose Equation (5.19) by one period and differentiate life-cycle resources with respect to n_t. It follows that baby-busters will gain through a drop in fertility, precisely when $(1-\pi)s_{t-1}(1+r) > \pi tr$. Put differently, when (1) bequests are predominantly accidental and exceed defined benefits of a pay-as-you-go scheme, (2) general equilibrium effects are

[6] With the endogenous variables other than bequests being so insensitive to an increase in μ, one might question, why it was not increased further in the baseline case to generate a bequest to GDP ratio of exactly 7.5 percent. The reason is that in the models incorporating other bequest motives a bequest to GDP ratio of 7.5 percent would produce unrealistic values for the other benchmark variables. To keep the different models comparable we therefore resort to a somewhat lower ratio.

negligible, and (3) social insurance contributions impose no work disincentives, baby-busters rather than facing a demographic burden will experience a demographic windfall profit. To see, whether this scenario is even close to probable, let us cast a glance at the corresponding figures for Germany.

Social Security expenditures in 1993 came to DM 309 billion (cf. [144], table 93). However, according to Börsch-Supan and Reil-Held [151] only 80 percent of these expenditures constitute intergenerational transfers, while the rest is mere *intra*generational redistribution. For lack of adequate data, let us further assume, that health and old-age insurance comprise pay-as-you-go elements of negligible magnitude. Accordingly, the adequate figure for public intergenerational transfers is DM 247 billion versus DM 183 billion for bequests.[7] In view of these figures it is highly improbable, that baby-busters are not adversely affected by a demographic transition. This is reinforced, when relaxing our assumptions. For one thing, public health insurance and old-age care certainly include a noteworthy fraction of intergenerational transfers, in which case the figure for public transfers has to be adjusted upward. For another thing, not all bequests observed in 1993 are accidental, implying that at least the fraction which is motivated by altruism may be adjusted downward as the number of heirs declines.

Let us next analyze the working of accidental bequests in a general equilibrium setting. Once more departing from the calibrated reference model of Section 5.2.1, which completely abstracts from private transfers, we gradually reduce π to below unity, this way introducing accidental bequests. Figure 5.3 presents the welfare of successive generations under varying degrees of private intergenerational linkage. The dotted line corresponds to the model without bequests and is a mere recapitulation of the doted line in Figure 5.2 and the solid line in Figure 5.1. Higher trajectories are associated with lower values of π and, thus, an increasing ratio of accidental bequests to GDP. We anew distinguish three polar cases. With bequests to GDP lying between zero and 0.8 percent, future generations are only partly compensated for the decline in net wages, let alone the decline in interest rates. They are, hence, worse off than baby-boomers. For a bequest to GDP ratio ranging between 0.8 and 4.6 percent, bequests are sufficient to offset the decline in net wages, though not the drop of interest. Future generations are, thus, better off than the generation working at present. Finally, with bequests amounting to more than 4.6 percent of GDP, future generations will even make up for the decline in interest income. In this case they will experience a higher welfare than today's retirees.

One way to gauge, which of the described segments is relevant for the German case is to inspect the actual ratio of bequests to GDP. Bequest of DM 183 billion and GDP of DM 3,169 yield a corresponding ratio of 5.8 per-

[7] Recall from Section 3.1, that the figure for bequests was derived exactly as detailed in Equation (5.19), namely by multiplying age-specific wealth $s_t(1+r)$ by age-specific mortality rates $(1-\pi)$.

Fig. 5.3. Welfare With Accidental Bequests

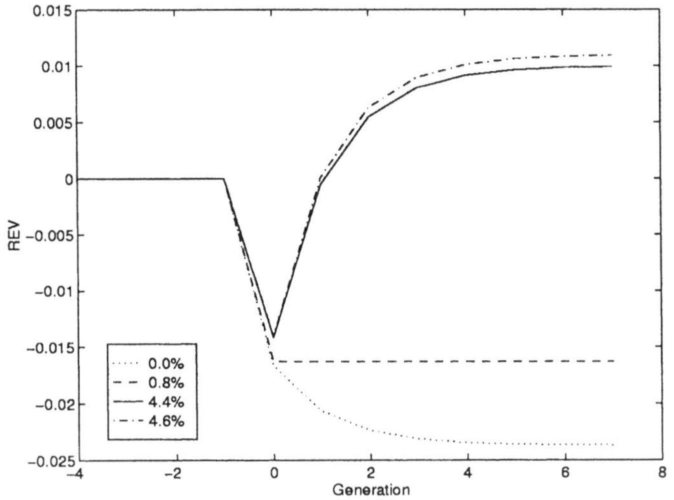

Note: The scenarios differ by the extent of private intergenerational transfers. The figures given in the legend refer to the ratio of bequests to GDP. The solid line depicts the baseline case. The complete simulations underlying the dotted, broken, solid, and broken-dotted line are reported in Appendix A.12, Tables A.3, A.9, A.8, and A.10, respectively.

cent in 1993. Following this approach Germany would range in the highest segment and one would project future generations to gain from the demographic transition. Contrary to the previous section, however, the ratio of bequests to GDP might not be a reasonable yardstick in the present context. To see this note that we are interested in the relative magnitude of public and private intergenerational transfers. It is this ratio which, in the first place, drives the qualitative outcome of compensation or non-compensation. In the case of bequests for joy-of-giving, τ, representing the extent of public intergenerational transfers, was insensitive to a variation of the bequest parameter. With τ calibrated to real world circumstances, it only remained to chose the correct extent of bequests. In the present model, however, the probability of survival π not only governs the volume of accidental bequests but also the extent of public intergenerational transfers. Specifically, a reduction in the probability of survival will cut down workers' contributions to the pay-as-you-go scheme, since the number of pensioners to be supported decreases. Therefore, increasing π until bequests amount to 5.8 percent of GDP, will wildly exaggerate the compensating effect of private transfers, given that we have, at the same time, reduced public intergenerational transfers.

To cope with the above objection, we use a different benchmark to generate the baseline case for accidental bequests. In particular, π is reduced until, in the initial steady-state, the ratio of private to public intergenerational transfers conforms to a realistic figure of 74 percent. This figure is obtained by dividing 1993 bequests of DM 183 billion by the 1993 pay-as-you-go share of Social Security expenditure, namely DM 247 billion.[8] This baseline case is depicted by the solid line in Figure 5.3. Note, that according to this calibration baby-buster will scarcely be affected by the demographic transtion. To the extent that public health and old-age care programs contain pay-as-you-go elements the ratio of 74 percent is too high. In this case the baseline trajectory would have to be adjusted downward. In any way, however, future generations are likely to be better off than today's working generation. Only if accidental bequests would fall to below 0.8 percent of GDP – this corresponds to a share in overall bequests of 14 percent – would future generations lose relative to baby-boomers.[9]

5.2.4 Bequests-as-Exchange

Finally, we explore the effects of a demographic transition on the condition that most private intergenerational transfers are motivated by exchange. This can be done by setting ν, μ, β to zero, π to unity and ϕ greater unity. The agent's utility function then boils down to

$$u_t = \left[(c_t^1)^{1-1/\gamma} + \frac{1}{1+\delta}(c_{t+1}^2)^{1-1/\gamma} + \frac{\phi}{1+\delta}(A_{t+1})^{1-1/\gamma}\right]^{\frac{1}{1-1/\gamma}} . \tag{5.20}$$

Combining Equations (5.2), (5.3), (5.4), (5.5), and (5.7) the agent's budget constraint comes to:

$$c_t^1 + \frac{c_{t+1}^2}{(1+r_{t+1})} + \frac{(1-\tau_{t+1})w_{t+1}}{(1+r_{t+1})}A_{t+1} = w_t - \frac{[(1+r_{t+1})-(1+n_{t-1})(1-a_t)]tr}{(1+n_{t-1})(1+r_{t+1})(1-a_t)} . \tag{5.21}$$

Recall that the agent 'purchases' attention from his offsprings by compensating them for earnings forgone while spending time with him. Therefore,

[8] Due to the trade-off between a realistic volume of bequests and a realistic contribution to social insurance, the baseline π generates bequests and contributions that are slightly too small.

[9] We found out earlier that overall bequest amount to 5.8 percent of GDP, thus GDP equals 17.24 times overall bequests. Consequently, accidental bequests equal to 0.8 percent of GDP – this is one of our polar cases – amount to 13.79 percent of overall bequests. These back-of-the-envelope calculations should, however, be considered with utmost caution, in that, so far, we have abstracted from labor disincentives caused by the pay-as-you-go system.

the price for attention is the offsprings' net wage, discounted to the present. Moreover, due to the compensation neither inheritances nor attention – apart from the appearance in net taxes – turn up as supplement or diminution of the agent's life-cycle earnings, respectively. According to Equation (5.4) inheritances received and attention provided just cancel out. Attention provided, however, enters the expression for the agent's social insurance liabilities in a positive fashion. The reason is obvious from Equation (5.7), with β and l_t set to zero and π equal to unity: as workers increase the share of time spent with their parents and, thus, reduce their supply of labor, contributions as percent of payroll are bound to increase. Once more, the model is closed by the factor and capital market equilibrium conditions.

The partial equilibrium effects of a drop in fertility can be outlined as follows. According to Equation (5.21), generation t, the first to have fewer children, does not face any change in life-cycle resources. Nonetheless, this generation experiences a welfare gain. Given that their children's net wage will decline – as is detailed below – they pay a lower price for attention. Baby-busters alike profit from a lower price for attention. In their case, however, the favorable effect is negligible as compared to the adverse effect induced by the pay-as-you-go scheme. Thus, contribution rates increase for two reasons. For one thing, the ratio of workers to pensioners has deteriorated. For another thing, labor supply has declined, as workers spend more time with their parents. The latter has become necessary as fewer siblings share the burden of taking care of their parents. Most important, and contrary to preceding transfer motives, there is no offsetting windfall profit in the form of inheritances. It is therefore impossible for future generations to be better off than presently living.

This result carries over to a general equilibrium setting, as is obvious from Figure 5.4. The dotted line, once more, refers to the reference model of Section 5.2.1 with ϕ and, thus, bequests equal to zero. As we increase the volume of exchange-motivated bequests relative to GDP, the welfare path comes to lie below the reference trajectory for every future generation. One of those trajectories is shown by the solid line. It corresponds to a bequest-to-GDP ratio of 6.0 percent and constitutes our baseline case for the bequest-as-exchange model.

Imagine, contributions to social insurance were levied on a lump-sum basis. To all of the models considered so far, this would make no difference, as labor supply was exogenous. In the present model, however, it would make a difference, since labor supply is somehow endogenous. To eliminate this effect of an endogenous labor supply – which actually is the subject of Section 5.4 – let us, for the moment, replace the flat rate contribution by a lump-sum contribution to social insurance. Again, the analysis of previous models is unaffected by this modification. In the present model, however, the agent's budget constraint reduces to

Fig. 5.4. Welfare With Bequests-as-Exchange

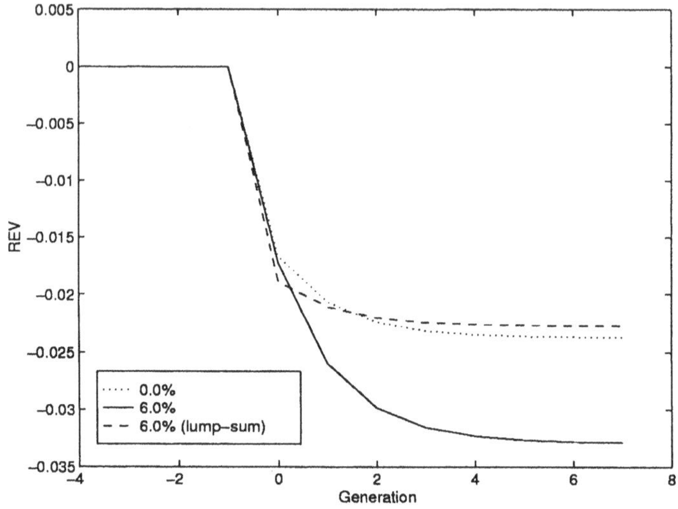

Note: The scenarios differ by the extent of private intergenerational transfers and by the way social insurance contributions are levied. The figures given in the legend refer to the ratio of bequests to GDP. The solid line depicts the baseline case. The complete simulations underlying the dotted, broken, and solid line are reported in Appendix A.12, Tables A.3, A.11, and A.12, respectively.

$$c_t^1 + \frac{c_{t+1}^2}{(1+r_{t+1})} + \frac{w_{t+1}}{(1+r_{t+1})}A_{t+1} = w_t - \frac{(r_{t+1}-n_{t-1})tr}{(1+n_{t-1})(1+r_{t+1})}.^{10} \tag{5.22}$$

This model, too, collapses to the reference model of Section 5.2.1 as ϕ is set to zero. In the limit, the model therefore exhibits a welfare path as depicted by the dotted line in Figure 5.4. Remarkable about the lump-sum version of the bequest-as-exchange model is the fact, that its welfare path is extremely insensitive to a variation of the volume of bequests. The broken line, for example, shows the welfare of successive generations, given the same parameterization as in the baseline case. However, even for much higher values of ϕ the welfare path closely tracks that of the reference model without bequests. Comparing Equation (5.22) and (5.13) this does not come as a surprise. The only difference between the two budget constraints is the third term in Equation (5.22) and, thus, an additional price effect, which is, though, of secondary order. It follows, that the bequest-as-exchange model in its essence – that is abstracting from the endogenous labor effect – does not feature private intergenerational transfers. Strictly speaking, the model does

[10] For the deduction, refer to Appendix A.6.

exhibit private intergenerational transfers – bequests and attention – that are, however, equal in value and opposite in direction and therefore have no distributional impact.

5.2.5 Summary

Figure 5.5 summarizes our findings by contrasting the baseline welfare paths of Sections 5.2.1 through 5.2.4. While the models underlying the trajectories differ, in the limit – that is, for $\mu = 0$, $\pi = 1$, and $\phi = 0$, respectively – they all collapse to the same non-bequest model as described in Section 5.2.1. Moreover, the models' parameterization, apart from the bequest parameter, is identical. Finally, the endogenous variables that serve for benchmarking the models to reality, exhibit fairly similar values across the models. All

Fig. 5.5. Comparing REV for Various Bequest Motives

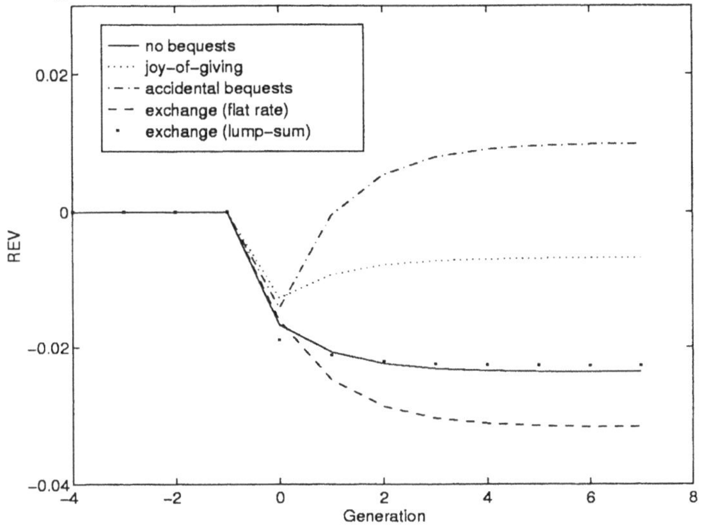

values of capital coefficient and real interest rate, for example, lie within a range of 3.4 to 4.2 and 3.5 to 4 percent, respectively. In view of the models' common features, the divergence in welfare paths can be safely attributed to the differences in bequest motives.

The role of private intergenerational transfers during a demographic transition greatly varies, depending on the underlying motive. With respect to their distributional implications, accidental bequests and exchange-motivated bequests can be regarded as the opposite poles of a spectrum. In the case of accidental bequests heirs appropriate the complete windfall gain resulting from a declining number of heirs relative to testators. In the case of bequests-as-exchange the demographic transition does not bring about any windfall profit. Nonetheless, when the pay-as-you-go scheme is financed through a flat rate tax, the demographic transition enables parents to extract resources from their offsprings. This works as follows. Providing attention is costly both in terms of forgone working time and in terms of lower net wages during working ours. While the first effect is made up for through inheritances, the second effect goes uncompensated. Thus, parents pay too low a price for attention purchased from their children.

One might question, why children consent to the exchange, when it makes them worse off. The answer is that they simply do not perceive the link between providing attention and reducing labor supply, on the one hand, and higher contributions to social insurance, on the other hand. This is especially likely for Germany, where on a microeconomic level the equivalence between contributions and benefits is far from perfect.

It is left to the reader to assess, how plausible such a setting is. To our mind, the essence of bequests-as-exchange is best captured in a model where the pay-as-you-go program is financed on a lump-sum basis. In such a model bequests constitute a payment rather than a transfer and, consequently, have no effect on intergenerational distribution. Bequests for joy-of-giving, finally, take an intermediate position, with the windfall gain shared equally between testators and heirs. From this ranking it follows that, if accidental bequests do not lead to a compensation – as, for example, in a partial equilibrium setting – none of the bequest motives will.[11]

With the exception of bequests-as-exchange, baby-busters and successive generations will be compensated for the fiscal burden associated with population aging. While bequests for joy-of-giving raise baby-busters above the welfare level of baby-boomers, accidental bequests even raise their welfare to the level experienced by generations completely unaffected by the demographic shock. Given that actual bequests are likely to be a mixture of the different forms of bequests discussed in this section, the prospect for future generations does not appear that gloomy.

5.3 Intergenerational Transfer Accounting and General Equilibrium

With the introduction of a general equilibrium model in Section 5.1 we are now in the position to review the earlier generational accounting exercise.

[11] A little caveat is in order. Accidental bequests can amount to DM 183 billion at most. Transfers induced by other motives, however, can amount to a maximum of DM 236 billion, including also transfer *inter vivos*. Being larger, transfers other than accidental bequests, could a priori still lead to a compensation. However, we have conducted the accidental bequest experiment also with a transfer volume of DM 236 billion and still did not obtain a compensation.

Recall that an accounting framework must necessarily abstract from both changes in relative prices as well as the adjustments of optimizing agents induced by those changes. In the present section we will therefore assess, whether the neglect of general equilibrium effects will bias our accounting results and, if this is the case, in which direction.

The reasoning behind conventional generational accounting is as follows. The conventional generational account GA^{pub} is supposed to be a good approximation of generations' net taxes. Furthermore, generations' welfare depends inversely on net taxes. Consequently, GA^{pub} is used as an inverse indicator for the effect of fiscal policy on generations' welfare. A corresponding line of argument can be made up for the extended accounting which takes into account both public and private intergenerational transfers. In particular, if GA^{tot} is a good approximation of the net public and private "bequest" a generation leaves to other generations and, moreover, this net overall bequest has a negative impact on the donor generations' welfare, GA^{tot} can serve as an inverse indicator for the effect of total intergenerational transfers on generations' welfare. For the moment assume that GA^{tot}, in fact, were a valid welfare indicator of public and private intergenerational transfers. In this case, we could complement our understanding of the welfare implications of population aging by using the extended accounts $GA^{\text{tot}} = GA^{\text{pub}} + GA^{\text{pri}}$ instead of the conventional accounts GA^{pub}.

In assessing the accurateness of the earlier accounting exercise we answer the following questions, first for public and subsequently for overall transfers: (1) Under which circumstances does generations' welfare depend inversely on net public and overall intergenerational transfers to other generations? (2) Are the public account GA^{pub} and the overall account GA^{tot}, as calculated in the general accounting framework, good predictors for net taxes and net overall transfers, respectively, as generated by a general equilibrium model?

5.3.1 Conventional Generational Accounting

For the moment we are only interested in public intergenerational transfers. Let us therefore resort to the most basic model abstracting from private intergenerational transfers altogether. This model is generated by setting ν, μ, ϕ, β to zero and π to unity and is restated for convenience. The agent maximizes the utility function

$$u_t = \left[\left(c_t^1\right)^{1-1/\gamma} + \frac{1}{1+\delta} \left(c_{t+1}^2\right)^{1-1\gamma} \right]^{\frac{1}{1-1/\gamma}} \tag{5.23}$$

subject to the budget constraint

$$c_t^1 + \frac{c_{t+1}^2}{(1+r_{t+1})} = w_t - \left[T_t - \frac{tr_{t+1}}{(1+r_{1+t})} \right] , \tag{5.24}$$

where the pay-as-you-go scheme is specified by

$$T_t = \frac{tr_t}{(1+n_{t-1})} \, . \tag{5.25}$$

For expository reasons we have replaced the payroll tax by a lump-sum tax. However, given an exogenous labor supply, this does not make any difference. Finally, factors are paid their marginal product and the capital stock evolves according to $k_{t+1} = s_t/(1+n_t)$.

As to the first question, it is immediately obvious that due to the income effect generational welfare depends negatively on net taxes as specified by the last term in Equation (5.24). Let us therefore move on to the second issue, namely the ability of conventional generational accounts GA^{pub} to predict net taxes.

Generational accounting usually begins by defining a base year for the calculation. In the present dynamic model we choose a base year that suits best the situation as presently observed in most industrialized countries. This situation is characterized by a still moderate dependency ratio but a dramatic deterioration of the ratio in the forthcoming decades. Recall that in the present model generation t, the one being born and working in period t, is the first generation exhibiting a lower fertility. Period t therefore conforms well to the present point in time and is chosen as base year.

With the base year defined, we can state the public generational account for a base year newborn $GA^{\text{pub}}_{t,t}$. This account is defined as the present value of life-cycle taxes minus transfers *per capita*. It is calculated by projecting age-specific taxes and transfers, as observed in the base year, into the future, where payments in the future are discounted at the base year interest rate. In the case of a defined benefit pay-as-you-go scheme $tr_t = tr_{t+1} = tr$, so that

$$GA^{\text{pub}}_{t,t} = T_t - \frac{tr}{(1+r_t)} = \frac{(r_t - n_{t-1})tr}{(1+n_{t-1})(1+r_t)} \quad \text{as opposed to} \tag{5.26}$$

$$NT_{t,t} = T_t - \frac{tr}{(1+r_{t+1})} = \frac{(r_{t+1} - n_{t-1})tr}{(1+n_{t-1})(1+r_{t+1})} \, , \tag{5.27}$$

the net taxes paid by a base year newborn. Obviously, generational accounting is quite good at depicting the net taxes of a base year newborn, with the exception of the discount rate which contrary to reality is assumed fixed.

To derive the public account of an individual born in the future, typically in period $t+1$, is slightly more arduous. We depart from the government's intertemporal budget constraint as specified in Equation (4.13). With the government being confined to providing a pay-as-you-go social insurance scheme this constraint boils down to

$$\sum_{s=0}^{D} N_{t,t-s} + \sum_{s=1}^{\infty} N_{t,t+s} = 0 \, , \tag{5.28}$$

where the two terms correspond to the aggregate accounts of presently living and future generations. Let L_t stand for the size of the cohort born in period t. Equation (5.28) can then be stated as:

$$-L_{t-1}tr + L_t T_t - \frac{L_t tr}{(1+r_t)} = -\sum_{s=1}^{\infty} N_{t,t+s} \, . \tag{5.29}$$

The first two terms denote aggregate pensions and contributions in the base year which according to Equation (5.25) add up to zero. It follows that the aggregate fiscal burden of future generations corresponds to the pension entitlements accumulated by today's working-aged. Assigning the aggregate burden evenly over future individuals yields the public account of a representative future individual. After some manipulations and assuming a constant base year interest rate one obtains

$$GA^{\text{pub}}_{t+1,t+1} = \frac{(r_t - n_t)tr}{(1+n_t)(1+r_t)} \quad \text{as opposed to} \tag{5.30}$$

$$NT_{t+1,t+1} = T_{t+1} - \frac{tr}{(1+r_{t+2})} = \frac{(r_{t+2} - n_t)tr}{(1+n_t)(1+r_{t+2})} \, , \tag{5.31}$$

the net tax of a representative future agent.[12] Again, the generational account appears to be a rather good approximation of net tax payments, as only the discount rate deviates from its real value.

A comparison of Equations (5.26) and (5.30) reveals that with $n_{t-1} > n_t$ the public account of a future individual exceeds the account of a representative living individual. Let us now compare, how well public generational accounts picture the development of net taxes. Figure 5.6 contrasts public accounts and net taxes simulated in the model discussed above and parameterized as detailed in Section 5.2.1. The accounting base year is zero. As to the generational accounts, we assume in correspondence with the steady state assumption that the accounts of base year newborns also apply to cohorts born prior to the base year.[13] While the increase in generational accounts reflects the deterioration of the dependency ratio holding everything else constant, the present value of net taxes also hinges on the development of interest rates. Interest rates decline as fertility drops, because capital becomes more abundant relative to labor. Hence, with $\partial NT/\partial r > 0$ net taxes must lie

[12] For a detailed derivation please refer to Appendix A.7, which owes to [149].

[13] This is somewhat in contrast to the practice in actual generational accounting studies. For lack of data those studies define the generational accounts of cohorts born prior to the base year as mere rest-of-life net taxes. In that the life span prior to the base year is not documented, those cohorts' accounts must therefore deviate from the accounts of base year newborns – even in a steady state. Since we face no data limitations in the present context, we can resort to the more general definition according to which generational accounts are constant in the steady state.

Fig. 5.6. Comparing Net Taxes and Public Accounts

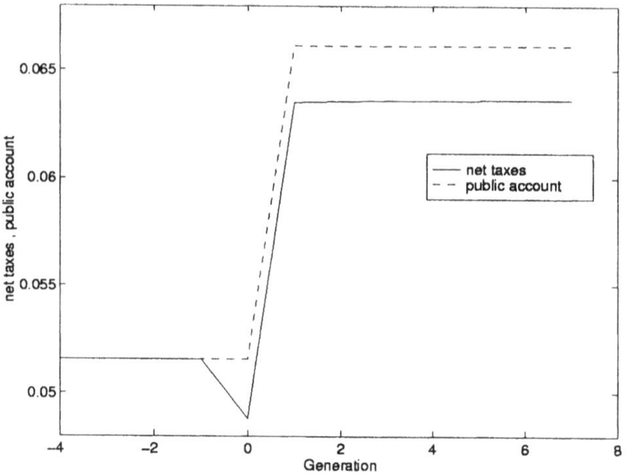

Note: A comprehensive overview of the simulation's trajectories is presented in Appendix A.12, Table A.3.

below generational accounts from generation 0 onwards. While generational accounts overestimate the fiscal burden of both current and future generations in the present demographic situation, the bias is of minor importance. For one thing, the bias is small relative to the fiscal imbalance. For another thing, both present and future accounts are biased in the same way. As a consequence, the absolute fiscal imbalance, our major concern, is correctly reported.

To summarize, we have shown that welfare depends positively on net taxes which are rather well approximated by public accounts. Consequently, public accounts can serve as welfare indicators for fiscal policy. At this point one might object that the result hinges on the neglect of distortionary taxes in our model. In principal, this is a valid argument. Generational accounting must *per* definition abstract from substitution effects. Therefore, incorporating substitution effects into our model by allowing for an endogenous labor supply and contributions proportional to payroll would drive an additional wedge between generational accounts and welfare. However, as Fehr and Kotlikoff [152] have shown, substitution effects are of negligible order relative to income effects and can therefore be safely ignored.

5.3.2 Extended Generational Accounting

In this section we investigate, whether the extended generational account GA^{tot} is suitable for indicating the joint welfare effect of both public and private intergenerational transfers. In doing this we again proceed along the lines of the above questions, namely (1) Does generational welfare depend on net overall transfers in an unambiguous fashion? (2) Is GA^{tot} a reasonable approximation of net overall transfers?

Let us begin with the first question. Net overall transfers are the sum of net taxes and net bequests to other generations. In the previous section we have already shown that welfare depends inversely on net taxes. It therefore remains to be shown that generational welfare also depends inversely on net bequests to other generations. We will argue that this is only the case in the accidental bequest model. To see why, combine Equations (5.2) and (5.3) to derive the expressions for net bequests under the different bequest motives:

$$NB^{\text{j}}_{t,t} = \frac{(1+n_t)}{(1+r_{t+1})} I^{\text{j}}_{t+1} - I^{\text{j}}_t \qquad \text{(joy-of-giving)} \tag{5.32}$$

$$NB^{\text{x}}_{t,t} = \frac{(1+n_t)}{(1+r_{t+1})} I^{\text{x}}_{t+1} - I^{\text{x}}_t \qquad \text{(exchange)} \tag{5.33}$$

$$NB^{\text{a}}_{t,t} = -I^{\text{a}}_t \qquad \text{(accidental)} \tag{5.34}$$

In the case of joy-of-giving and exchange motivated bequests the relation between net bequests and welfare is ambiguous. Thus, a decline in net bequests can imply a welfare loss, when the decline is brought about by fewer bequests left behind I_{t+1}.[14] At the same time, a decline in net bequests can imply a welfare gain, when the decline is caused by an increase in the inheritances received I_t. Only in the case of accidental bequests is there an unambiguous negative relationship between net bequests and welfare. A decline in net bequests is always generated by an increase in received inheritances and, hence, associated with raising welfare. Let us summarize our interim result by stating that the net overall transfer to other generations only constitutes a meaningful welfare indicator on the condition that most bequests are accidental. Put differently, when generations derive utility from leaving a bequest to their children, the net bequest – defined as the bequest left minus the inheritance received – is misleading as welfare indicator.

In the following analysis we use the accidental bequest model as benchmark which is restated here for convenience. Recall that it is generated by setting ν, μ, ϕ, β to zero and π lower than unity. The agent maximizes the utility function

[14] In the case of exchange-motivated bequests it is not immediately obvious from the utility function (cf. Equation (5.1)) that welfare increases in I^{x}_{t+1}. However, if one replaces A_{t+1} by means of Equations (5.5) and (5.4), the relationship becomes evident.

$$u_t = \left[\left(c_t^1\right)^{1-1\gamma} + \frac{\pi}{1+\delta} \left(c_{t+1}^2\right)^{1-1\gamma} \right]^{\frac{1}{1-1\gamma}} \tag{5.35}$$

subject to the budget constraints

$$c_t^1 = I_t + w_t - T_t - s_t \tag{5.36}$$

$$c_{t+1}^2 = s_t(1 + r_{t+1}) + tr_{t+1} \ , \tag{5.37}$$

where the accidental bequest and pay-as-you-go scheme are specified by

$$I_t = \frac{(1-\pi)s_{t-1}(1+r_t)}{(1+n_{t-1})} \quad \text{and} \tag{5.38}$$

$$T_t = \frac{\pi tr_t}{(1+n_{t-1})} \ , \tag{5.39}$$

respectively. Once more we substitute a lump-sum tax for the payroll tax introduced in Section 5.1. As stated earlier, however, the two are equivalent with labor supply being exogenous. Factors are paid their marginal product and capital market equilibrium is defined by:

$$k_{t+1} = \frac{s_t}{(1+n_t)} \ . \tag{5.40}$$

Combining Equations (5.36) and (5.37) to yield the agent's life-cycle budget constraint

$$c_t^1 + \frac{c_{t+1}^2}{(1+r_{t+1})} = w_t - \left[\left(T_t - \frac{tr_{t+1}}{(1+r_{1+t})} \right) + \left(- I_t \right) \right] \tag{5.41}$$

makes our earlier point immediately obvious. The first term in the square bracket are net taxes accruing to other generations, the second term are net bequests left to other generations (which are negative because received inheritances outweigh). Both have a negative impact on the agent's utility via the income effect. Consequently, also their sum which we called ***net overall transfer*** has a negative impact on the agent's utility.

In what follows we attempt to answer the second question, that is whether the GA^{tot} as calculated in Section 4.4.2 is an acceptable approximation of the net overall transfers as generated by the general equilibrium model. Note, however, that we cannot immediately compare net overall transfers as specified in Equation (5.41) and GA^{tot}, as derived in generational accounting. The reason is that the unit of reference in the general equilibrium model is the ***representative*** individual, while in generational accounting, being a macroeconomic framework, it is the ***average*** individual. The representative individual in the general equilibrium model lives for two periods. This is obvious from Equation (5.41), where second period consumption enters with probability 1 and accidental bequests accruing to other generations do not appear at all. In contrast, the life-span of an average individual falls below two periods, since only a fraction of the population survives to the end of the second period. Hence, a comparison of net overall bequests and overall generational accounts requires to reformulate Equation (5.41) in terms of an average individual.[15] This can be done as follows. Weight the *per capita* Equations (5.36), (5.37), and (5.38) by the respective cohort size, combine them, and divide by the initial cohort size. As a result one obtains the life-cycle budget constraint of an average individual:[16]

$$c_t^1 + \frac{\pi c_{t+1}^2}{(1+r_{t+1})} = w_t - \left[\left(T_t - \frac{\pi tr_{t+1}}{(1+r_{t+1})}\right) + \left(\frac{(1+n_t)I_{t+1}}{(1+r_{t+1})} - I_t\right)\right] . \tag{5.42}$$

The term in the square bracket denotes net overall transfers in terms of an average individual and serves as benchmark for assessing the accurateness of GA^{tot}. Note, that the overall transfer can also be stated as the difference between life-cycle earnings and consumption – a fact that is exploited by the comprehensive accounting framework, as earnings and consumption are easier to observe.

Let us next recapitulate, how the overall generational accounts of a representative living and future individual were calculated. As to the account of a base year newborn, we subtracted life-cycle consumption from life-cycle earnings – both stated in terms of present value. In doing this, we assumed that age-specific flows of consumption and earnings in the base year stayed constant over time, as is only the case under steady state conditions.[17] In the same way, we projected the base year interest rate into the future. Thus the overall account of a base year newborn reads

$$GA_{t,t}^{\text{tot}} = w_t - c_t^1 - \frac{\pi c_t^2}{(1+r_t)} \qquad \text{as opposed to} \tag{5.43}$$

$$TT_{t,t} = w_t - c_t^1 - \frac{\pi c_{t+1}^2}{(1+r_{t+1})} , \tag{5.44}$$

the total net transfer predicted by a general equilibrium model. Of course, the steady state assumption is not valid during a demographic transition. Consequently, the account and actual transfer deviate with respect to the interest rate and second period consumption. As outlined earlier, the interest rate is going to fall during the demographic transition. Insofar $GA_{t,t}^{\text{tot}}$ by holding the interest rate constant overstates the total transfer left to other

---

[15] In the previous section this reformulation could be avoided. Given that the former model economy featured only one sort of individual, average and representative individual were equivalent expressions.

[16] The transformation is detailed in Appendix A.8.

[17] To be precise, we assumed that flows *per capita* grow at a constant rate equivalent to the rate of technical progress. In the present framework, however, the rate of technical progress is taken account of in the population growth rate. It can therefore be ignored here.

generations and understates the welfare position of living generations. On the other hand, baby-boomers, faced with a lower interest rate, will reduce their second period consumption. On this account, $GA_{t,t}^{\text{tot}}$ by holding second period consumption constant understates the total transfer of living generations or, equivalently, overstates their welfare. In view of these counteracting effects, it is impossible to determine the bias of $GA_{t,t}^{\text{tot}}$ on merely analytical grounds. We will later answer this question by way of simulation, but let us first derive an expression for the overall account of a representative future individual.

As in conventional generational accounting, the net burden of a future individual is calculated as residual by means of an intertemporal budget constraint. In the case of the extended accounting version this is the economy's intertemporal budget constraint

$$W_t^{\text{p}} + \sum_{s=0}^{D} L_{t,t-s} - \sum_{s=0}^{D} N_{t,t-s} - \sum_{s=0}^{D} C_{t,t-s} + \sum_{s=1}^{\infty} L_{t,t+s} - \sum_{s=1}^{\infty} N_{t,t+s} - \sum_{s=1}^{\infty} C_{t,t+s} = 0, \tag{5.45}$$

as introduced in Section 4.4.2. Recall that in this accounting identity W_t^{p} depicts net private wealth in base year t. $L_{t,k}$, $N_{t,k}$, and $C_{t,k}$ stand for the present value of future labor income, net taxes, and consumption attributed to all members of the generation born in year k. Finally, D is the maximum life-expectancy. Next, it is assumed that the government's intertemporal budget constraint is satisfied, as specified by Equation (5.28). Consequently, Equation (5.45) reduces to:

$$W_t^{\text{p}} + \sum_{s=0}^{D} L_{t,t-s} - \sum_{s=0}^{D} C_{t,t-s} = -\left[\sum_{s=1}^{\infty} L_{t,t+s} - \sum_{s=1}^{\infty} C_{t,t+s}\right] . \tag{5.46}$$

Now, the left hand side is supposed to depict the net overall transfer of living generations, which is equal in magnitude but opposite in sign to the net overall transfer of future generations, shown on the right hand side. In terms of our two-generation-world this constraint can be written as

$$L_t k_t(1+r_t) + L_t w_t - \left(\pi L_{t-1} c_t^2 + L_t c_t^1 + \frac{\pi L_t c_t^2}{(1+r_t)}\right) = -\sum_{s=1}^{\infty} \frac{L_{t+s}}{(1+r_t)^s}\left[w_t - \left(c_t^1 + \frac{\pi c_t^2}{(1+r_t)}\right)\right] , \tag{5.47}$$

where in steady state fashion base year interest rate and *per capita* magnitudes are projected into the future. An equivalent expression is:

$$L_t I_t - L_t T_t + L_t w_t - L_t c_t^1 - \frac{\pi L_t c_t^2}{(1+r_t)} = -\sum_{s=1}^{\infty} \frac{L_{t+s}}{(1+r_t)^s}\left[w_t - \left(c_t^1 + \frac{\pi c_t^2}{(1+r_t)}\right)\right] , \tag{5.48}$$

stating that the part of base year newborns' income – from both intergenerational transfers and work – which is not consumed, is left to future generations.[18] In correspondence with conventional generational accounting we assume that this "bequest" is distributed evenly over future generations. Thus, dividing by L_t yields

$$I_t - T_t + w_t - c_t^1 - \frac{\pi c_t^2}{(1+r_t)} = -GA_{t+1,t+1}^{\text{tot}} \sum_{s=1}^{\infty} \left(\frac{1+n_t}{1+r_t}\right)^s . \tag{5.49}$$

Finally, after simplifying the geometric series and some rearrangement, the future generations' overall account comes to

$$GA_{t+1,t+1}^{tot} = -\frac{r_t - n_t}{(1+n_t)} \left(I_t - T_t + w_t - c_t^1 - \frac{\pi c_t^2}{(1+r_t)}\right) \tag{5.50}$$

as opposed to

$$TT_{t+1,t+1} = w_{t+1} - c_{t+1}^1 - \frac{\pi c_{t+2}^2}{(1+r_{t+2})} , \tag{5.51}$$

the net total transfer generated by the general equilibrium model. At first sight the two do not appear to have much in common. It can be shown once more, however, that $GA_{t+1,t+1}^{\text{tot}}$ and $TT_{t+1,t+1}$ are equivalent on the steady state assumption.[19]

Interest rates and *per capita* magnitudes happen not to be constant over time – especially with a demographic transition under way. This is why the accounting framework is bound to make mistakes in assessing generational burdens. In conventional accounting the only source of bias is the assumed constancy of the interest rate. In the present context there is an additional source of error, namely the assumed constancy of wages and *per capita* consumption. Let us now investigate by means of simulation, whether this error is likely to be large. The solid line in Figure 5.7 depicts generations' net total transfers to other generations as specified by Equations (5.44) or (5.51). Again period 0 corresponds to the present point in time and generation 0 and 1 denote baby-boomers and baby-busters, respectively. The simulation is carried out in the accidental bequest model which is numerically specified as detailed in Section 5.2.3. In particular, bequests in the initial steady state amount to 74 percent of public intergenerational transfers, as presently observed in Germany. With respect to future generations, the adverse effect of a defined benefit system therefore outweighs the favorable effect of increased inheritances and net overall transfers increase.

The broken line illustrates the overall accounts of present and future generations as specified by Equations (5.43) and (5.50). Obviously, the account

[18] For a detailed derivation of future generations' total account please refer to Appendix A.9.

[19] The proof is relegated to Appendix A.10.

Fig. 5.7. Comparing Net Total Transfers and Total Accounts

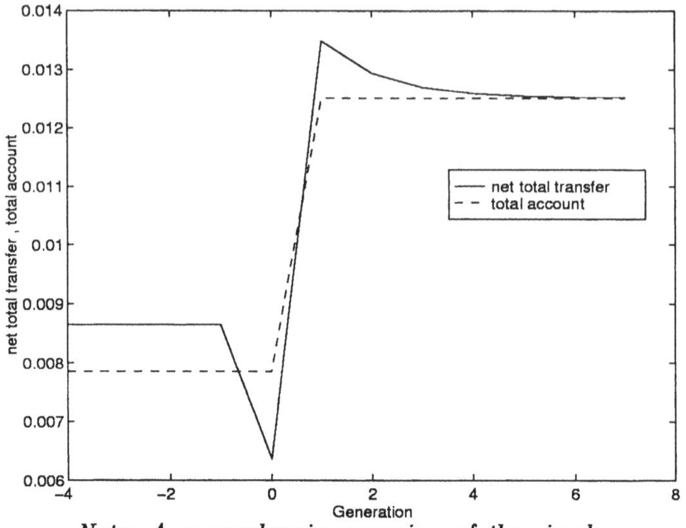

Note: A comprehensive overview of the simulation's trajectories is given in Appendix A.12, Table A.8.

is not too bad an approximation of actual transfers. Not only does the accounting framework correctly predict the qualitative outcome according to which inheritances are not sufficient to make up for increased contributions to social insurance. In addition, the accounting exercise appears suitable for gauging the transition's quantitative impact on intergenerational transfers. The reason is that general equilibrium effects and individuals' adjustments, as illustrated by the two peaks in the net transfer's trajectory, are small relative to the impact of falling fertility on intergenerational transfers. Put differently, in order to assess the quantitative impact of a shock as severe as the demographic transition a tool as crude as accounting is just sufficient.[20]

5.3.3 Summary

On the preceding pages we have made explicit the economic theory underlying the extended version of generational accounting. As in conventional generational accounting the basic framework is an overlapping generations model, in which only the present value of annual flows matters for generations' wel-

[20] One might question, why the account of living generations does not coincide with net transfers in the initial steady state, as was the case in Figure 5.6. The explanation is that in the base year c_t^1 already deviates from its steady state value.

fare. In addition to life-cycle net taxes, however, the extended version also takes account of private intergenerational transfers accruing over a lifetime.

By subtracting net received private transfers from net taxes paid, extended accounting implicitly assumes that generations' welfare depends positively on the former. Among the bequests models we have reviewed, this only holds for the accidental bequest model. It is however safer to make this point by way of negation, since it is by no way clear, whether the bequests models known so far are exhaustive. Thus, private intergenerational transfers make no sense as welfare indicators, if they are motivated by altruism or exchange, as under these circumstances both the donor and recipient generation profit from private transfers.[21]

Alike conventional generational accounting the extended version works on the steady state hypothesis implying that base year values prevail in the future. As to public sector accounting this is not too bold an assumption. First, there is no general theory describing the 'behavior' of fiscal policy in the same way as microeconomic theory describes the behavior of private households. It is therefore straightforward to assume that base year fiscal policy prevails for some time into the future. Second, the lion's share of government expenditure is not discretionary but, in fact, predetermined for some years. The most popular example are pension rights that bear much resemblance with 'nicely printed bonds'. Finally, the assumed constancy of the interest rate, while being a shortcoming, is corrected for by extended sensitivity analysis.

In the case of comprehensive generational accounting the steady state assumption is more open to criticism. In addition to interest rates and fiscal policy, this framework requires constancy of wages and *per capita* consumption. Given that private households react to changes in relative prices and given that population aging will certainly bring forth such changes, this seems to be an heroic assumption. It could be illustrated, however, that the change in relative prices and the induced adjustments of private households are likely to be small relative to the dependency ratio's direct impact on intergenerational transfers.

Some might question, what advantage the formidably arduous generational accounting exercise has vis-à-vis a back-on-the-envelope calculation as carried out on page 109. Indeed, overall generational accounts can be expressed as $GA^{tot}_{u,u} = -\frac{r-n_{u-1}}{(1+n_{u-1})}\left((1-\pi)s - \frac{\pi tr}{(1+r)}\right)$ for $u = t, t+1$. Therefore, the question of whether private transfers compensate for fiscal burdens hinges on the relative magnitude of base year public transfers πtr and base year private transfers $(1-\pi)s(1+r)$, just as developed in Section 5.2.3.[22] The alleged equivalence between the two approaches, however, owes to the

[21] With parent's reaping off the entire windfall profit from exchange motivated bequests, recipients do not profit from these bequests. In a more general formulation, however, both children and parents benefit from the exchange.

[22] For a derivation please refer to Appendix A.11.

simplified model we use for analysis. A more realistic model incorporating also transfers *inter vivos* would reveal that the accounting framework has a crucial advantage, namely the calculation of private transfers as residual. As made clear at several occasions, private intergenerational transfers, especially when made before the donor's death, are hard to observe. Hence, the reporting of net transfers as income not consumed has a greater chance of giving comprehensive account of all intergenerational transfers.[23]

Comprehensive generational accounting complements our understanding of the impact of the demographic transition by netting out the welfare effects of public and private intergenerational transfers. It should be stressed, however, that even the extended version of general accounting is not a comprehensive indicator for generation's welfare during a demographic transition. Thus, overall accounts suggest that future generations are adversely affected by the fertility shock. On the other hand, recall from Section 5.2.3 that future generations will experience a higher welfare than today's working-aged and about the same welfare as today's old. The reason for this divergence is that intergenerational transfers are not the only factors influencing generations' welfare. In addition, factor incomes, that is wages and interest rates, have a major impact on generations' well-being and they too will change in the course of population aging. Most important, wages will increase as outlined in Section 5.2, and thus counteract transfers' impact on intergenerational distribution.

5.4 The Taxation of Private Intergenerational Transfers

Up to now, we have abstracted from distortionary taxation. However, the increase in contribution rates to social insurance in the course of population aging might entail significant labor disincentive effects, which add to the burden of future generations. This has considerable bearing on both the empirical investigation of Section 4.4 as well as the theoretical analysis of Sections 5.2 and 5.3.

To begin with, conventional generational accounting, by definition, disregards substitution effects, which can only be captured in a model of optimizing agents. Fehr and Kotlikoff [152] maintain that the substitution effects induced by fiscal policy are of secondary order as compared to income effects.

[23] Here the attentive reader might perceive a logical contradiction. How can transfers *inter vivos* possibly be accidental? That is the reason, why earlier we qualified our use of the accidental bequest model. Among the bequest motives used in the literature so far the accidental bequest model is the only one being compatible with the extended accounting exercise. This does not necessarily mean, that there are no other motives, not yet taken up by the literature, which are consistent with both comprehensive accounting and transfers *inter vivos*. One could, e.g., think of parents bequeathing because they abide to some social norm rather than deriving utility from the bequest.

This argument is underpinned by simulating a couple of policy experiments in a general equilibrium model of 55 overlapping generations. It should be stressed, however, that their demonstration is of little relevance in the present context. In that they only consider fiscal policy shocks, the substitution effects are feedback or second-round effects which necessarily are of negligible magnitude relative to the first-round effects documented by generational accounting. In contrast, a demographic shock is a truly exogenous shock with respect to fiscal policy. It has a bearing on both generational accounts and the extent of substitution and there is nothing to ensure that substitution effects are negligible relative to income effects. This is reinforced when taking into account that the excess burden of distortionary taxes increases more than proportional with the tax rate. If, however, substitution effects are of any significance, the generational accounts calculated in Section 4.4 underestimate the burden of future generations.

With the same line of argument, the welfare paths derived in Section 5.2 are too favorable with respect to future generations. Put differently, the potential of private intergenerational transfers to make up for fiscal burdens might be significantly lower in the presence of distortionary taxes.

These considerations are integrated into the analysis by rendering labor supply endogenous in the models considered so far. In combination with a flat rate tax, this allows for the distortions hitherto neglected. We will then focus on the following questions. First, is the excess burden induced by distortionary contributions to social insurance likely to be significant? If so, are there means of reducing this excess burden? Second, do the qualitative results of Section 5.2 carry over to a more realistic setting with distortionary taxes? Finally, are inheritance taxes less distortionary than payroll taxes? If so, could the excess burden be reduced by financing part of the social insurance benefits out of inheritance rather than payroll taxation.

5.4.1 The Impact of Distortionary Social Insurance Contributions

Once more, we begin our analysis with the most basic model abstracting from private intergenerational transfers altogether. This model incorporates an endogenous labor supply and is a natural extension of the reference model presented in Section 5.2.1. In particular, all parameter values correspond to those of the reference model, with the exception of ν, which is set to a value greater zero, namely 0.1. The latter also requires the choice of a parameter value for the elasticity of substitution between first period consumption and leisure. In correspondence with Auerbach and Kotlikoff [103] ρ is set to 0.83.

This parameterization generates a value for the capital coefficient (interest rate) that is slightly too low (high), but fairly close to that of the reference model, namely 3.0 (0.042) as compared to 3.4 (0.04). The deviation from real world values should not bother too much, given that the model, by abstracting from private intergenerational transfers, is a poor description of reality, anyhow. When making allowances for bequests, as is done in the following sections, the capital coefficient returns to realistic levels. Of greater importance is the proximity to the reference model's values. This guarantees that any deviations in the two model's welfare paths exclusively stem from labor disincentive effects.

The model comprises the usual factor and capital market equilibrium conditions as well as the utility function

$$u_t = \left[\left((c_t^1)^{1-1/\rho} + \nu (l_t)^{1-1/\rho} \right)^{\frac{1-1/\gamma}{1-1/\rho}} + \frac{1}{1+\delta} (c_{t+1}^2)^{1-1/\gamma} \right]^{\frac{1}{1-1/\gamma}} , \tag{5.52}$$

the government budget constraint

$$\tau_t = \frac{tr}{(1+n_{t-1})(1-l_t)w_t} , \tag{5.53}$$

and the household budget constraint

$$c_t^1 + (1-\tau_t)w_t l_t + \frac{c_{t+1}^2}{(1+r_{t+1})} = w_t - \frac{[(1+r_{t+1}) - (1+n_{t-1})(1-l_t)]tr}{(1+n_{t-1})(1+r_{t+1})(1-l_t)} , \tag{5.54}$$

obtained from Equations (5.2), (5.3), and (5.7). Let us again begin with a partial equilibrium consideration. As is obvious from Equation (5.54), a drop in fertility will not affect the first generation to have fewer children, say generation t. This generation still faces an unchanged dependency ratio during working years and, therefore, experiences neither price nor income shocks. In contrast, generation $t+1$ is hit in various ways. First, as indicated by Equation (5.53), this generation will see its contributions to social insurance increase, owing to a worsened ratio of workers to pensioners. The falling net wage, in turn, will induce baby-busters to reduce their labor supply, this way further boosting contributions to social security. Future generations will therefore be worse off than presently living.

The crucial question of this section, however, is whether the welfare loss of future relative to present generations is larger than in Section 5.2.1, where labor disincentive effects were left out of account. To figure that out, note that agents, due to the insurance scheme's lacking equivalence of contributions and benefits, do not perceive the link between their work effort $(1-l)$ and their contribution rate τ_t, as specified by Equation (5.53). As a consequence, when deciding, how much time to spend on leisure, they disregard their action's negative effect on net wages. The result is a sub-optimal supply of labor.[24]

[24] Note, the analogy to the model with exchange-motivated bequests, where offsprings are not aware of the link between labor supply and contribution rates either. This analogy is reflected in the similar expressions for life-cycle resources in Equation (5.21) and (5.54).

While an economy incorporating distortions obviously departs from a lower welfare level as compared to an economy without such distortions, we have not yet shown that the relative welfare loss induced by population aging is larger in the former economy. This only holds, if the distortion caused by social insurance increases as the population grows older. To see, whether this is the case, we proceed as follows. All terms of Equation (5.54) are brought on the left hand side and differentiated with respect to l_t, while taking into account the dependency $\partial\tau_t/\partial l_t > 0$ as specified by Equation (5.53). This way we derive the real opportunity cost of a marginal increase in the demand for leisure:

$$MC_l = (1-\tau_t)w_t + \frac{tr}{(1+n_{t-1})(1-l_t)} \, . \tag{5.55}$$

Note, that the first term on the right hand side denotes the marginal cost as perceived by the agent. Consequently, the pay-as-you-go scheme drives a wedge between true and perceived marginal costs and, hence, causes the inefficiency. What is more important, this wedge increases as the population growth rate declines. With this adverse effect coming on top of the income effect, the welfare loss of future relative to presently living generations must be larger in a setting with endogenous labor supply.

As illustrated by Figure 5.8 this analysis carries over to a general equilibrium setting. While in a setting of exogenous labor supply future generations in the long-run suffer a welfare loss equivalent to 2.4 percent of life-cycle resources, this loss raises to 3.2 percent, when allowing for endogenous labor supply. Accordingly, the welfare loss due to labor-disincentive effects accounts for one fourth of the overall welfare loss induced by a fertility shock. Of course, these figures should not be taken too literally. For one thing, the model both in structure and parameterization is a poor characterization of reality. For another thing, at least the Social Security component of the German pay-as-you-go scheme does incorporate a substantial degree of equivalence between contributions and benefits. The distortion generated by our model is therefore exaggerated. With this caveats in mind, the labor-disincentive effect seems nevertheless substantial.

From the analysis of this section it follows that future generations' fiscal burden can be reduced without, at the same time, increasing present generations' net taxes. This can be done by strengthening the link between what people pay into the public coffers and what they get in return. This beneficial effect, however, is already included in the generational accounts presented in Section 4.4, since generational accounting abstracts from disincentives, anyhow. It should also be stressed that this policy measure, while being neutral with respect to intergenerational distribution, restricts the scope for *intra*generational distribution. Its political feasibility is therefore limited.

Before turning to models that include private intergenerational transfers, let us clarify a question left over from Section 5.2.1. Figure 5.1 made us believe that the real issue to be concerned about during a demographic transition

Fig. 5.8. The Impact of Distortionary Contributions to Social Insurance

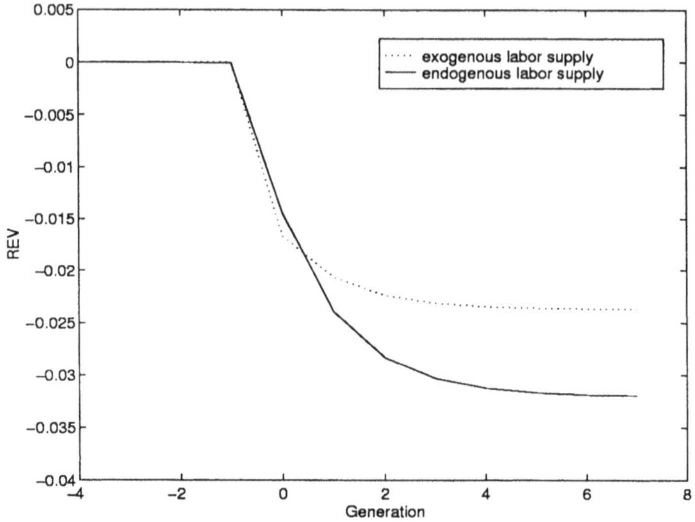

Note: The welfare paths correspond to $\nu = 0$ (broken line) and $\nu > 0$ (solid line). The complete simulations underlying the broken and doted lines are reported in Appendix A.12, Tables A.3 and A.13, respectively.

was the drop of baby-boomers' interest income. Taking into account labor disincentive effects somewhat modifies this finding. While still amounting to 1.5 percent, the welfare loss of baby-boomers seems relatively modest compared to the 3.2 suffered by future generations and even in proportion to the 2.4 percent experienced by baby-busters.

5.4.2 Joy-of-Giving

This section departs from the model of Section 5.2.2, featuring bequests for joy-of-giving. In contrast to the previous model, however, the labor supply is endogenized by setting ν to 0.1 and ρ to 0.83. With respect to the bequest parameter μ we stick to the baseline callibration of Section 5.2.2. The modified model generates values for the benchmark variables that deviate only slightly from previous figures. Thus, in the initial steady state the capital coefficient comes to 3.9 (previously 4.2), the interest rate to 3.7 (3.5) percent, the bequest-to-GDP ratio to 6.2 (6.7) percent, and the contribution rate to 25.6 (22.7) percent.[25] In addition, the present model permits to switch the tax base of the pay-as-you-go scheme. By increasing β_t from initially zero,

[25] As stated earlier, the close correspondence of benchmark variables guarantees that any deviation in the welfare paths of the two models is solely attributable

an increasing share of social insurance benefits is financed out of inheritance instead of payroll taxes. The model therefore comprises the agent's utility function

$$u_t = \left[\left((c_t^1)^{1-1/\rho} + \nu(l_t)^{1-1/\rho}\right)^{1-1/\gamma} + \frac{1}{1+\delta}(c_{t+1}^2)^{1-1/\gamma} + \frac{\mu}{1+\delta}(I_{t+1})^{1-1/\gamma}\right]^{\frac{1}{1-1/\gamma}}, \tag{5.56}$$

the government budget constraints

$$(1-\beta_t)\frac{tr}{(1+n_{t-1})} = (1-l_t)w_t\tau_t \tag{5.57}$$

$$\beta_t\frac{tr}{(1+n_{t-1})} = I_t\tau_t^{\mathrm{i}}, \tag{5.58}$$

the household budget constraint

$$c_t^1 + (1-\tau_t)w_t l_t + \frac{c_{t+1}^2}{(1+r_{t+1})} + \frac{(1+n_t)(1+\tau_{t+1}^{\mathrm{i}})I_{t+1}}{(1+r_{t+1})} = I_t + (1-\tau_t)w_t + \frac{tr}{(1+r_{t+1})}, \tag{5.59}$$

based on Equations (5.2), (5.3), (5.7), and (5.8), as well as the usual capital and factor market equilibrium conditions. To begin with, we investigate whether making allowances for distortionary taxes changes the qualitative outcomes of Section 5.2.2. For this purpose, β_t is set to zero for all t. As illustrated by the broken lines in Figure 5.9, taking into account distortionary taxes does make a difference. In particular, the increase in inheritances received by baby-busters is no longer sufficient to make up for both higher contributions and greater distortions relative to baby-busters. Future generations are therefore worse off than presently living.

Let us next inspect, whether the government can, in any efficient way, exploit inheritances to ease the distributional conflict between present and future generations. The government could, for example, tax private transfers and use the proceeds to reduce contributions to social insurance. This experiment is depicted by the solid line in Figure 5.9. Specifically, we assume that 10 percent of social insurance expenditures are financed by inheritance taxation, starting with bequests from boomers to busters. Obviously, this policy affects both intergenerational distribution and overall efficiency. Baby-boomers participate in the fiscal burden induced by population aging through a higher price of inheritances. However, the effect on efficiency may be adverse, and with the model's present parameterization, in fact, is.[26] Given that we substitute one distortionary tax for another, the effect on allocation depends on the

to labor-disincentive effects. Although not explicitly reported, we have further submitted ν to an extensive sensitivity test, in order to ensure that welfare paths change monotonously over the whole parameter range.

[26] This qualitative finding is robust with respect to timing and magnitude of the inheritance tax.

Fig. 5.9. The Taxation of Bequests for Joy-of-Giving

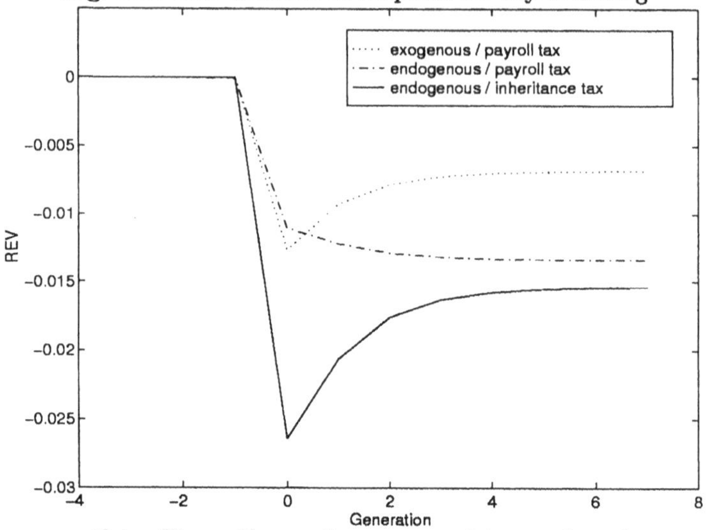

Note: The welfare paths correspond to $\nu = 0$ and $\beta = 0$ (broken-dotted line), $\nu > 0$ and $\beta = 0$ (broken line), as well as $\nu > 0$ and $\beta_t = 0.1$ for $t \geq 1$ (solid line). The complete simulations underlying the broken-dotted, broken, and solid line are given in Appendix A.12, Tables A.5, A.14, and A.15, respectively.

corresponding elasticities of substitution and, consequently, is an empirical question in the first place. This is underpinned by Figure 5.10, which illustrates the tax switch for a slightly different parameterization of the model. Thus, γ is reduced to 0.5 and the share of expenditure to be financed out of inheritance taxation is set to 1 percent. Under these circumstances the tax switch not only leads to a more even sharing of the demographic burden, but also improves efficiency. This is not immediately obvious, since baby-boomers are adversely affected by the policy. However, by means of a lump-sum redistribution authority of the Auerbach/Kotlikoff [103]-type, it can be shown that future generations are able to compensate baby-boomers and still be better-off.

In view of the empirical imbonderabilities, the case for the taxation of bequests for joy-of-giving is not particularly strong. From a dynamic perspective, though, this assessment might change. In contrast to a payroll tax, the distortion of an inheritance tax does not increase in the course of population aging. To see this proceed as in Section 5.4.1. Bring all terms of Equation (5.59) on the left hand side and differentiate with respect to I_{t+1} while, at the same time, taking into account the relation $\partial \tau^{\mathrm{i}}_{t+1}/\partial I_{t+1} < 0$ as

Fig. 5.10. The Taxation of Bequests with $\gamma = 0.5$

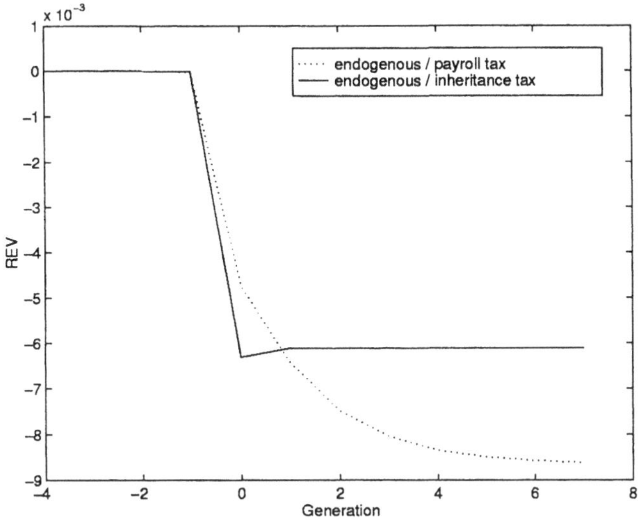

Note: The welfare paths correspond to $\nu > 0$ and $\beta = 0$ (dotted line) and $\nu > 0$ and $\beta_t = 0.01$ for $t \geq 1$ (solid line). Contrary to Figure 5.9, γ is set to 0.5. The complete simulations underlying the dotted and solid line are given in Appendix A.12, Tables A.16 and A.17, respectively.

specified by Equation (5.58). This yields the marginal cost of bequeathing in terms of forgone resources:

$$MC_I = \frac{(1+n_t)(1+\tau^{i}_{t+1})}{(1+r_{t+1})} - \beta_{t+1}\frac{tr}{(1+r_{t+1})I_{t+1}} \,. \tag{5.60}$$

The agent only perceives the first term on the right hand side and, therefore, too high a marginal cost if inheritance taxes are in effect, that is $\beta_{t+1} > 0$. Taxes on bequests for joy-of-giving, consequently, lead to sub-optimal inheritances and excessive consumption on the part of the testator. The wedge between true and perceived marginal costs, though, is independent of the population growth rate. To the extent that old-age benefits are financed through inheritance taxation, they do not any longer constitute intergenerational transfers and, thus, are unaffected by the old-age dependency ratio.

From this reasoning one might deduce the following proposition. If the mix of payroll and inheritance taxes, as presently observed in Germany, is optimal (in the sense that the actual β maximizes agents' utility), the share of old-age benefits that is financed out of inheritance taxes must increase for this policy to remain optimal during a demographic transition. In that the distortion of inheritance relative to payroll taxation declines in the course of population aging, overall excess burden can be minimized by shifting a larger part of the demographic burden onto inheritance taxation.

Of course, this argument is subject to the qualifications put forth by the theory of the second best. A rigorous treatment is therefore recommended and relegated to further research.

5.4.3 Accidental Bequests

In what follows we add to the model of Section 5.2.3 an endogenous labor supply by raising ν above zero. The otherwise identical model generates benchmark variables in the initial steady state that are in the neighborhood of previous values, namely 3.3 (previously 3.6) for the capital coefficient, 4.1 (3.8) percent for the interest rate, 20.1 (17.5) percent for the contribution rate to social insurance, and 4.0 (4.4) for bequests relative to GDP. As in the previous section one can also opt for inheritance versus payroll taxes. The model is therefore given by the utility function

$$u_t = \left[\left((c_t^1)^{1-1/\rho} + \nu(l_t)^{1-1/\rho}\right)^{1-1/\gamma} + \frac{\pi}{1+\delta}(c_{t+1}^2)^{1-1/\gamma}\right]^{\frac{1}{1-1/\gamma}}, \tag{5.61}$$

the government budget constraints

$$(1-\beta_t)\frac{\pi tr}{(1+n_{t-1})} = (1-l_t)w_t\tau_t \tag{5.62}$$

$$\beta_t \pi tr = \frac{(1-\pi)s_{t-1}(1+r_t)\tau_t^{\mathrm{i}}}{(1+\tau_t^{\mathrm{i}})}, \tag{5.63}$$

the household budget constraint

$$c_t^1 + (1-\tau_t)w_t l_t + \frac{c_{t+1}^2}{(1+r_{t+1})} = \frac{(1-\pi)s_{t-1}(1+r_t)}{(1+n_{t-1})(1+\tau_t^{\mathrm{i}})} + (1-\tau_t)w_t + \frac{tr}{(1+r_{t+1})}, \tag{5.64}$$

according to Equations (5.2), (5.3), (5.6), (5.7), and (5.8), and the usual equations specifying factor and capital market equilibrium. First, let us inspect how robust are the qualitative implications of our earlier analysis of accidental bequests to the inclusion of distortionary taxes. We found that the increase in accidental bequests is sufficient to make up for the negative income effect of social security contributions. As recapitulated by the dotted line in Figure 5.11, baby-busters are therefore better off as compared to baby-boomers and even close to the welfare level of their grand-parents, who are spared the drop in interest income. If one makes allowances for labor-disincentive effects, the welfare advantage vis-à-vis baby-boomers is cut in half but still prevails, as illustrated by the broken line.

Let us next consider the rationale for shifting part of the tax burden onto inheritances. A glance at the household's budget constraint reveals that the taxation of accidental bequests entails no distortion of relative prices and, as a consequence, no welfare loss. A switch from the distortionary payroll tax towards a lump-sum taxation of accidental bequests is therefore always and at any time recommendable. This is illustrated by the solid line in Figure 5.11, which depicts generations' welfare on the condition, that, with immediate effect, 60 percent of social insurance benefits are financed through inheritance

Fig. 5.11. The Taxation of Accidental Bequests

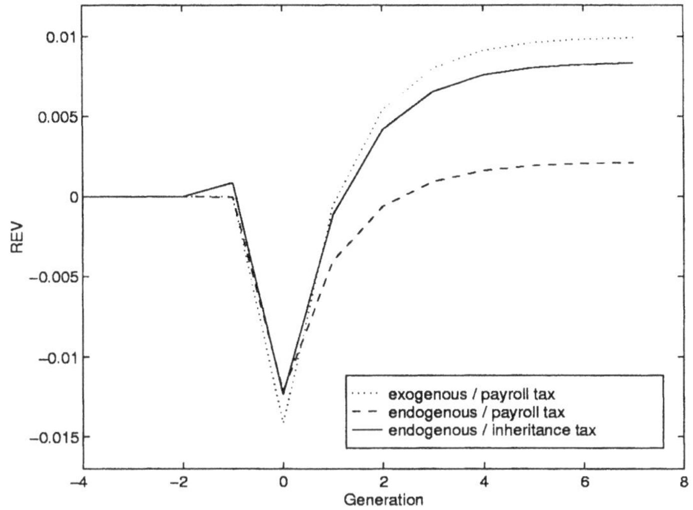

Note: The welfare paths correspond to $\nu = 0$ and $\beta = 0$ (dotted line), $\nu > 0$ and $\beta = 0$ (broken line), as well as $\nu > 0$ and $\beta_t = 0.6$ for $t \geq 0$ (solid line). The complete simulations underlying the dotted, broken, and solid line are given in Appendix A.12, Tables A.8, A.18, and A.19, respectively.

taxation.[27] The new trajectory at no point moves below the old one and, thus, indicates a pareto-improvement. Furthermore, it does not come as a surprise, that with a large part of the distortion eliminated the welfare path closely tracks that of Section 5.2.3.

While it is always advisable to increase the share of government revenue levied through the taxation of accidental bequests, the case for such a policy shift is reinforced with the demographic transition ahead of us. This is because the distortions of payroll taxes will increase in the course of population aging, as was demonstrated earlier.

[27] This policy implies that inheritances are completely taxed away. Rather than claiming realism, this scenario illustrates that, given exclusively accidental bequests, the more tax shifting the better.

5.4.4 Bequests-as-Exchange

We finally review the effects and policy implications of bequests-as-exchange when labor supply is endogenous. Apart from ν the model is parameterized as in Section 5.2.4 and, in particular, generates similar benchmark values. In the initial steady state the capital coefficient comes to 3.2 (previously 3.5), the interest rate to 4.1 (3.9) percent, the ratio of bequests to GDP amounts to 6.0 (6.0) percent, and the contribution rate to social insurance equals 29.4 (26.1) percent. Furthermore and in correspondence with previous sections, one can levy a share β_t of overall tax revenue by inheritance taxation. In the initial steady state this share is set to zero. The model of this section comprises the utility function

$$u_t = \left[\left((c_t^1)^{1-1/\rho} + \nu (l_t)^{1-1/\rho} \right)^{1-1/\gamma} + \frac{1}{1+\delta} (c_{t+1}^2)^{1-1/\gamma} + \frac{\phi}{1+\delta} (A_{t+1})^{1-1/\gamma} \right]^{\frac{1}{1-1/\gamma}}, \tag{5.65}$$

the government budget constraints

$$(1-\beta_t) \frac{tr}{(1+n_{t-1})} = (1-l_t)(1-a_t) w_t \tau_t \tag{5.66}$$

$$\beta_t \frac{tr}{(1+n_{t-1})} = \tau_t^{\mathrm{i}} I_t = \tau_t^{\mathrm{i}} (1-\tau_t) w_t a_t \,, \tag{5.67}$$

the household budget constraint

$$c_t^1 + (1-\tau_t)(1-a_t) w_t l_t + \frac{c_{t+1}^2}{(1+r_{t+1})} + \frac{(1+\tau_{t+1}^{\mathrm{i}})(1-\tau_{t+1}) w_{t+1}}{(1+r_{t+1})} A_{t+1}$$

$$= I_t + (1-\tau_t)(1-a_t) w_t + \frac{tr}{(1+r_{t+1})} \tag{5.68}$$

derived from Equations (5.2), (5.3), (5.4), (5.5), (5.7), and (5.8), the exchange relationship

$$I_t = (1-\tau_t) w_t a_t \,, \tag{5.69}$$

the factor and capital market equilibrium conditions, as well as the equation $A_{t+1} = (1+n_t) a_{t+1}$.

To begin with, we set $\beta_t = 0$ for all t and investigate how an increase in ν affects generations' welfare during a demographic transition. This is illustrated in Figure 5.12, which contrasts the welfare trajectories for an exogenous (dotted line) and endogenous labor supply (broken line). Not surprisingly, future generations are worse off when adding labor disincentive effects to the negative income effect induced by a worsening dependency ratio. Consequently, the non-compensation outcome of our earlier analysis is reinforced in a more realistic setting. Let us next inspect, whether inheritance taxation

Fig. 5.12. The Taxation of Bequests-as-Exchange

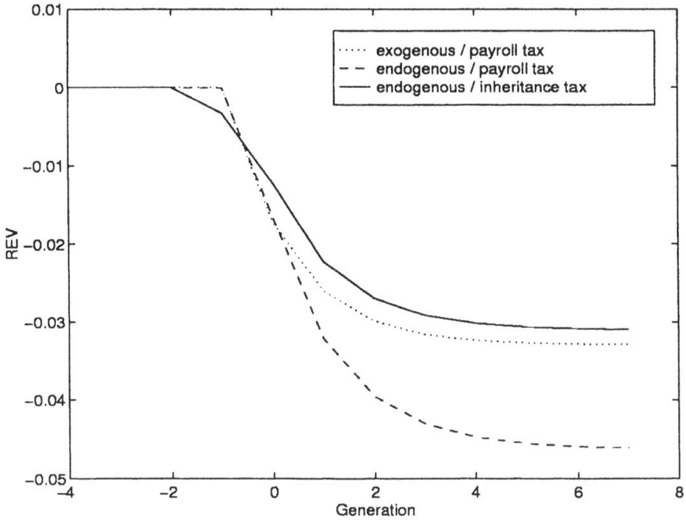

Note: The welfare paths correspond to $\nu = 0$ and $\beta = 0$ (dotted line), $\nu > 0$ and $\beta = 0$ (broken line), as well as $\nu > 0$ and $\beta_t = 0.02$ for $t \geq 0$ (solid line). The complete simulations underlying the dotted, broken, and solid line are given in Appendix A.12, Tables A.11, A.20, and A.21, respectively.

can improve efficiency or intergenerational distribution, or both. The solid line in Figure 5.12 depicts generations' welfare on the condition that the government, with immediate effect, switches from pure payroll taxation to a hybrid scheme with 2 percent of tax revenue levied by inheritance taxation. With respect to distributional objectives this measure is certainly advisable. While today's old, that is generation -1, suffer a slight welfare loss due to the increasing price of attention, the welfare loss of successive generations is much less pronounced than under a pure payroll tax scheme. As a consequence, the welfare path is much smother when taxing inheritances. At least equally important is the fact that a tax switch – whenever enacted – improves efficiency. This will be established in what follows.

To begin with, the cutting down of payroll taxes reduces distortions. This becomes apparent when contrasting true and perceived marginal costs of reducing the labor supply. Once more, bring all terms in Equation (5.68) on the left hand side and substitute I_t by means of Equation (5.69). Then differentiate with respect to l_t, while making allowances for the relation $\partial \tau_t / \partial l_t > 0$ as given by Equation (5.66). The true opportunity cost of a marginal reduction of labor supply equals:

$$MC_l = (1-\tau_t)(1-a_t)w_t + (1-\beta_t)\frac{(1-(1-a_t)l_t)tr}{(1+n_{t-1})(1-a_t)(1-l_t)^2}\,. \tag{5.70}$$

Another time the social insurance scheme drives a wedge (henceforth WE_t) between true and perceived marginal costs as specified by the last term. This wedge can be reduced by raising the share of tax revenue β_t levied through inheritance taxation. The problem's dynamic dimension becomes obvious, when taking into account that $\partial WE_t/\partial n_{t-1} < 0$ and $\partial WE_t/\partial a_t > 0$. Thus, while it is always welfare-enhancing to increase the share of inheritance tax revenue, it is especially pressing when faced with a demographic transition, as it magnifies the initial distortion. Furthermore, in the presence of bequests-as-exchange the deterioration is greater than in the previous models. As was made clear in Section 5.2.4, a baby-buster spends more time with his parents, since the burden of taking care of ones parents is shared by fewer siblings. In addition to the direct effect, a drop in fertility therefore raises the distortion via $\partial WE_t/\partial a_t > 0$. Given that $... = n_{t-1} > n_t = n_{t+1} = ...$ and $... = a_{t-1} = a_t < a_{t+1} ...$, inheritances should be taxed in the following period at the latest, that is when baby-boomers decease and inheritances increase.

So far we have only considered the beneficial effect of reducing payroll taxes. What about the welfare effect of increasing the inheritance tax? While in the case of joy-of-giving and accidental bequests inheritance taxation was harmful or neutral, respectively, it is welfare-enhancing when bequests are motivated by exchange. As shown earlier, children do not perceive that providing attention to their parents is costly in terms of higher contribution rates, the reason being the lack of equivalence between contributions and benefits. Consequently, they charge too low a price for attention this way spurring excessive demand on the part of the parents. Inheritance taxation, at least partly, corrects for this distortion by rising the price for attention. This mechanism can be illustrated in the usual way. Bring all terms of Equation (5.68) on the left hand side and differentiate with respect to a_t, while making allowances for $\partial\tau_t/a_t > 0$ as specified by Equation (5.66). The true opportunity cost of providing a marginal unit of attention comes to:

$$MC_a = -(1-\tau_t)w_t l_t + (1-\tau_t)w_t + \frac{(1-\beta_t)tr}{(1+n_{t-1})(1-a_t)}\,. \tag{5.71}$$

The first term on the right hand depicts the effect that providing attention reduces the price of leisure, the second term stands for the reduction in the endowment of labor income. Strictly speaking, both effects would have to be taken into account by children when pricing attention. Recall however, that we have abstracted from the former effect in order to keep the model tractable (cf. FN page 101). The third term gives the cost of higher contribution rates and, in that it is not passed on in prices, constitutes the distortion. Children charge too low a price of $(1-\tau_t)w_t$. Parents pay a price of $(1+\tau_t^i)(1-\tau_t)w_t$.[28]

[28] This can be seen, when transposing Equation (5.68) by one period: the fourth term on the left hand side becomes $\frac{(1+\tau_t^i)(1-\tau_t)w_t}{(1+\tau_t)}(1+n_{t-1})a_t$.

Consequently, by approximating prices to marginal costs the inheritance tax partially offsets the distortion. As before, the distortion increases in the course of population aging. Although welfare-enhancing at any time, the taxation of bequests-as-exchange should therefore be increased in the following period at the latest.

Also, the favorable distributional effect of higher inheritance tax rates can now be understood more clearly. Bequests-as-exchange allow parents to extract resources from their children by paying too low a price for attention. In that inheritance taxation discourages bequests-as-exchange it restricts the redistribution from those already hit hard to those relatively well off.

Among the three prominent transfer motives the case for inheritance taxation is strongest for bequests-as-exchange. Under this transfer motive both the reduction of payroll taxes and the taxing of inheritances diminish distortions. Let us finally, investigate, to which extent this result is driven by simplifying assumptions. First, consider the simplification just noted, namely the neglect of the leisure price effect in the compensation scheme. With children charging parents $(1 - l_t)(1 - \tau_t)w_t$ instead of $(1 - \tau_t)w_t$, the wedge between price and marginal costs would be even greater and the finding of our simulation reinforced. Second, we have – in correspondence with Cox [41]– made the simplifying assumption that parents reap off all gains from the exchange. Modelling the exchange as a Nash bargain, instead, would not change the results. Still, children would perceive the wrong cost of providing attention, which could be corrected by inheritance taxation.

Finally, following Davies [18] we have modelled the cost of providing attention in terms of forgone time. This assumption does drive our results. Using a more general formulation as in Cox [41], the wedge between true and perceived marginal costs as specified by the last term in Equation (5.71) would disappear and taxing inheritances would introduce, rather than correct for a distortion. It should be stressed, however, that this distortion is independent of the population growth rate. Insofar one might resort to the weaker proposition, already stated in the context of bequests for joy-of-giving: If the mix of payroll and inheritance taxation is optimal at present, population aging will necessitate a shift towards inheritance taxation for fiscal policy to remain optimal. As before, however, this proposition is subject to the qualifications of the theory of the second best and still requires a rigorous treatment.

5.4.5 Summary

First we have reviewed the distributive implications of private intergenerational transfers in a more realistic setting that makes allowances for labor-disincentive effects. Taking into account both the income effect and the excess burden induced by higher contributions to social insurance, it is most unlikely that inheritances will be sufficient to compensate future generations. With the exception of accidental bequests, we find that baby-busters and subsequent generations have fewer life-cycle resources as compared to baby-boomers.

While accidental bequests put baby-busters ahead of baby-boomers, they do not suffice for raising busters' welfare to the level experienced by generations entirely unaffected by the fertility shock.

Next we have investigated the allocative implications of private intergenerational transfers or, stated differently, the scope for inheritance taxation. On the one hand inheritance taxes are very popular in that they promote intergenerational mobility and equal opportunity. On the other hand governments have been very cautious in taxing private intergenerational transfers lacking adequate evidence on the underlying motives. While it is well understood that accidental bequests can be taxed at no efficiency cost, the taxing of altruistic bequests leads to excessive consumption on the part of testators and, thus, to sub-optimal capital accumulation and growth.

While we could not establish a predominant bequest motive and, as a consequence, were unable to suggest the optimal extent of inheritance taxation, we could nevertheless highlight an important advantage of inheritance taxes vis-à-vis payroll taxes in financing a pay-as-you-go scheme. In contrast to payroll taxes, the distortion of inheritance taxation, if any, is independent of the dependency ratio. The distortion of inheritance taxes relative to payroll taxes will therefore decline as the population grows older. Whether or not this suggest that a growing share of tax revenue be financed by inheritance rather than payroll taxation is left to further research. Among other things, the answer to this question hinges on the efficiency of the tax mix in the initial steady state.

In any way, there are other – probably more efficient – measures that can be undertaken in order to reduce tax distortions induced by population aging. As stated earlier, one can strengthen the link between contributions and benefits. Furthermore, one can reduce the extent of the pay-as-you-go scheme by partially funding pension benefits. While these measures are certainly necessary they too have their shortcomings. Strengthening the link between contributions and benefits, for example, limits the scope for *intra*generational distribution. Funding Social Security is certainly an option in the long-run. In the short-run, though, existing pension entitlements must be honored, so that public intergenerational transfers will be around for still some time.

Never should inheritances taxation be viewed as a substitute for other measures. If anything, it is a further component in the piecemeal effort to cope with population aging. However, a clear understanding of the consequences of increased inheritance taxation is indispensable, given that the present design of the tax will have exactly this effect during a demographic transition. Since in most countries inheritances *per capita* are taxed at a progressive tariff, the average tax rate will increase during the bequest wave.

6. Summary

The principal purpose of this study has been to clarify the impact of population aging on generational distribution, where special attention has been given to private intergenerational transfers. In view of the critical role of the transfer motive we have begun by presenting competing transfer models as well as their empirical implications. Subsequently, we have reviewed empirical research aimed at identifying a predominant motive for bequests and transfers *inter vivos*. As documented in Chapter 2, empirical evidence in favor of a specific transfer motive is inconclusive. If anything, it has been proved that the volume of transfers *inter vivos* is significant. Given that transfers before the donor's death are by definition intentional, this is strong evidence against the standard life-cycle model without a transfer motive as proposed by Modigliani and Brumberg [77]. In addition, it has been established by the literature that Ricardian Neutrality and unequal sharing of bequests is rejected by the data, both strong evidence against pure altruism.

Chapter 3 has presented empirical evidence on transfer patterns in Germany drawing from two micro data sources the Income and Expenditure Survey 1993 and the Socio-Economic Panel. Subject to the qualification that the surveys either implicitly or explicitly underreport transfers by the very well-to-do, the following stylized facts could be identified. First, transfers *inter vivos* are positively correlated to donors' economic status. Since this finding is compatible with all of the common transfer motives, it is unfortunately not suited for discriminating between competing models. Second, the size distribution of intergenerational transfers is highly skewed with bequests being even more concentrated than transfers *inter vivos*. This is in perfect correspondence with the previous finding, given that donors' income and wealth is also highly concentrated. Moreover, it lends support to the notion that bequests and transfer *inter vivos* are governed by distinct motives. Third, the vast majority of intergenerational transfers is directed from old to young. Fourth, the predominant form of bequests in Germany are real estate. Finally, in the case of Germany we see confirmed the earlier finding according to which *inter vivos* and, consequently, intentional transfers are significant.

Although we were not able to identify a predominant transfer motive, the empirical investigation undertaken in Chapters 2 and 3 has served some important purposes. By providing clear evidence against pure life-cycle saving, these chapters have reinforced the principal aim of this study, namely to increase our understanding of private intergenerational transfers. The empirical investigation has further suggested that in view of their relative importance any analysis should focus on intergenerational transfers directed from old to young. The equilibrium model of Chapter 5 therefore abstracts from alternative forms of private transfers. In addition, the model's parameters governing the volume of private intergenerational transfers have been chosen on the basis of the German figures derived in Chapter 3. The inconclusive evidence on a predominant transfer motive, finally, has had an important bearing on the further course of our inquiry. Specifically, each conclusion subsequently drawn had to be tested with respect to all of the common transfer motives.

For the time being, however, Chapter 4 presented some demographic and accounting exercises, which have taken a largely agnostic view with respect to the transfer motive. First, Section 4.1 has given facts and forecasts on the demographic transition. It has been shown that low fertility and mortality will lead to a dramatic aging of the population characterized by an increase in the median age from 38 years in 1995 to 48 years by 2050. Even massive immigration of on average younger cohorts is not able to break this trend, as has been demonstrated by counterfactual population projections. In Section 4.2 the impact of this demographic development on pay-as-you-go social insurance schemes has been illustrated by means of the dependency ratio. Thus, the ratio of pensioners to workers will double within the next 50 years. The dependency ratio has subsequently been contrasted to the evolution of a so-called inheritance index, the ratio of testators to heirs. This index by and large tracks the dependency ratio with the following exceptions. While the dependency ratio increases from the outset, the number of testators relative to heirs falls initially due to a further increase in life-expectancy. Moreover, the inheritance index lags behind the dependency ratio owing to the fact that death occurs about 15 years after retirement. The latter could be an impediment to the compensating role of inheritances, if recipients face binding liquidity constraints. Finally, the increase in the inheritance index falls short of the dependency ratio's peak by 40 percentage points implying that cohorts burdened by excessive contributions to social insurance and those profiting from higher inheritances are not perfectly equivalent.

Of course, a necessary condition for compensation is that transfer receipts *per capita* increase as the number of recipients declines. This has been confirmed, irrespective of the transfer motive, in Section 4.3. Even more striking, under three transfer motives, namely accidental bequests, exchange, and a specific version of joy-of-giving (with the overall bequest entering the testator's utility function), the fertility drop leaves the overall donation unaffected thus translating into a one-by-one increase in the receipt *per capita*. The inverse relation between receipts and number of recipients is further confirmed by the literature and casual evidence from the Socio-Economic Panel.

Section 4.4 has approached the question of compensation by means of a generational accounting exercise referring to 1995 as base year. With respect to public intergenerational transfers we have found that true government debt amounts to almost 140 percent of GDP. This implies a net tax burden for a representative future individual of DM 440,000, which is double the amount to be paid by a representative living individual. Subsequently, the conventional accounting has been complemented by a private transfer accounting yielding the following insights. Over most of the life cycle private and public transfers, measured over the remaining lifespan and in present value, run in opposite direction. This means a net recipient of public transfers usually is a net donor of private transfers and *vice versa*. We have further shown that both current and future generations receive a life-cycle 'inheritance' of about DM 320,000. Consequently, inheritances while alleviating the fiscal imbalance in relative terms are not capable of compensating future generations altogether. Unfortunately, this qualitative outcome is not robust to alternative specifications of the discount rate. In particular, if the interest rate is increased from its baseline value of 5 to 7 percent, inheritances will reverse the generational imbalance. It should, however, be kept in mind that population aging will rather push the interest rate below its baseline value, making this scenario most improbable.

Chapter 5 has investigated the impact of population aging on generation's welfare. In doing this we have gradually broadened our perspective by departing from a partial equilibrium analysis with exogenous labor supply, moving on to general equilibrium and finally making the labor supply endogenous. The partial equilibrium setting with exogenous labor supply conforms quite well with the assumptions underlying the accounting exercise. In such a setting intergenerational transfers are the sole determinants of generations' welfare affected by a drop in fertility. Consequently, they perfectly serve as welfare indicator. By allowing for general equilibrium and endogenous labor supply we have taken into account welfare determinants ignored so far, namely factor price movements and excess burden.

The main findings of Section 5.2 have been as follows. First, if all bequests observed in Germany are accidental, if general equilibrium effects are negligible, and if the labor supply is exogenous, there will be no compensation of fiscal burdens. Second, given that among the transfer motives introduced accidental bequests are most favorable for future generations, none of the transfer motives will lead to a compensation. Note, that this is in perfect correspondence with the accounting results. Third, turning to general equilibrium and allowing for factor price movements somewhat modifies this result. A drop in fertility increases the relative scarceness of labor, increases wages, and in this way works in favor of future generations. The welfare effects of factor price movements and intergenerational transfers therefore run in opposite direction. While under joy-of-giving and exchange the factor price effect is not sufficient to change the qualitative outcome, in the case of accidental bequests it produces a compensation.

Section 5.3 has been some kind of an excursus. In particular, we have used the general equilibrium model with exogenous labor supply as benchmark for assessing the accurateness of the comprehensive generational accounting exercise. For one thing, we have shown that the accidental bequest model is the theoretical foundation underlying the extended accounting exercise, since it is the only model known to date that does not include transfers in the donor's utility function. For another thing, we have demonstrated that although extended accounts are calculated on the inappropriate steady state assumption they are rather good approximations of generations' public and private transfers. This hinges on the fact that the transition's direct effect on generations' life-cycle resources is large relative to adjustments induced by the transition.

In Section 5.4 we have continued to extend the general equilibrium model allowing for an endogenous labor supply. In such a setting flat rate taxes entail labor disincentive effects this way further adding to the fiscal burden of future generations. Therefore taking into account excess burden we again arrive at the non-compensation result, irrespective of the underlying transfer motive. Subsequently, we have inspected into whether private transfers may in some other way alleviate the fiscal burden of future generations, namely by financing social insurance in a more efficient way. Our findings have been as follows. Shifting part of the tax burden from payroll onto inheritance taxes is recommendable without any reservation in the case of accidental bequests. With other motives being operative all that could be said is that the distortions of inheritance taxes relative to payroll taxes decline during a demographic transition.

Let us conclude by pointing out some directions for further research. As has become clear in the course of Chapter 5, factor price movements induced by population aging are crucial determinants for generations' welfare. Since the common tool for assessing generational distribution, generational accounting, leaves factor price movements out of account, further empirical research should be dedicated to this issue. Another important aspect altogether ignored in this study is the impact of population aging on *intra*generational distribution. In that large inheritance are commonly viewed as impediment to intergenerational mobility and equal opportunity, population aging could have unfavorable distributive side effects. This issue, however, would have to be addressed in a model of heterogenous agents. Finally, we have over the entire sequence of the study assumed full employment. It would be important to specify in which manner population aging affects the employment level and, via this route, generational welfare.

A. Appendix

A.1 The Implications of Altruistic Bequests

To show, how parent's earnings, child's earnings, and the degree of altruism affect the size of bequests, the Marshall demand function for bequests is differentiated with respect to the respective variables. The parent's maximization problem is stated as follows:

$$\max_{c_t, c_{t+1}} \; u_t(c_t, u_{t+1}(c_{t+1}))$$

$$\text{s.t.} \quad c_t = w_t - b \tag{A.1}$$

$$c_{t+1} = (1+r)\, b + w_{t+1} \tag{A.2}$$

$$b \geq 0\,, \tag{A.3}$$

with well-behaved utility functions, i.e. $\partial u_i / \partial c_i > 0$, $\partial^2 u_i / \partial c_i^2 < 0$, and $\partial u_i / \partial c_i \to \infty$ as $c_i \to 0$, for $i = t, t+1$. Furthermore, it is assumed that the parent's utility function is separable in its arguments, $\partial u_t / \partial u_{t+1} = \psi > 0$. By substituting c_t and c_{t+1} and maximizing with respect to b one derives

$$\frac{\partial u_t}{\partial c_t}(c_t) \geq (1+r)\, \psi \, \frac{\partial u_{t+1}}{\partial c_{t+1}}(c_{t+1})\,, \tag{A.4}$$

holding with equality if $b > 0$. Since the analysis is restricted to operational bequests, this is the case. Note, that due to the separability the derivative of the parent's utility function with respect to c_t is solely dependant on c_t. By once more substituting c_t and c_{t+1} with the help of Equations (A.1) and (A.2) one derives the Marshall demand function for bequests in implicit form. Differentiated totally it reads:

$$\underbrace{\left[(1+r)^2 \psi \, \frac{\partial^2 u_{t+1}}{\partial c_{t+1}^2} + \frac{\partial^2 u_t}{\partial c_t^2}\right]}_{(-)} db$$

$$= \underbrace{\frac{\partial^2 u_t}{\partial c_t^2}}_{(-)} dw_t - (1+r) \underbrace{\frac{\partial u_{t+1}}{\partial c_{t+1}}}_{(+)} d\psi - (1+r)\, \psi \, \underbrace{\frac{\partial^2 u_{t+1}}{\partial c_{t+1}^2}}_{(-)} dw_{t+1}\,,$$

with the signs of the respective terms denoted underneath. Concentrating on the variation of one exogenous variable at a time, yields the derivatives in question:

$$\frac{db}{dw_t} > 0 \quad , \quad \frac{db}{dw_{t+1}} < 0 \quad , \quad \frac{db}{d\psi} > 0 \, . \tag{A.5}$$

Next, it is shown that the main implications of altruistic bequests carry over to an overlapping generations model. In particular, one finds that heir's and testator's stock of life-cycle resources takes on the role of periodical earnings. The problem can be stated as

$$\max_{c_t^1, c_{t+1}^2, c_{t+1}^1, c_{t+2}^2} \quad u_t(c_t^1, c_{t+1}^2, u_{t+1}(c_{t+1}^1, c_{t+2}^2))$$

$$\text{s.t.} \quad c_t^1 = w_t - s_t \tag{A.6}$$

$$c_{t+1}^2 = w_{t+1} + (1+r)\, s_t - b \tag{A.7}$$

$$c_{t+1}^1 = w_{t+1} - s_{t+1} \tag{A.8}$$

$$c_{t+2}^2 = w_{t+2} + (s_{t+1} + b)(1+r) \tag{A.9}$$

$$b \geq 0 \, , \tag{A.10}$$

where c_j^i stands for consumption of an agent in his i-th period of life as of year j and s_j depicts saving in year j. Once more the utility functions are well-behaved and $\partial u_t / \partial u_{t+1} = \psi > 0$. Note, that Equations (A.6) and (A.7) for one thing and Equations (A.8) and (A.9) for another thing can be combined to

$$c_t^1 + \frac{c_{t+1}^2}{(1+r)} + \frac{b}{(1+r)} = w_t + \frac{w_{t+1}}{(1+r)} \quad \text{and} \tag{A.11}$$

$$c_{t+1}^1 + \frac{c_{t+2}^2}{(1+r)} = b + w_{t+1} + \frac{w_{t+2}}{(1+r)} \, , \tag{A.12}$$

respectively. Due to Hicks' composite commodity theorem, if r is fixed, the problem can be reformulated as follows:

$$\max_{\bar{c}_t, \bar{c}_{t+1}} \; u_t(\bar{c}_t, u_{t+1}(\bar{c}_{t+1}))$$

$$\text{s.t.} \quad \bar{c}_t = \bar{w}_t - \frac{b}{(1+r)} \tag{A.13}$$

$$\bar{c}_{t+1} = b + \bar{w}_{t+1} \tag{A.14}$$

$$b \geq 0 \, , \tag{A.15}$$

where $\bar{c}_t = c_t^1 + c_{t+1}^2/(1+r)$ and $\bar{c}_{t+1} = c_{t+1}^1 + c_{t+2}^2/(1+r)$ denote composite commodities and $\bar{w}_t = w_t + w_{t+1}/(1+r)$ and $\bar{w}_{t+1} = w_{t+1} + w_{t+2}/(1+r)$ stand for life-cycle resources. This is in essence the problem we have dealt with already. Consequently,

$$\frac{db}{d\bar{w}_t} > 0 \quad , \quad \frac{db}{d\bar{w}_{t+1}} < 0 \,. \tag{A.16}$$

Finally, it is proved that Ricardian Neutrality holds, if agents are altruistic towards their offsprings. Recall, that this requires ***operational*** bequests before and after government redistribution is carried out. Suppose, the generation born in year t benefits from a government transfer tr which is financed by borrowing abroad. If the economy lasts for only two periods, it follows from the government's intertemporal budget constraint that the following generation faces a tax increase of $(1+r)tr$. If one further assumes that the economy is populated by one agent at a time, the generation t maximization problem can be stated as follows:

$$\max_{c_t, c_{t+1}} \; u_t(c_t, u_{t+1}(c_{t+1}))$$

$$\text{s.t.} \quad c_t = w_t + tr - b \tag{A.17}$$

$$c_{t+1} = (1+r)\,b + w_{t+1} - (1+r)tr \tag{A.18}$$

$$b \geq 0\,, \tag{A.19}$$

where the utility functions exhibit the common properties and the parent's utility function, in addition, is separable in its arguments. Substituting c_t as well as c_{t+1} and maximizing with respect to b yields the usual Euler equation, if bequests are operational:

$$\frac{\partial u_t}{\partial c_t}(w_t + tr - b) = \psi\,(1+r)\frac{\partial u_{t+1}}{\partial c_{t+1}}((1+r)\,b + w_{t+1} - (1+r)\,tr)\,. \tag{A.20}$$

Totally differentiating this Marshall demand function with respect to b and tr results in

$$\left[\frac{\partial^2 u_t}{\partial c_t^2} + \psi(1+r)^2\,\frac{\partial^2 u_{t+1}}{c_{t+1}^2}\right] dtr = \left[\frac{\partial^2 u_t}{\partial c_t^2} + \psi(1+r)^2\,\frac{\partial^2 u_{t+1}}{c_{t+1}^2}\right] db\,. \tag{A.21}$$

Thus, any redistribution by means of public intergenerational transfers is offset one-by-one through private intergenerational transfers in the opposite direction, $db/dtr = 1$.

A.2 The Impact of Social Security on Accidental Bequests

To begin with, we investigate how a fully funded Social Security program affects accidental bequests. In doing so, one has to distinguish two polar cases with respect to the efficiency of public pension themes. Either, they face the same transaction costs as private annuity markets, in which case their return does not exceed the return of common bonds, or they overcome market imperfections and offer actuarially fair annuity returns. These two cases will be considered in turn.

First, assume that any surviving member of a generation receives as pension his contribution t plus accrued interest. Note, that in the absence of any transaction costs, Social Security would make a budget surplus which augments to the interest bearing contributions of short-lived members. In the present case, though, we assume that transaction costs eat up this surplus. The maximization problem of a representative agent can then be stated as

$$\max_{c_t, c_{t+1}} \; u_t = u(c_t) + \pi u(c_{t+1})$$

$$\text{s.t.} \quad c_t = w_t - s - t \tag{A.22}$$

$$c_{t+1} = (1+r)\, s + (1+r)\, t \tag{A.23}$$

$$s \geq 0\,, \tag{A.24}$$

with constraint (A.24) assumed to be non-binding for convenience. Combining the first two constraints yields $c_t + c_{t+1}/(1+r) = w_t$ from which it follows that life-cycle resources and, thus, consumption is not affected by this kind of Social Security theme. According to Equation (A.22) its introduction therefore depresses private saving and accidental bequests.

Next, suppose public pension themes overcome annuity market imperfections. In this case contributions of short-lived members are distributed to surviving members, implying that the latter receive $(1+r)/\pi$ dollars for any dollar contributed. A representative individual then solves the problem:

$$\max_{c_t, c_{t+1}} \; u_t = u(c_t) + \pi u(c_{t+1})$$

$$\text{s.t.} \quad c_t = w_t - s - t \tag{A.25}$$

$$c_{t+1} = (1+r)\, s + \frac{(1+r)}{\pi}\, t \tag{A.26}$$

$$s \geq 0\,. \tag{A.27}$$

This time combining the first two constraints, one finds that the introduction of a funded Social Security program raises life-cycle income by $t(1-\pi)/\pi$, the reason being higher returns. Consequently, not only t but also c_t increases, which according to Equation (A.25) results in a stronger decline of private saving and accidental bequests than in the previous scenario.

Furthermore, while private saving declines by $t + c_t$, public saving only increases by t. Hence, the introduction of an actuarially fair, funded pension theme depresses national saving. Note, the analogy to a pay-as-you-go pension theme. The introduction of funded Social Security reduces accidental bequests to the young generation and, in this way, works like a transfer of purchasing power across generations.

Accidental bequests are also negatively affected by a pay-as-you-go Social Security program. The program's budget constraint reads $t(1+n) = \pi\, tr$, with t, tr, n denoting contributions, pensions, and population growth rate, respectively. The agent's problem can be stated as

$$\max_{c_t, c_{t+1}} u_t = u(c_t) + \pi u(c_{t+1})$$

$$\text{s.t.} \quad c_t = w_t - s - \frac{\pi}{(1+n)} tr \tag{A.28}$$

$$c_{t+1} = (1+r)\, s + tr \tag{A.29}$$

$$s \geq 0\,. \tag{A.30}$$

Again, combining the first and second period constraints, one derives the life-cycle budget constraint

$$c_t + \frac{c_{t+1}}{(1+r)} = w_t + \frac{(1+n)tr - (1+r)\pi\, tr}{(1+n)(1+r)}\,. \tag{A.31}$$

Obviously, life-cycle income and consumption c_t will increase, stay constant, or decline when $(1+n)$ is greater, equal, or smaller $(1+r)\pi$, respectively. From Equation (A.28) it is directly evident, that private saving and accidental bequests decrease, when c_t increases or stays constant. To see that the same holds for c_t declining, realize that the decline in c_t is smaller than the increase in t, because the cut in life-cycle resources is spread over two periods.

A.3 The Impact of the Number of Children on Inheritances *Per Capita*

The inverse relation between the number of offspring and the size of the inheritance per child can be demonstrated by partially differentiating the parent's Marshall demand function for inheritances with respect to n. First consider the case, where parent's utility depends on their children's utility *per capita*. The parent's maximization problem can then be stated as follows:

$$\max_{c_t, c_{t+1}} u_t(c_t, u_{t+1}(c_{t+1}))$$

$$\text{s.t.} \quad c_t = w_t - (1+n)I \tag{A.32}$$

$$c_{t+1} = (1+r)\, I \tag{A.33}$$

$$I \geq 0\,, \tag{A.34}$$

with well-behaved utility functions, i.e. $\partial u_i/\partial c_i > 0$, $\partial^2 u_i/\partial c_i^2 < 0$, and $\partial u_i/\partial c_i \to \infty$ as $c_i \to 0$, for $i = t, t+1$. Furthermore, it is assumed that the parent's utility function is separable in its arguments, $\partial u_t/\partial u_{t+1} = \psi > 0$. Substituting c_t and c_{t+1} by means of Equations (A.32) and (A.33) and differentiating with respect to I, yields the first order condition

$$(1+n)\frac{\partial u_t}{\partial c_t}(c_t) \geq \psi(1+r)\frac{\partial u_{t+1}}{\partial c_{t+1}}(c_{t+1})\,, \tag{A.35}$$

holding with equality, if $I > 0$, as previously assumed. Once more substituting c_t and c_{t+1} in Equation (A.35), one derives the Marshall demand function for inheritances in implicit form. Totally differentiating this function with respect to I and n yields

$$\left[(1+n)^2 \frac{\partial^2 u_t}{\partial c_t^2} + \psi(1+r)^2 \frac{\partial^2 u_{t+1}}{\partial c_{t+1}^2}\right] dI = \left[\frac{\partial u_t}{\partial c_t} - (1+n)\frac{\partial^2 u_t}{c_t^2} I\right] dn ,$$

$$(-) \qquad\qquad\qquad\qquad (+)$$

with the signs of the terms indicated underneath. It follows that $\partial I/\partial n < 0$.

If one assumes instead that the sum of children's utility enters parent's utility, $u_t(c_t, (1+n)u_{t+1}(c_{t+1}))$, the term $(1+n)$ drops out in the first order condition and the total differential reduces to

$$\left[(1+n)\frac{\partial^2 u_t}{\partial c_t^2} + \psi(1+r)^2 \frac{\partial^2 u_{t+1}}{\partial c_{t+1}^2}\right] dI = \left[-\frac{\partial^2 u_t}{c_t^2} I\right] dn ,$$

$$(-) \qquad\qquad\qquad\qquad (+)$$

still implying $\partial I/\partial n < 0$.

Next, consider the joy-of-giving model, where parents derive utility from the inheritance *per capita*. The parent's optimization problem reads

$$\max_{c_t, I} \; u_t(c_t, I)$$

$$\text{s.t.} \quad c_t = w_t - (1+n)I , \tag{A.36}$$

leading to the following first order condition:

$$(1+n)\frac{\partial u_t}{\partial c_t}(c_t, I) = \frac{\partial u_t}{\partial I}(c_t, I) . \tag{A.37}$$

Totally differentiating the first order condition with respect to I and n, after substituting c_t by means of Equation A.36 yields

$$\left[\frac{\partial^2 u_t}{\partial I^2} - n\frac{\partial u_t}{\partial I \partial c_t} + (1+n)^2 \frac{\partial^2 u_t}{\partial c_t} - (1+n)\frac{\partial u_t}{\partial c_t \partial I}\right] dI$$

$$(-)$$

$$= \left[\frac{\partial u_t}{\partial c_t} - (1+n)I\frac{\partial^2 u_t}{\partial c_t^2} + I\frac{\partial u_t}{\partial I \partial c_t}\right] dn .$$

$$(+)$$

implying $\partial I/\partial n < 0$.

Where, instead, parents derive utility from the overall bequest, the maximization problem has to be formulated as

$$\begin{aligned}
&\max_{c_t, I} \; u_t(c_t, (1+n)I) \\
&\text{s.t.} \quad c_t = w_t - (1+n)I \; , \qquad \text{(A.38)}
\end{aligned}$$

implying the first order condition

$$\frac{\partial u_t}{\partial c_t}(c_t, (1+n)I) = \frac{\partial u_t}{\partial b}(c_t, (1+n)I) \qquad \text{(A.39)}$$

and the total differential of the implicit Marshall demand function

$$n\underbrace{\left[-\frac{\partial u_t}{\partial b \partial c_t} + \frac{\partial^2 u_t}{\partial b^2} + \frac{\partial^2 u_t}{\partial c_t^2} - \frac{\partial u_t}{\partial c_t \partial b}\right]}_{(-)} dI = I\underbrace{\left[-\frac{\partial^2 u_t}{\partial I^2} + \frac{\partial u_t}{\partial c_t \partial b} + \frac{\partial u_t}{\partial b \partial c_t} - \frac{\partial^2 u_t}{\partial b^2}\right]}_{(+)} dn \; .$$

Consequently, $\partial I/\partial n < 0$.

Finally, the maximization problem in the case of exchange motivated transfers reads

$$\begin{aligned}
&\max_{c_t, a} \; u_t(c_t, (1+n)a) \\
&\text{s.t.} \quad c_t = w_t - (1+n)I \qquad \text{(A.40)} \\
&\qquad\; I = w_{t+1}a \qquad \text{(A.41)} \\
&\qquad\; 0 \leq a \leq 1 \; . \qquad \text{(A.42)}
\end{aligned}$$

Inserting Equation (A.41) into Equation (A.40) and assuming that Constraint (A.42) does not bind, the first order condition becomes

$$w_{t+1}\frac{\partial u_t}{\partial c_t}(c_t, (1+n)a) = \frac{\partial u_t}{\partial A}(c_t, (1+n)a) \; . \qquad \text{(A.43)}$$

Totally differentiating the implicit Marshall demand function with respect to a and n yields $\partial a/\partial n = -a/(1+n)$. The impact of fertility on the size of the inheritance ***per capita*** can now be derived by differentiating Equation (A.41) with respect to n: $\partial I/\partial n = -w_{t+1}a/(1+n) = -I/(1+n) < 0$. Furthermore, integrating $\partial I/\partial n = -I/(1+n)$ with respect to n yields $(1+n)I = const.$ and thus proves that parents do not adjust overall bequests as the number of children varies.

A.4 Sensitivity Analysis of Public and Private Accounts

Table A.1. Sensitivity Analysis, Public Transfers ($GA_{t,t}^{\text{pub}}$; $GA_{t+1,t+1}^{\text{pub}}$)

		Growth Rate 0.01	Growth Rate 0.015	Growth Rate 0.02
	0.03	341.4 ; 570.0	391.0 ; 621.9	442.6 ; 671.3
Interest Rate	0.05	190.2 ; 411.6	222.3 ; 443.8	258.8 ; 481.8
	0.07	103.2 ; 336.6	121.3 ; 349.8	142.4 ; 367.2
		Migration Low	**Migration Baseline**	**Migration High**
Relative Imm.	0	222.3 ; 475.9	222.3 ; 443.8	222.3 ; 414.5
Wealth	1	222.3 ; 475.9	222.3 ; 443.8	222.3 ; 414.5

In thousands of German Marks.

Table A.2. Sensitivity Analysis, Private Transfers ($GA_{t,t}^{\text{pri}}$; $GA_{t+1,t+1}^{\text{pri}}$)

		Growth Rate 0.01	Growth Rate 0.015	Growth Rate 0.02
	0.03	-392.0 ; -183.3	-422.8 ; -143.5	-458.7 ; -111.5
Interest Rate	0.05	-304.6 ; -385.2	-323.4 ; -327.8	-344.3 ; -274.1
	0.07	-247.5 ; -628.5	-260.6 ; -561.7	-274.9 ; -497.2
		Migration Low	**Migration Baseline**	**Migration High**
Relative Imm.	0	-323.4 ; -355.3	-323.4 ; -327.8	-323.4 ; -295.1
Wealth	1	-323.4 ; -372.4	-323.4 ; -352.0	-323.4 ; -324.9

In thousands of German Marks.

A.5 The Unified General Equilibrium Model

Representative Individual's Utility Function

$$u_t = \left[\left(\left(c_t^1\right)^{1-1/\rho} + \nu(l_t)^{1-1/\rho} \right)^{\frac{1-1/\gamma}{1-1/\rho}} + \frac{\pi}{1+\delta}\left(c_{t+1}^2\right)^{1-1/\gamma} + \frac{\pi\mu}{1+\delta}\left(I_{t+1}^j\right)^{1-1/\gamma} + \frac{\pi\phi}{1+\delta}\left(A_{t+1}\right)^{1-1/\gamma} \right]^{\frac{1}{1-1/\gamma}}$$

Representative Individual's Budget Constraints

$$c_t^1 = I_t^{\mathrm{a}} + (1-a_t)(1-l_t)(1-\tau_t)w_t - s_t$$

$$c_{t+1}^2 = (s_t + I_t^{\mathrm{j}} + I_t^{\mathrm{x}})(1+r_{t+1}) + tr_{t+1} - (1+n_t)(1+\tau_{t+1}^{\mathrm{i}})(I_{t+1}^{\mathrm{j}} + I_{t+1}^{\mathrm{x}})$$

$$I_t^{\mathrm{a}} = \frac{(1-\pi)s_{t-1}(1+r_t)}{(1+n_{t-1})(1+\tau_t^{\mathrm{i}})}$$

$$I_{t+1}^{\mathrm{x}} = (1-\tau_{t+1})w_{t+1}a_{t+1}$$

$$A_{t+1} = (1+n_t)a_{t+1}$$

Government Budget Constraints

$$(1-\beta_t)\frac{\pi tr_t}{1+n_{t-1}} = (1-l_t)(1-a_t)w_t\tau_t$$

$$\beta_t\frac{\pi tr_t}{1+n_{t-1}} = \pi I_t^{\mathrm{j}}\tau_t^{\mathrm{i}} + \pi I_t^{\mathrm{x}}\tau_t^{\mathrm{i}} + \frac{(1-\pi)s_{t-1}(1+r_t)\tau_t^{\mathrm{i}}}{(1+n_{t-1})(1+\tau_t^{\mathrm{i}})}$$

Factor Market Equilibrium

$$w_t = (1-\alpha)k_t^{\alpha}$$

$$r_t = \alpha k_t^{(\alpha-1)}$$

Capital Market Equilibrium

$$k_{t+1} = \frac{s_t + \pi I_t^{\mathrm{j}} + \pi I_t^{\mathrm{x}}}{(1+n_t)(1-l_{t+1})}$$

A.6 Bequests-as-Exchange and Lump-Sum Taxation

The first four equations constitute the agent's budget constraints, where T_t denotes the lump-sum contribution to the pay-as-you-go scheme. The last equation shows the government budget constraint.

$$\begin{aligned} c_t^1 &= (1-a_t)w_t - T_t - s_t \\ c_{t+1}^2 &= (s_t + I_t)(1+r_{t+1}) + tr_{t+1} - (1+n_t)I_{t+1} \\ I_{t+1} &= w_{t+1}a_{t+1} \\ A_{t+1} &= (1+n_t)a_{t+1} \\ T_t &= \frac{tr}{1+n_{t-1}} \end{aligned}$$

Substituting and rearranging these equations yields Equation (5.22).

A.7 The Derivation of Future Generations' Public Generational Account

In order to derive the public generational account of a representative future individual – typically born in period $t+1$ – we depart from the government's intertemporal budget constraint

$$\sum_{s=0}^{D} N_{t,t-s} + \sum_{s=1}^{\infty} N_{t,t+s} = 0\,, \tag{A.44}$$

with the two terms denoting the aggregate accounts of presently living and future generations, respectively. Let L_t stand for the size of the cohort born in period t and assume – as is common procedure in generational accounting – that the interest rate as observed in the base year stays constant over time. Equation (A.44) can then be rearranged to yield:

$$-L_{t-1}tr + L_tT_t - \frac{L_t tr}{(1+r_t)} = -\sum_{s=1}^{\infty} N_{t,t+s}\,. \tag{A.45}$$

The first two terms symbolize the aggregate pensions and contributions in the base year and add up to zero according to Equation (5.25). Thus, the aggregate fiscal burden of future generations equals the pension liabilities accumulated by today's working aged. In order to derive the fiscal burden *per capita*, the overall burden is shared equally among future generations. Thus, it is assumed that $GA_{t+s,t+s} = GA_{t+1,t+1}\ \forall\ s > 1$ and Equation (A.45) can be transformed as follows:

$$
\begin{aligned}
\frac{L_t tr}{(1+r_t)} &= \sum_{s=1}^{\infty} N_{t,t+s} \\
&= \sum_{s=1}^{\infty} \frac{N_{t+s,t+s}}{L_{t+s}} \frac{L_{t+s}}{(1+r_t)^s} \\
&= \sum_{s=1}^{\infty} GA^{\text{pub}}_{t+s,t+s} \frac{L_{t+s}}{(1+r_t)^s} \\
&= GA^{\text{pub}}_{t+1,t+1} \sum_{s=1}^{\infty} \frac{L_{t+s}}{(1+r_t)^s} \,. \qquad \text{(A.46)}
\end{aligned}
$$

Dividing by L_t and assuming that the fertility rate drops once and for all, that is $n_{t-1} > n_t = n_{t+s} \;\forall\; s > 1$, Equation (A.46) reduces to

$$
\begin{aligned}
\frac{tr}{(1+r_t)} &= GA^{\text{pub}}_{t+1,t+1} \sum_{s=1}^{\infty} \left(\frac{1+n_t}{1+r_t}\right)^s \\
&= GA^{\text{pub}}_{t+1,t+1} \frac{(1+n_t)}{(r_t-n_t)} \,, \qquad \text{(A.47)}
\end{aligned}
$$

where the infinite geometric series can be simplified on the condition $r_t > n_t$. From here it follows directly that

$$
GA^{\text{pub}}_{t+1,t+1} = \frac{(r_t-n_t)tr}{(1+n_t)(1+r_t)} \,. \qquad \text{(A.48)}
$$

A.8 The Derivation of the Life-Cycle Budget Constraint of an Average Individual

Let L_t stand for the size of a cohort born in period t. The *per capita* Equation (5.36) weighted with population size then yields:

$$
L_t c_t^1 = L_t I_t + L_t w_t - L_t T_t - L_t s_t \,. \qquad \text{(A.49)}
$$

The last term can be specified by weighting Equations (5.37) and (5.38) with the respective cohort size

$$
\begin{aligned}
\pi L_t s_t (1+r_{t+1}) &= \pi L_t c_{t+1}^2 - \pi L_t tr_{t+1} \qquad \text{(A.50)} \\
(1-\pi) L_t s_t (1+r_{t+1}) &= L_{t+1} I_{t+1} \,, \qquad \text{(A.51)}
\end{aligned}
$$

adding up, and solving for $L_t s_t$:

$$
L_t s_t = \frac{\pi L_t c_{t+1}^2}{(1+r_{t+1})} - \frac{\pi L_t tr_{t+1}}{(1+r_{t+1})} + \frac{L_{t+1} I_{t+1}}{(1+r_{t+1})} \,. \qquad \text{(A.52)}
$$

After substitution of $L_t s_t$ in Equation (A.49) by means of Equation (A.52), division by L_t, and some rearrangements, we obtain the life-cycle budget constraint in terms of an average individual:

$$c_t^1 + \frac{\pi c_{t+1}^2}{(1+r_{t+1})} = w_t - \left[\left(T_t - \frac{\pi tr_{t+1}}{(1+r_{t+1})}\right) + \left(\frac{(1+n_t)I_{t+1}}{(1+r_{t+1})} - I_t\right)\right] . \tag{A.53}$$

A.9 The Calculation of Future Generations' Total Generational Account

We depart from the economy's overall budget constraint

$$W_t^p + \sum_{s=0}^{D} L_{t,t-s} - \sum_{s=0}^{D} N_{t,t-s} - \sum_{s=0}^{D} C_{t,t-s} + \sum_{s=1}^{\infty} L_{t,t+s} - \sum_{s=1}^{\infty} N_{t,t+s} - \sum_{s=1}^{\infty} C_{t,t+s} = 0 , \tag{A.54}$$

already introduced in Section 4.4.2. With the government's intertemporal budget constraint being satisfied (cf. Equation (5.28)), net taxes cancel out and the constraint reduces to:

$$W_t^p + \sum_{s=0}^{D} L_{t,t-s} - \sum_{s=0}^{D} C_{t,t-s} = - \left[\sum_{s=1}^{\infty} L_{t,t+s} - \sum_{s=1}^{\infty} C_{t,t+s}\right] . \tag{A.55}$$

In a two-generation-world and on the accounting-specific steady state assumption the constraint can be restated as:

$$L_t k_t (1+r_t) + L_t w_t - \left(\pi L_{t-1} c_t^2 + L_t c_t^1 + \frac{\pi L_t c_t^2}{(1+r_t)}\right)$$
$$= - \sum_{s=1}^{\infty} \frac{L_{t+s}}{(1+r_t)^s} \left[w_t - \left(c_t^1 + \frac{\pi c_t^2}{(1+r_t)}\right)\right] . \tag{A.56}$$

With U denoting $L_t w_t - L_t c_t^1 - (\pi L_t c_t^2)/(1+r_t)$ the left hand side of Equation (A.56) can be transformed as follows:

$$
\begin{aligned}
& L_t k_t(1+r_t) - \pi L_{t-1} c_t^2 + U \\
&= L_{t-1} s_{t-1}(1+r_t) - \pi L_{t-1} c_t^2 + U && \text{(acc. to Eq. (5.40))} \\
&= \pi L_{t-1} s_{t-1}(1+r_t) + (1-\pi) L_{t-1} s_{t-1}(1+r_t) - \pi L_{t-1} c_t^2 + U \\
&= \pi L_{t-1} s_{t-1}(1+r_t) - \pi L_{t-1} c_t^2 + (1-\pi) L_{t-1} s_{t-1}(1+r_t) + U \\
&= -\pi L_{t-1} tr_t + (1-\pi) L_{t-1} s_{t-1}(1+r_t) + U && \text{(acc. to Eq. (5.37))} \\
&= -L_t T_t + (1-\pi) L_{t-1} s_{t-1}(1+r_t) + U && \text{(acc. to Eq. (5.39))} \\
&= -L_t T_t + L_t I_t + U && \text{(acc. to Eq. (5.38))} \\
&= -L_t T_t + L_t I_t + L_t w_t - L_t c_t^1 - \frac{\pi L_t c_t^2}{(1+r_t)} \, . && \text{(A.57)}
\end{aligned}
$$

Furthermore, dividing by L_t and assuming that the fertility rate drops once and for all, that is $n_{t-1} > n_t = n_{t+s} \ \forall \ s > 1$, Equation (A.56) reduces to:

$$
I_t - T_t + w_t - c_t^1 - \frac{\pi c_t^2}{(1+r_t)} = -\sum_{s=1}^{\infty} \left(\frac{1+n_t}{1+r_t}\right)^s \left[w_t - \left(c_t^1 + \frac{\pi c_t^2}{(1+r_t)} \right) \right] . \tag{A.58}
$$

The term in the square bracket is the GA^{tot} of all future generations, which initially is equal to the GA^{tot} of the base year newborn (cf. Equation (5.43)). However, numerically specifying future accounts in this way, will practically never satisfy the intertemporal budget constraint. We therefore treat the account of future generations $GA^{tot}_{t+1,t+1}$ as an endogenous variable which is solved for on the condition that the intertemporal budget constraint *is* satisfied. Provided that $r_t > n_t$ the infinite geometrical series boils down to $(1+n_t)/(r_t - n_t)$ and future generations' account equals

$$
GA^{tot}_{t+1,t+1} = -\frac{r_t - n_t}{(1+n_t)} \left(I_t - T_t + w_t - c_t^1 - \frac{\pi c_t^2}{(1+r_t)} \right) . \tag{A.59}
$$

A.10 The Equivalence of $GA^{tot}_{t+1,t+1}$ and $TT_{t+1,t+1}$ under Steady State Conditions

In order to demonstrate that

$$
GA^{tot}_{t+1,t+1} = -\frac{r_t - n_t}{(1+n_t)} \left(I_t - T_t + w_t - c_t^1 - \frac{\pi c_t^2}{(1+r_t)} \right) \text{ equals} \tag{A.60}
$$

$$
TT_{t+1,t+1} = w_{t+1} - c_{t+1}^1 - \frac{\pi c_{t+2}^2}{(1+r_{t+2})} \tag{A.61}
$$

under steady state circumstances, reformulate net overall transfers according to Equation (5.42):

$$TT_{t+1,t+1} = T_{t+1} - \frac{\pi tr_{t+2}}{(1+r_{t+2})} + \frac{(1+n_{t+1})I_{t+2}}{(1+r_{t+2})} - I_{t+1} \,. \tag{A.62}$$

Substituting inheritances and the tax by means of Equations (5.38) and (5.39) and further taking into account the defined benefit character of the pay-as-you-go scheme yields:

$$TT_{t+1,t+1} = \frac{(r_{t+2}-n_t)\pi tr}{(1+n_t)(1+r_{t+2})} + (1-\pi)s_{t+1} - \frac{(1-\pi)s_t(1+r_{t+1})}{(1+n_t)} \,. \tag{A.63}$$

Imposing the steady state assumption, Equation (A.63) boils down to

$$TT'_{t+1,t+1} = -\frac{r_t - n_t}{(1+n_t)}\left((1-\pi)s_t - \frac{\pi tr}{(1+r_t)}\right) , \tag{A.64}$$

where the apostrophe indicates our departure from the general equilibrium model in assuming constant variables over time. Substituting savings by help of Equation (5.38) yields:

$$TT'_{t+1,t+1} = -\frac{r_t - n_t}{(1+n_t)}\left(\frac{(1+n_t)I_{t+1}}{(1+r_{t+1})} - \frac{\pi tr}{(1+r_t)}\right) , \tag{A.65}$$

which according to Equation (5.42) on the steady state assumption is equivalent to:

$$TT'_{t+1,t+1} = -\frac{r_t - n_t}{(1+n_t)}\left(I_t - T_t + w_t - c_t^1 - \frac{\pi c_t^2}{(1+r_t)}\right) = GA^{tot}_{t+1,t+1} \,. \tag{A.66}$$

A.11 The Equivalence of Extended Generational Accounting and the Back-of-the-Envelope Calculation

Imposing the accounting-specific steady state assumption, the overall accounts of a representative living and future individual can be reformulated as follows:

$$GA_{t,t}^{\text{tot}} = w_t - c_t^1 - \frac{\pi c_t^2}{(1+r_t)} \qquad \text{(Eq. (5.43))}$$

$$= \frac{(r-n_{t-1})\pi tr}{(1+n_{t-1})(1+r)} + \frac{(1+n_t)I_{t+1}}{(1+r_{t+1})} - I_t \qquad \text{(Eq. (5.42))}$$

$$= \frac{(r-n_{t-1})\pi tr}{(1+n_{t-1})(1+r)} + (1-\pi)s - \frac{(1-\pi)s(1+r)}{(1+n_{t-1})} \qquad \text{(Eq. (5.38))}$$

$$= -\frac{(r-n_{t-1})}{(1+n_{t-1})}\left((1-\pi)s - \frac{\pi tr}{(1+r)}\right) \tag{A.67}$$

$$GA_{t+1,t+1}^{\text{tot}} = -\frac{r_t - n_t}{(1+n_t)}\left(I_t - T_t + w_t - c_t^1 - \frac{\pi c_t^2}{(1+r_t)}\right) \qquad \text{(Eq. (5.50))}$$

$$= -\frac{(r-n_t)}{(1+n_t)}\left(\frac{(1+n_t)I_{t+1}}{(1+r)} - \frac{\pi tr}{(1+r)}\right) \qquad \text{(Eq. (5.42))}$$

$$= -\frac{(r-n_t)}{(1+n_t)}\left((1-\pi)s - \frac{\pi tr}{(1+r)}\right) \qquad \text{(Eq. (5.38))}\,. \tag{A.68}$$

As is obvious from Equations (A.67) and (A.68), the accounts only differ by the population growth rate. Thus, intuitively speaking, overall accounting investigates the impact of a changing dependency ratio $1/(1+n)$ on intergenerational transfers, holding all else constant. Whether future generations are better or worse of than presently living depends on the relative magnitude of private and public transfers: $\partial GA^{\text{tot}}/\partial n > 0$ if $(1-\pi)s(1+r) > \pi tr$ and $\partial GA^{\text{tot}}/\partial n < 0$ if $(1-\pi)s(1+r) < \pi tr$. Note that this perfectly corresponds to the condition derived on page 109.

A.12 Complete Simulation Results

Table A.3. Demographic Transition without Private Transfers, Full-Scale Social Insurance (Section 5.2.1)

t	$k(t)$	$k(t)/y(t) p.a.$	$r(t) p.a.$	$w(t)$	$\tau(t)$	$c^1(t)$	$c^2(t)$	$s(t)$	$REV(t)$[a]
-4	0.0545	3.3839	0.0397	0.3624	0.2453	0.1999	0.3566	0.0736	0.0000
-3	0.0545	3.3839	0.0397	0.3624	0.2453	0.1999	0.3566	0.0736	0.0000
-2	0.0545	3.3839	0.0397	0.3624	0.2453	0.1999	0.3566	0.0736	0.0000
-1	0.0545	3.3839	0.0397	0.3624	0.2453	0.1999	0.3566	0.0736	0.0000
0	0.0545	3.3839	0.0397	0.3624	0.2453	0.2007	0.3566	0.0728	-0.0167
1	0.0628	3.7625	0.0372	0.3754	0.2756	0.1997	0.3380	0.0723	-0.0207
2	0.0623	3.7428	0.0373	0.3748	0.2760	0.1992	0.3372	0.0721	-0.0224
3	0.0622	3.7343	0.0374	0.3745	0.2762	0.1990	0.3369	0.0720	-0.0231
4	0.0621	3.7306	0.0374	0.3744	0.2763	0.1989	0.3368	0.0720	-0.0235
5	0.0620	3.7290	0.0374	0.3743	0.2764	0.1989	0.3367	0.0719	-0.0236
6	0.0620	3.7283	0.0374	0.3743	0.2764	0.1989	0.3367	0.0719	-0.0237
7	0.0620	3.7280	0.0374	0.3743	0.2764	0.1989	0.3367	0.0719	-0.0237
8	0.0620	3.7279	0.0374	0.3743	0.2764	0.1989	0.3366	0.0719	-0.0237
.	.	.	.	.	.	.	.	.	.
.	.	.	.	.	.	.	.	.	.
∞	0.0620	3.7278	0.0374	0.3743	0.2764	0.1989	0.3366	0.0719	-0.0237

[a] In the context of REV t is a generation rather than a time index.

Table A.4. Demographic Transition without Private Transfers, Low-Scale Social Insurance (Section 5.2.1)

t	$k(t)$	$k(t)/y(t)p.a.$	$r(t)p.a.$	$w(t)$	$\tau(t)$	$c^1(t)$	$c^2(t)$	$s(t)$	$REV(t)^a$
-4	0.0768	4.3749	0.0338	0.3948	0.1500	0.2319	0.3612	0.1036	0.0000
-3	0.0768	4.3749	0.0338	0.3948	0.1500	0.2319	0.3612	0.1036	0.0000
-2	0.0768	4.3749	0.0338	0.3948	0.1500	0.2319	0.3612	0.1036	0.0000
-1	0.0768	4.3749	0.0338	0.3948	0.1500	0.2319	0.3612	0.1036	0.0000
0	0.0768	4.3749	0.0338	0.3948	0.1500	0.2321	0.3612	0.1035	-0.0195
1	0.0892	4.8962	0.0314	0.4099	0.1682	0.2355	0.3419	0.1054	-0.0075
2	0.0909	4.9657	0.0312	0.4118	0.1674	0.2367	0.3446	0.1061	-0.0032
3	0.0915	4.9905	0.0311	0.4125	0.1671	0.2372	0.3456	0.1064	-0.0017
4	0.0917	4.9993	0.0310	0.4127	0.1670	0.2373	0.3459	0.1065	-0.0011
5	0.0918	5.0024	0.0310	0.4128	0.1670	0.2374	0.3460	0.1065	-0.0009
6	0.0918	5.0035	0.0310	0.4128	0.1669	0.2374	0.3461	0.1065	-0.0009
7	0.0918	5.0039	0.0310	0.4128	0.1669	0.2374	0.3461	0.1065	-0.0008
8	0.0918	5.0040	0.0310	0.4129	0.1669	0.2374	0.3461	0.1065	-0.0008
.	.	.	.	.	.	.	.	.	.
.	.	.	.	.	.	.	.	.	.
∞	0.0918	5.0041	0.0310	0.4129	0.1669	0.2374	0.3461	0.1065	-0.0008

[a] In the context of REV t is a generation rather than a time index.

Table A.5. Demographic Transition with Joy-of Giving Transfers, Baseline (Section 5.2.2)

t	$k(t)$	$k(t)/y(t)p.a.$	$r(t)p.a.$	$w(t)$	$\tau(t)$	$c^1(t)$	$c^2(t)$	$I(t)$	$I(t)/y(t)$	$s(t)$	$REV(t)$[a]
-4	0.0738	4.2494	0.0345	0.3910	0.2274	0.2282	0.3607	0.0258	0.0669	0.0739	0.0000
-3	0.0738	4.2494	0.0345	0.3910	0.2274	0.2282	0.3607	0.0258	0.0669	0.0739	0.0000
-2	0.0738	4.2494	0.0345	0.3910	0.2274	0.2282	0.3607	0.0258	0.0669	0.0739	0.0000
-1	0.0738	4.2494	0.0345	0.3910	0.2274	0.2282	0.3607	0.0258	0.0669	0.0739	0.0000
0	0.0738	4.2494	0.0345	0.3910	0.2274	0.2291	0.3607	0.0258	0.0669	0.0730	-0.0127
1	0.0852	4.7294	0.0322	0.4052	0.2553	0.2301	0.3433	0.0277	0.0596	0.0716	-0.0092
2	0.0857	4.7501	0.0321	0.4057	0.2550	0.2305	0.3440	0.0278	0.0596	0.0718	-0.0078
3	0.0859	4.7587	0.0320	0.4060	0.2548	0.2307	0.3443	0.0278	0.0596	0.0719	-0.0072
4	0.0860	4.7622	0.0320	0.4061	0.2547	0.2307	0.3444	0.0278	0.0596	0.0719	-0.0070
5	0.0860	4.7637	0.0320	0.4061	0.2547	0.2308	0.3445	0.0278	0.0597	0.0719	-0.0069
6	0.0860	4.7643	0.0320	0.4062	0.2547	0.2308	0.3445	0.0278	0.0597	0.0719	-0.0068
7	0.0860	4.7646	0.0320	0.4062	0.2547	0.2308	0.3445	0.0278	0.0597	0.0719	-0.0068
8	0.0860	4.7647	0.0320	0.4062	0.2547	0.2308	0.3445	0.0278	0.0597	0.0719	-0.0068
.	.	.	.	.	.	.	.	.	.	.	.
.	.	.	.	.	.	.	.	.	.	.	.
∞	0.0860	4.7648	0.0320	0.4062	0.2547	0.2308	0.3445	0.0278	0.0597	0.0719	-0.0068

[a] In the context of REV t is a generation rather than a time index.

Table A.6. Demographic Transition with Joy-of Giving Transfers, 3.4% Bequest to GDP (Section 5.2.2)

t	$k(t)$	$k(t)/y(t) p.a.$	$r(t) p.a.$	$w(t)$	$\tau(t)$	$c^1(t)$	$c^2(t)$	$I(t)$	$I(t)/y(t)$	$s(t)$	$REV(t)$[a]
-4	0.0639	3.8142	0.0369	0.3771	0.2357	0.2146	0.3589	0.0127	0.0341	0.0736	0.0000
-3	0.0639	3.8142	0.0369	0.3771	0.2357	0.2146	0.3589	0.0127	0.0341	0.0736	0.0000
-2	0.0639	3.8142	0.0369	0.3771	0.2357	0.2146	0.3589	0.0127	0.0341	0.0736	0.0000
-1	0.0639	3.8142	0.0369	0.3771	0.2357	0.2146	0.3589	0.0127	0.0341	0.0736	0.0000
0	0.0639	3.8142	0.0369	0.3771	0.2357	0.2154	0.3589	0.0127	0.0341	0.0728	-0.0147
1	0.0737	4.2433	0.0345	0.3908	0.2647	0.2154	0.3408	0.0136	0.0303	0.0719	-0.0147
2	0.0737	4.2432	0.0345	0.3908	0.2647	0.2154	0.3408	0.0136	0.0303	0.0719	-0.0147
3	0.0737	4.2432	0.0345	0.3908	0.2647	0.2154	0.3408	0.0136	0.0303	0.0719	-0.0147
4	0.0737	4.2432	0.0345	0.3908	0.2647	0.2154	0.3408	0.0136	0.0303	0.0719	-0.0147
5	0.0737	4.2432	0.0345	0.3908	0.2647	0.2154	0.3408	0.0136	0.0303	0.0719	-0.0147
6	0.0737	4.2432	0.0345	0.3908	0.2647	0.2154	0.3408	0.0136	0.0303	0.0719	-0.0147
7	0.0737	4.2432	0.0345	0.3908	0.2647	0.2154	0.3408	0.0136	0.0303	0.0719	-0.0147
8	0.0737	4.2432	0.0345	0.3908	0.2647	0.2154	0.3408	0.0136	0.0303	0.0719	-0.0147
.	.	.	.	.	.	.	.	.	.	.	.
.	.	.	.	.	.	.	.	.	.	.	.
∞	0.0737	4.2432	0.0345	0.3908	0.2647	0.2154	0.3408	0.0136	0.0303	0.0719	-0.0147

[a] In the context of REV t is a generation rather than a time index.

Table A.7. Demographic Transition with Joy-of Giving Transfers, 12.4% Bequest to GDP (Section 5.2.2)

t	$k(t)$	$k(t)/y(t)p.a.$	$r(t)p.a.$	$w(t)$	$\tau(t)$	$c^1(t)$	$c^2(t)$	$I(t)$	$I(t)/y(t)$	$s(t)$	$REV(t)$[a]
-4	0.0930	5.0502	0.0308	0.4141	0.2146	0.2504	0.3634	0.0507	0.1239	0.0748	0.0000
-3	0.0930	5.0502	0.0308	0.4141	0.2146	0.2504	0.3634	0.0507	0.1239	0.0748	0.0000
-2	0.0930	5.0502	0.0308	0.4141	0.2146	0.2504	0.3634	0.0507	0.1239	0.0748	0.0000
-1	0.0930	5.0502	0.0308	0.4141	0.2146	0.2504	0.3634	0.0507	0.1239	0.0748	0.0000
0	0.0930	5.0502	0.0308	0.4141	0.2146	0.2515	0.3634	0.0507	0.1239	0.0738	-0.0087
1	0.1073	5.6235	0.0287	0.4292	0.2410	0.2542	0.3470	0.0546	0.1107	0.0716	0.0000
2	0.1088	5.6843	0.0284	0.4308	0.2401	0.2553	0.3491	0.0549	0.1110	0.0720	0.0036
3	0.1095	5.7094	0.0284	0.4314	0.2398	0.2557	0.3499	0.0551	0.1111	0.0722	0.0050
4	0.1097	5.7197	0.0283	0.4317	0.2397	0.2559	0.3503	0.0551	0.1111	0.0723	0.0056
5	0.1098	5.7239	0.0283	0.4318	0.2396	0.2560	0.3504	0.0551	0.1111	0.0723	0.0059
6	0.1099	5.7256	0.0283	0.4318	0.2396	0.2560	0.3504	0.0552	0.1111	0.0723	0.0060
7	0.1099	5.7263	0.0283	0.4318	0.2396	0.2560	0.3505	0.0552	0.1111	0.0723	0.0060
8	0.1099	5.7266	0.0283	0.4318	0.2396	0.2561	0.3505	0.0552	0.1111	0.0723	0.0060
.	.	.	.	.	.	.	.	.	.	.	.
.	.	.	.	.	.	.	.	.	.	.	.
∞	0.1099	5.7268	0.0283	0.4318	0.2396	0.2561	0.3505	0.0552	0.1111	0.0723	0.0060

[a] In the context of REV t is a generation rather than a time index.

Table A.8. Demographic Transition with Accidental Bequests, Baseline (Section 5.2.3)

t	$k(t)$	$k(t)/y(t)p.a.$	$r(t)p.a.$	$w(t)$	$\tau(t)$	$c^1(t)$	$c^2(t)$	$I(t)$	$I(t)/y(t)$	$s(t)$	$REV(t)$[a]
-4	0.0596	3.6191	0.0381	0.3706	0.1751	0.2747	0.3672	0.0494	0.0440	0.0805	0.0000
-3	0.0596	3.6191	0.0381	0.3706	0.1751	0.2747	0.3672	0.0494	0.0440	0.0805	0.0000
-2	0.0596	3.6191	0.0381	0.3706	0.1751	0.2747	0.3672	0.0494	0.0440	0.0805	0.0000
-1	0.0596	3.6191	0.0381	0.3706	0.1751	0.2747	0.3672	0.0494	0.0440	0.0805	0.0000
0	0.0596	3.6191	0.0381	0.3706	0.1751	0.2755	0.3672	0.0494	0.0440	0.0797	-0.0142
1	0.0687	4.0249	0.0357	0.3839	0.1967	0.2800	0.3481	0.0531	0.0420	0.0815	-0.0005
2	0.0703	4.0938	0.0353	0.3861	0.1956	0.2820	0.3508	0.0537	0.0427	0.0823	0.0054
3	0.0709	4.1239	0.0351	0.3871	0.1951	0.2829	0.3520	0.0540	0.0431	0.0826	0.0080
4	0.0712	4.1370	0.0351	0.3875	0.1949	0.2833	0.3525	0.0541	0.0432	0.0828	0.0091
5	0.0714	4.1426	0.0350	0.3877	0.1948	0.2834	0.3527	0.0542	0.0432	0.0829	0.0096
6	0.0714	4.1451	0.0350	0.3877	0.1948	0.2835	0.3528	0.0542	0.0433	0.0829	0.0098
7	0.0715	4.1461	0.0350	0.3878	0.1947	0.2835	0.3528	0.0542	0.0433	0.0829	0.0099
8	0.0715	4.1466	0.0350	0.3878	0.1947	0.2836	0.3528	0.0542	0.0433	0.0829	0.0100
.	.	.	.	.	.	.	.	.	.	.	.
.	.	.	.	.	.	.	.	.	.	.	.
∞	0.0715	4.1469	0.0350	0.3878	0.1947	0.2836	0.3529	0.0542	0.0433	0.0829	0.0100

[a] In the context of REV t is a generation rather than a time index.

Table A.9. Demographic Transition with Accidental Bequests, 0.8% Bequest to GDP (Section 5.2.3)

t	$k(t)$	$k(t)/y(t) p.a.$	$r(t) p.a.$	$w(t)$	$\tau(t)$	$c^1(t)$	$c^2(t)$	$I(t)$	$I(t)/y(t)$	$s(t)$	$REV(t)$[a]
-4	0.0565	3.4762	0.0391	0.3656	0.2309	0.2139	0.3608	0.0089	0.0078	0.0763	0.0000
-3	0.0565	3.4762	0.0391	0.3656	0.2309	0.2139	0.3608	0.0089	0.0078	0.0763	0.0000
-2	0.0565	3.4762	0.0391	0.3656	0.2309	0.2139	0.3608	0.0089	0.0078	0.0763	0.0000
-1	0.0565	3.4762	0.0391	0.3656	0.2309	0.2139	0.3608	0.0089	0.0078	0.0763	0.0000
0	0.0565	3.4762	0.0391	0.3656	0.2309	0.2146	0.3608	0.0089	0.0078	0.0755	-0.0163
1	0.0651	3.8660	0.0366	0.3788	0.2594	0.2146	0.3420	0.0096	0.0075	0.0755	-0.0163
2	0.0651	3.8660	0.0366	0.3788	0.2594	0.2146	0.3420	0.0096	0.0075	0.0755	-0.0163
3	0.0651	3.8661	0.0366	0.3788	0.2594	0.2146	0.3420	0.0096	0.0075	0.0755	-0.0163
4	0.0651	3.8661	0.0366	0.3788	0.2594	0.2146	0.3420	0.0096	0.0075	0.0755	-0.0163
5	0.0651	3.8661	0.0366	0.3788	0.2594	0.2146	0.3420	0.0096	0.0075	0.0755	-0.0163
6	0.0651	3.8661	0.0366	0.3788	0.2594	0.2146	0.3420	0.0096	0.0075	0.0755	-0.0163
7	0.0651	3.8661	0.0366	0.3788	0.2594	0.2146	0.3420	0.0096	0.0075	0.0755	-0.0163
8	0.0651	3.8661	0.0366	0.3788	0.2594	0.2146	0.3420	0.0096	0.0075	0.0755	-0.0163
.	.	.	.	.	.	.	.	.	.	.	.
.	.	.	.	.	.	.	.	.	.	.	.
∞	0.0651	3.8661	0.0366	0.3788	0.2594	0.2146	0.3420	0.0096	0.0075	0.0755	-0.0163

[a] In the context of REV t is a generation rather than a time index.

Table A.10. Demographic Transition with Accidental Bequests, 4.6% Bequest to GDP (Section 5.2.3)

t	$k(t)$	$k(t)/y(t)p.a.$	$r(t)p.a.$	$w(t)$	$\tau(t)$	$c^1(t)$	$c^2(t)$	$I(t)$	$I(t)/y(t)$	$s(t)$	$REV(t)^a$
-4	0.0595	3.6138	0.0382	0.3704	0.1728	0.2773	0.3670	0.0512	0.0455	0.0803	0.0000
-3	0.0595	3.6138	0.0382	0.3704	0.1728	0.2773	0.3670	0.0512	0.0455	0.0803	0.0000
-2	0.0595	3.6138	0.0382	0.3704	0.1728	0.2773	0.3670	0.0512	0.0455	0.0803	0.0000
-1	0.0595	3.6138	0.0382	0.3704	0.1728	0.2773	0.3670	0.0512	0.0455	0.0803	0.0000
0	0.0595	3.6138	0.0382	0.3704	0.1728	0.2781	0.3670	0.0512	0.0455	0.0795	-0.0140
1	0.0685	4.0188	0.0357	0.3838	0.1941	0.2829	0.3479	0.0550	0.0435	0.0814	0.0000
2	0.0702	4.0900	0.0353	0.3860	0.1930	0.2850	0.3506	0.0557	0.0443	0.0822	0.0063
3	0.0709	4.1211	0.0352	0.3870	0.1925	0.2859	0.3519	0.0560	0.0446	0.0826	0.0089
4	0.0712	4.1346	0.0351	0.3874	0.1923	0.2863	0.3524	0.0561	0.0448	0.0827	0.0101
5	0.0713	4.1405	0.0351	0.3876	0.1922	0.2864	0.3526	0.0561	0.0448	0.0828	0.0106
6	0.0714	4.1430	0.0350	0.3877	0.1921	0.2865	0.3527	0.0562	0.0449	0.0828	0.0108
7	0.0714	4.1441	0.0350	0.3877	0.1921	0.2866	0.3527	0.0562	0.0449	0.0828	0.0109
8	0.0714	4.1446	0.0350	0.3877	0.1921	0.2866	0.3528	0.0562	0.0449	0.0829	0.0110
.	.	.	.	.	.	.	.	.	.	.	.
.	.	.	.	.	.	.	.	.	.	.	.
∞	0.0714	4.1450	0.0350	0.3877	0.1921	0.2866	0.3528	0.0562	0.0449	0.0829	0.0110

[a] In the context of REV t is a generation rather than a time index.

Table A.11. Demographic Transition with Bequests-as-Exchange, Baseline (Section 5.2.4)

t	$k(t)$	$k(t)/y(t)p.a.$	$r(t)p.a.$	$w(t)$	$\tau(t)$	$c^1(t)$	$c^2(t)$	$I(t)$	$I(t)/y(t)$	$a(t)$	$s(t)$	$REV(t)^a$
-4	0.0581	3.5490	0.0386	0.3682	0.2608	0.1937	0.3367	0.0203	0.0602	0.0744	0.0581	0.0000
-3	0.0581	3.5490	0.0386	0.3682	0.2608	0.1937	0.3367	0.0203	0.0602	0.0744	0.0581	0.0000
-2	0.0581	3.5490	0.0386	0.3682	0.2608	0.1937	0.3367	0.0203	0.0602	0.0744	0.0581	0.0000
-1	0.0581	3.5490	0.0386	0.3682	0.2608	0.1937	0.3367	0.0203	0.0602	0.0744	0.0581	0.0000
0	0.0581	3.5490	0.0386	0.3682	0.2608	0.1945	0.3367	0.0203	0.0602	0.0744	0.0574	-0.0173
1	0.0670	3.9485	0.0361	0.3815	0.2957	0.1923	0.3193	0.0223	0.0554	0.0830	0.0541	-0.0260
2	0.0659	3.9016	0.0364	0.3800	0.2969	0.1913	0.3177	0.0222	0.0553	0.0829	0.0537	-0.0299
3	0.0654	3.8810	0.0365	0.3793	0.2974	0.1909	0.3169	0.0221	0.0552	0.0829	0.0536	-0.0316
4	0.0652	3.8719	0.0366	0.3790	0.2976	0.1907	0.3166	0.0221	0.0552	0.0829	0.0535	-0.0323
5	0.0651	3.8679	0.0366	0.3789	0.2977	0.1906	0.3165	0.0221	0.0552	0.0829	0.0535	-0.0327
6	0.0651	3.8661	0.0366	0.3788	0.2977	0.1905	0.3164	0.0220	0.0552	0.0829	0.0534	-0.0328
7	0.0651	3.8653	0.0366	0.3788	0.2978	0.1905	0.3164	0.0220	0.0552	0.0829	0.0534	-0.0329
8	0.0651	3.8650	0.0366	0.3788	0.2978	0.1905	0.3164	0.0220	0.0552	0.0829	0.0534	-0.0329
.	.	.	.	.	.	.	.	.	.	.	.	.
.	.	.	.	.	.	.	.	.	.	.	.	.
0	0.0651	3.8647	0.0366	0.3788	0.2978	0.1905	0.3164	0.0220	0.0552	0.0829	0.0534	-0.0329

[a] In the context of REV t is a generation rather than a time index.

Table A.12. Demographic Transition with Bequests-as-Exchange, Lump-sum Contribution (Section 5.2.4)

t	$k(t)$	$k(t)/y(t) p.a.$	$r(t) p.a.$	$w(t)$	$T(t)/w(t)$	$c^1(t)$	$c^2(t)$	$I(t)$	$I(t)/y(t)$	$a(t)$	$s(t)$	$REV(t)$[a]
-4	0.0617	3.7142	0.0375	0.3738	0.2378	0.2016	0.3419	0.0219	0.0593	0.0586	0.0614	0.0000
-3	0.0617	3.7142	0.0375	0.3738	0.2378	0.2016	0.3419	0.0219	0.0593	0.0586	0.0614	0.0000
-2	0.0617	3.7142	0.0375	0.3738	0.2378	0.2016	0.3419	0.0219	0.0593	0.0586	0.0614	0.0000
-1	0.0617	3.7142	0.0375	0.3738	0.2378	0.2016	0.3419	0.0219	0.0593	0.0586	0.0614	0.0000
0	0.0617	3.7142	0.0375	0.3738	0.2378	0.2023	0.3419	0.0219	0.0593	0.0586	0.0607	-0.0189
1	0.0712	4.1365	0.0351	0.3875	0.2670	0.2017	0.3242	0.0244	0.0547	0.0628	0.0580	-0.0211
2	0.0710	4.1243	0.0351	0.3871	0.2673	0.2015	0.3238	0.0243	0.0546	0.0628	0.0579	-0.0220
3	0.0708	4.1191	0.0352	0.3869	0.2674	0.2014	0.3236	0.0243	0.0546	0.0628	0.0578	-0.0224
4	0.0708	4.1169	0.0352	0.3869	0.2674	0.2013	0.3235	0.0243	0.0546	0.0628	0.0578	-0.0226
5	0.0708	4.1160	0.0352	0.3868	0.2674	0.2013	0.3235	0.0243	0.0546	0.0628	0.0578	-0.0227
6	0.0708	4.1156	0.0352	0.3868	0.2674	0.2013	0.3235	0.0243	0.0546	0.0628	0.0578	-0.0227
7	0.0708	4.1155	0.0352	0.3868	0.2674	0.2013	0.3235	0.0243	0.0546	0.0628	0.0578	-0.0227
8	0.0707	4.1154	0.0352	0.3868	0.2674	0.2013	0.3235	0.0243	0.0546	0.0628	0.0578	-0.0227
.	.	.	.	.	.	.	.	.	.	.	.	.
.	.	.	.	.	.	.	.	.	.	.	.	.
∞	0.0707	4.1153	0.0352	0.3868	0.2674	0.2013	0.3235	0.0243	0.0546	0.0628	0.0578	-0.0227

[a] In the context of REV t is a generation rather than a time index.

Table A.13. Demographic Transition without Private Transfers, Endogenous Labor Supply (Section 5.4.1)

t	$k(t)$	$k(t)/y(t)p.a.$	$r(t)p.a.$	$w(t)$	$\tau(t)$	$c^1(t)$	$l(t)$	$c^2(t)$	$s(t)$	$REV(t)^a$
-4	0.0472	3.0385	0.0423	0.3496	0.2765	0.1740	0.0805	0.3233	0.0586	0.0000
-3	0.0472	3.0385	0.0423	0.3496	0.2765	0.1740	0.0805	0.3233	0.0586	0.0000
-2	0.0472	3.0385	0.0423	0.3496	0.2765	0.1740	0.0805	0.3233	0.0586	0.0000
-1	0.0472	3.0385	0.0423	0.3496	0.2765	0.1740	0.0805	0.3233	0.0586	0.0000
0	0.0472	3.0393	0.0423	0.3496	0.2766	0.1747	0.0809	0.3232	0.0578	-0.0145
1	0.0542	3.3689	0.0398	0.3618	0.3110	0.1724	0.0808	0.3064	0.0567	-0.0240
2	0.0532	3.3228	0.0401	0.3602	0.3124	0.1714	0.0808	0.3047	0.0562	-0.0283
3	0.0527	3.3018	0.0403	0.3594	0.3131	0.1709	0.0807	0.3040	0.0560	-0.0303
4	0.0525	3.2921	0.0404	0.3591	0.3134	0.1707	0.0807	0.3037	0.0559	-0.0312
5	0.0524	3.2876	0.0404	0.3589	0.3135	0.1706	0.0807	0.3035	0.0559	-0.0317
6	0.0524	3.2855	0.0404	0.3588	0.3136	0.1706	0.0807	0.3034	0.0559	-0.0319
7	0.0524	3.2845	0.0404	0.3588	0.3136	0.1705	0.0807	0.3034	0.0558	-0.0319
8	0.0524	3.2841	0.0404	0.3588	0.3137	0.1705	0.0807	0.3034	0.0558	-0.0320
.	.	.	.	.	.	.	.	.	.	.
.	.	.	.	.	.	.	.	.	.	.
∞	0.0524	3.2837	0.0404	0.3588	0.3137	0.1705	0.0807	0.3034	0.0558	-0.0320

[a] In the context of REV t is a generation rather than a time index.

Table A.14. Demographic Transition, Joy-of-Giving, and Endogenous Labor Supply (Section 5.4.2)

t	$k(t)$	$k(t)/y(t) p.a.$	$r(t) p.a.$	$w(t)$	$\tau(t)$	$c^1(t)$	$l(t)$	$c^2(t)$	$I(t)$	$I(t)/y(t)$	$s(t)$	$REV(t)$[a]
-4	0.0656	3.8872	0.0365	0.3795	0.2559	0.2008	0.0848	0.3258	0.0233	0.0622	0.0577	0.0000
-3	0.0656	3.8872	0.0365	0.3795	0.2559	0.2008	0.0848	0.3258	0.0233	0.0622	0.0577	0.0000
-2	0.0656	3.8872	0.0365	0.3795	0.2559	0.2008	0.0848	0.3258	0.0233	0.0622	0.0577	0.0000
-1	0.0656	3.8872	0.0365	0.3795	0.2559	0.2008	0.0848	0.3258	0.0233	0.0622	0.0577	0.0000
0	0.0656	3.8883	0.0365	0.3796	0.2560	0.2016	0.0852	0.3258	0.0233	0.0622	0.0567	-0.0110
1	0.0754	4.3182	0.0341	0.3931	0.2878	0.2012	0.0856	0.3099	0.0251	0.0555	0.0547	-0.0122
2	0.0752	4.3089	0.0342	0.3928	0.2880	0.2010	0.0856	0.3096	0.0250	0.0554	0.0547	-0.0129
3	0.0751	4.3048	0.0342	0.3927	0.2881	0.2010	0.0856	0.3095	0.0250	0.0554	0.0546	-0.0132
4	0.0751	4.3031	0.0342	0.3926	0.2882	0.2009	0.0856	0.3094	0.0250	0.0554	0.0546	-0.0133
5	0.0751	4.3023	0.0342	0.3926	0.2882	0.2009	0.0856	0.3094	0.0250	0.0554	0.0546	-0.0134
6	0.0751	4.3020	0.0342	0.3926	0.2882	0.2009	0.0856	0.3094	0.0250	0.0554	0.0546	-0.0134
7	0.0751	4.3018	0.0342	0.3926	0.2882	0.2009	0.0856	0.3094	0.0250	0.0554	0.0546	-0.0134
8	0.0751	4.3018	0.0342	0.3926	0.2882	0.2009	0.0856	0.3094	0.0250	0.0554	0.0546	-0.0134
.	.	.	.	.	.	.	.	.	.	.	.	.
.	.	.	.	.	.	.	.	.	.	.	.	.
∞	0.0751	4.3017	0.0342	0.3926	0.2882	0.2009	0.0856	0.3094	0.0250	0.0554	0.0546	-0.0134

[a] In the context of REV t is a generation rather than a time index.

Table A.15. Demographic Transition, Joy-of-Giving, Endogenous Labor Supply, and Inheritance Taxation (Section 5.4.2)

t	$k(t)$	$k(t)/y(t)p.a.$	$r(t)p.a.$	$w(t)$	$\tau(t)$	$\tau^i(t)$	$c^1(t)$	$l(t)$	$c^2(t)$	$I(t)$	$I(t)/y(t)$	$s(t)$	$REV(t)$[a]
-4	0.0656	3.8872	0.0365	0.3795	0.2559	0.0000	0.2008	0.0848	0.3258	0.0233	0.0622	0.0577	0.0000
-3	0.0656	3.8872	0.0365	0.3795	0.2559	0.0000	0.2008	0.0848	0.3258	0.0233	0.0622	0.0577	0.0000
-2	0.0656	3.8872	0.0365	0.3795	0.2559	0.0000	0.2008	0.0848	0.3258	0.0233	0.0622	0.0577	0.0000
-1	0.0656	3.8872	0.0365	0.3795	0.2559	0.0000	0.2008	0.0848	0.3258	0.0233	0.0622	0.0577	0.0000
0	0.0656	3.8875	0.0365	0.3795	0.2559	0.0000	0.2011	0.0849	0.3258	0.0233	0.0622	0.0573	-0.0264
1	0.0759	4.3365	0.0340	0.3936	0.2581	0.6063	0.2030	0.0834	0.3084	0.0171	0.0606	0.0647	-0.0206
2	0.0769	4.3796	0.0338	0.3949	0.2572	0.6024	0.2038	0.0834	0.3098	0.0172	0.0606	0.0650	-0.0176
3	0.0773	4.3981	0.0337	0.3955	0.2569	0.6008	0.2042	0.0835	0.3104	0.0172	0.0606	0.0652	-0.0163
4	0.0775	4.4060	0.0337	0.3957	0.2567	0.6001	0.2043	0.0835	0.3106	0.0172	0.0606	0.0652	-0.0157
5	0.0776	4.4094	0.0337	0.3958	0.2566	0.5998	0.2044	0.0835	0.3107	0.0172	0.0607	0.0653	-0.0155
6	0.0776	4.4108	0.0337	0.3958	0.2566	0.5996	0.2044	0.0835	0.3108	0.0173	0.0607	0.0653	-0.0154
7	0.0776	4.4114	0.0337	0.3959	0.2566	0.5996	0.2044	0.0835	0.3108	0.0173	0.0607	0.0653	-0.0154
8	0.0776	4.4117	0.0337	0.3959	0.2566	0.5996	0.2045	0.0835	0.3108	0.0173	0.0607	0.0653	-0.0154
.	.	.	.	.	.	.	.	.	.	.	.	.	.
.	.	.	.	.	.	.	.	.	.	.	.	.	.
∞	0.0776	4.4119	0.0337	0.3959	0.2566	0.5995	0.2045	0.0835	0.3108	0.0173	0.0607	0.0653	-0.0153

[a] In the context of REV t is a generation rather than a time index.

Table A.16. Demographic Transition and Joy-of-Giving Transfers with $\gamma = 0.5$ (Section 5.4.2)

t	$k(t)$	$k(t)/y(t)p.a.$	$r(t)p.a.$	$w(t)$	$\tau(t)$	$c^1(t)$	$l(t)$	$c^2(t)$	$I(t)$	$I(t)/y(t)$	$s(t)$	$REV(t)^a$
-4	0.0509	3.2139	0.0410	0.3562	0.2773	0.2196	0.1002	0.2588	0.0498	0.1416	0.0120	0.0000
-3	0.0509	3.2139	0.0410	0.3562	0.2773	0.2196	0.1002	0.2588	0.0498	0.1416	0.0120	0.0000
-2	0.0509	3.2139	0.0410	0.3562	0.2773	0.2196	0.1002	0.2588	0.0498	0.1416	0.0120	0.0000
-1	0.0509	3.2139	0.0410	0.3562	0.2773	0.2196	0.1002	0.2588	0.0498	0.1416	0.0120	0.0000
0	0.0509	3.2144	0.0409	0.3562	0.2774	0.2200	0.1004	0.2588	0.0498	0.1416	0.0116	-0.0047
1	0.0589	3.5854	0.0383	0.3694	0.3115	0.2194	0.1011	0.2497	0.0518	0.1221	0.0093	-0.0064
2	0.0586	3.5734	0.0384	0.3690	0.3119	0.2191	0.1011	0.2493	0.0518	0.1220	0.0092	-0.0075
3	0.0585	3.5671	0.0385	0.3688	0.3120	0.2189	0.1011	0.2492	0.0517	0.1220	0.0092	-0.0081
4	0.0584	3.5638	0.0385	0.3687	0.3121	0.2188	0.1011	0.2491	0.0517	0.1220	0.0091	-0.0083
5	0.0584	3.5621	0.0385	0.3686	0.3122	0.2188	0.1011	0.2490	0.0517	0.1220	0.0091	-0.0085
6	0.0583	3.5612	0.0385	0.3686	0.3122	0.2188	0.1011	0.2490	0.0517	0.1220	0.0091	-0.0086
7	0.0583	3.5607	0.0385	0.3686	0.3122	0.2188	0.1011	0.2490	0.0517	0.1220	0.0091	-0.0086
8	0.0583	3.5604	0.0385	0.3686	0.3122	0.2187	0.1011	0.2490	0.0517	0.1220	0.0091	-0.0086
.	.	.	.	.	.	.	.	.	.	.	.	.
.	.	.	.	.	.	.	.	.	.	.	.	.
∞	0.0583	3.5602	0.0385	0.3686	0.3122	0.2187	0.1011	0.2490	0.0517	0.1220	0.0091	-0.0087

[a] In the context of REV t is a generation rather than a time index.

Table A.17. Demographic Transition, Joy-of-Giving, and Inheritance Taxation with $\gamma = 0.5$ (Section 5.4.2)

t	$k(t)$	$k(t)/y(t) p.a.$	$r(t) p.a.$	$w(t)$	$\tau(t)$	$\tau^i(t)$	$c^1(t)$	$l(t)$	$c^2(t)$	$I(t)$	$I(t)/y(t)$	$s(t)$	$REV(t)$[a]
-4	0.0509	3.2139	0.0410	0.3562	0.2773	0.0000	0.2196	0.1002	0.2588	0.0498	0.1416	0.0120	0.0000
-3	0.0509	3.2139	0.0410	0.3562	0.2773	0.0000	0.2196	0.1002	0.2588	0.0498	0.1416	0.0120	0.0000
-2	0.0509	3.2139	0.0410	0.3562	0.2773	0.0000	0.2196	0.1002	0.2588	0.0498	0.1416	0.0120	0.0000
-1	0.0509	3.2139	0.0410	0.3562	0.2773	0.0000	0.2196	0.1002	0.2588	0.0498	0.1416	0.0120	0.0000
0	0.0509	3.2142	0.0409	0.3562	0.2774	0.0000	0.2198	0.1003	0.2588	0.0498	0.1416	0.0118	-0.0063
1	0.0590	3.5921	0.0383	0.3697	0.3075	0.0243	0.2198	0.1007	0.2493	0.0511	0.1233	0.0104	-0.0061
2	0.0590	3.5921	0.0383	0.3697	0.3075	0.0243	0.2198	0.1007	0.2493	0.0511	0.1233	0.0104	-0.0061
3	0.0590	3.5921	0.0383	0.3697	0.3075	0.0243	0.2198	0.1007	0.2493	0.0511	0.1233	0.0104	-0.0061
4	0.0590	3.5921	0.0383	0.3697	0.3075	0.0243	0.2198	0.1007	0.2493	0.0511	0.1233	0.0104	-0.0061
5	0.0590	3.5921	0.0383	0.3697	0.3075	0.0243	0.2198	0.1007	0.2493	0.0511	0.1233	0.0104	-0.0061
6	0.0590	3.5921	0.0383	0.3697	0.3075	0.0243	0.2198	0.1007	0.2493	0.0511	0.1233	0.0104	-0.0061
7	0.0590	3.5921	0.0383	0.3697	0.3075	0.0243	0.2198	0.1007	0.2493	0.0511	0.1233	0.0104	-0.0061
8	0.0590	3.5921	0.0383	0.3697	0.3075	0.0243	0.2198	0.1007	0.2493	0.0511	0.1233	0.0104	-0.0061
.	.	.	.	.	.	.	.	.	.	.	.	.	.
.	.	.	.	.	.	.	.	.	.	.	.	.	.
∞	0.0590	3.5921	0.0383	0.3697	0.3075	0.0243	0.2198	0.1007	0.2493	0.0511	0.1233	0.0104	-0.0061

[a] In the context of REV t is a generation rather than a time index.

Table A.18. Demographic Transition, Accidental Bequests, and Endogenous Labor Supply (Section 5.4.3)

t	$k(t)$	$k(t)/y(t)p.a.$	$r(t)p.a.$	$w(t)$	$\tau(t)$	$c^1(t)$	$l(t)$	$c^2(t)$	$I(t)$	$I(t)/y(t)$	$s(t)$	$REV(t)$[a]
-4	0.0517	3.2550	0.0406	0.3577	0.2013	0.2361	0.0988	0.3280	0.0416	0.0395	0.0630	0.0000
-3	0.0517	3.2550	0.0406	0.3577	0.2013	0.2361	0.0988	0.3280	0.0416	0.0395	0.0630	0.0000
-2	0.0517	3.2550	0.0406	0.3577	0.2013	0.2361	0.0988	0.3280	0.0416	0.0395	0.0630	0.0000
-1	0.0517	3.2550	0.0406	0.3577	0.2013	0.2361	0.0988	0.3280	0.0416	0.0395	0.0630	0.0000
0	0.0518	3.2558	0.0406	0.3577	0.2013	0.2369	0.0991	0.3280	0.0416	0.0396	0.0620	-0.0121
1	0.0594	3.6109	0.0382	0.3703	0.2266	0.2393	0.0999	0.3109	0.0444	0.0377	0.0629	-0.0040
2	0.0603	3.6491	0.0379	0.3716	0.2258	0.2404	0.1000	0.3122	0.0447	0.0381	0.0633	-0.0006
3	0.0606	3.6663	0.0378	0.3722	0.2254	0.2408	0.1000	0.3128	0.0449	0.0383	0.0635	0.0010
4	0.0608	3.6740	0.0378	0.3724	0.2253	0.2411	0.1000	0.3131	0.0449	0.0384	0.0636	0.0016
5	0.0609	3.6774	0.0378	0.3726	0.2252	0.2411	0.1000	0.3132	0.0450	0.0384	0.0636	0.0019
6	0.0609	3.6789	0.0377	0.3726	0.2252	0.2412	0.1000	0.3133	0.0450	0.0384	0.0636	0.0021
7	0.0609	3.6796	0.0377	0.3726	0.2252	0.2412	0.1000	0.3133	0.0450	0.0384	0.0636	0.0021
8	0.0609	3.6799	0.0377	0.3726	0.2252	0.2412	0.1000	0.3133	0.0450	0.0384	0.0636	0.0022
.	.	.	.	.	.	.	.	.	.	.	.	.
.	.	.	.	.	.	.	.	.	.	.	.	.
∞	0.0610	3.6801	0.0377	0.3727	0.2252	0.2412	0.1000	0.3133	0.0450	0.0384	0.0636	0.0022

[a] In the context of REV t is a generation rather than a time index.

Table A.19. Demographic Transition, Accidental Bequests, Endogenous Labor Supply, and Inheritance Taxation (Section 5.4.3)

t	$k(t)$	$k(t)/y(t) p.a.$	$r(t) p.a.$	$w(t)$	$\tau(t)$	$\tau^i(t)$	$c^1(t)$	$l(t)$	$c^2(t)$	$I(t)$	$I(t)/y(t)$	$s(t)$	$REV(t)$[a]
-4	0.0517	3.2550	0.0406	0.3577	0.2013	0.0000	0.2361	0.0988	0.3280	0.0416	0.0395	0.0630	0.0000
-3	0.0517	3.2550	0.0406	0.3577	0.2013	0.0000	0.2361	0.0988	0.3280	0.0416	0.0395	0.0630	0.0000
-2	0.0517	3.2550	0.0406	0.3577	0.2013	0.0000	0.2361	0.0988	0.3280	0.0416	0.0395	0.0630	0.0000
-1	0.0517	3.2549	0.0406	0.3577	0.2013	0.0000	0.2361	0.0988	0.3280	0.0416	0.0395	0.0630	0.0009
0	0.0513	3.2315	0.0408	0.3569	0.0809	11.8913	0.2391	0.0892	0.3293	0.0032	0.0393	0.0629	-0.0123
1	0.0595	3.6142	0.0382	0.3704	0.0906	487.6998	0.2428	0.0886	0.3134	0.0001	0.0377	0.0643	-0.0011
2	0.0608	3.6739	0.0378	0.3724	0.0901	78.2713	0.2445	0.0888	0.3155	0.0006	0.0384	0.0649	0.0042
3	0.0614	3.7005	0.0376	0.3733	0.0899	56.9973	0.2452	0.0888	0.3164	0.0008	0.0386	0.0652	0.0066
4	0.0617	3.7122	0.0375	0.3737	0.0898	50.8892	0.2455	0.0889	0.3168	0.0009	0.0388	0.0653	0.0076
5	0.0618	3.7174	0.0375	0.3739	0.0898	48.5963	0.2457	0.0889	0.3170	0.0009	0.0388	0.0653	0.0081
6	0.0618	3.7197	0.0375	0.3740	0.0898	47.6522	0.2457	0.0889	0.3171	0.0009	0.0388	0.0654	0.0083
7	0.0618	3.7206	0.0375	0.3740	0.0898	47.2488	0.2458	0.0889	0.3171	0.0010	0.0388	0.0654	0.0083
8	0.0619	3.7211	0.0375	0.3740	0.0897	47.0737	0.2458	0.0889	0.3171	0.0010	0.0388	0.0654	0.0084
.	.	.	.	.	.	.	.	.	.	.	.	.	.
.	.	.	.	.	.	.	.	.	.	.	.	.	.
∞	0.0619	3.7214	0.0375	0.3740	0.0897	46.9374	0.2458	0.0889	0.3172	0.0010	0.0389	0.0654	0.0084

[a] In the context of REV t is a generation rather than a time index.

Table A.20. Demographic Transition, Bequests-as-Exchange, and Endogenous Labor Supply (Section 5.4.4)

t	$k(t)$	$k(t)/y(t)p.a.$	$r(t)p.a.$	$w(t)$	$\tau(t)$	$c^1(t)$	$l(t)$	$c^2(t)$	$I(t)$	$I(t)/y(t)$	$a(t)$	$s(t)$	$REV(t)$[a]
-4	0.0507	3.2043	0.0410	0.3559	0.2937	0.1691	0.0837	0.3050	0.0181	0.0604	0.0718	0.0446	0.0000
-3	0.0507	3.2043	0.0410	0.3559	0.2937	0.1691	0.0837	0.3050	0.0181	0.0604	0.0718	0.0446	0.0000
-2	0.0507	3.2043	0.0410	0.3559	0.2937	0.1691	0.0837	0.3050	0.0181	0.0604	0.0718	0.0446	0.0000
-1	0.0507	3.2043	0.0410	0.3559	0.2937	0.1691	0.0837	0.3050	0.0181	0.0604	0.0718	0.0446	0.0000
0	0.0507	3.2052	0.0410	0.3559	0.2938	0.1699	0.0841	0.3050	0.0181	0.0604	0.0718	0.0438	-0.0166
1	0.0582	3.5569	0.0385	0.3684	0.3337	0.1664	0.0847	0.2892	0.0198	0.0557	0.0808	0.0402	-0.0322
2	0.0565	3.4788	0.0391	0.3657	0.3361	0.1647	0.0846	0.2867	0.0196	0.0555	0.0808	0.0396	-0.0395
3	0.0558	3.4422	0.0393	0.3644	0.3373	0.1639	0.0846	0.2856	0.0195	0.0554	0.0808	0.0393	-0.0430
4	0.0554	3.4247	0.0394	0.3638	0.3379	0.1636	0.0846	0.2850	0.0195	0.0553	0.0808	0.0392	-0.0447
5	0.0552	3.4164	0.0395	0.3635	0.3382	0.1634	0.0845	0.2847	0.0194	0.0553	0.0808	0.0391	-0.0455
6	0.0551	3.4124	0.0395	0.3634	0.3383	0.1633	0.0845	0.2846	0.0194	0.0553	0.0808	0.0391	-0.0459
7	0.0551	3.4105	0.0395	0.3633	0.3384	0.1632	0.0845	0.2846	0.0194	0.0553	0.0808	0.0390	-0.0461
8	0.0551	3.4096	0.0395	0.3633	0.3384	0.1632	0.0845	0.2845	0.0194	0.0553	0.0808	0.0390	-0.0462
.	.	.	.	.	.	.	.	.	.	.	.	.	.
.	.	.	.	.	.	.	.	.	.	.	.	.	.
∞	0.0550	3.4087	0.0395	0.3633	0.3384	0.1632	0.0845	0.2845	0.0194	0.0553	0.0808	0.0390	-0.0463

[a] In the context of REV t is a generation rather than a time index.

Table A.21. Demographic Transition, Bequests-as-Exchange, Endogenous Labor Supply, and Inheritance Taxation (Section 5.4.4)

t	$k(t)$	$k(t)/y(t)p.a.$	$r(t)p.a.$	$w(t)$	$\tau(t)$	$\tau^i(t)$	$c^1(t)$	$l(t)$	$c^2(t)$	$I(t)$	$I(t)/y(t)$	$a(t)$	$s(t)$	$REV(t)$[a]
-4	0.0507	3.2043	0.0410	0.3559	0.2937	0.0000	0.1691	0.0837	0.3050	0.0181	0.0604	0.0718	0.0446	0.0000
-3	0.0507	3.2043	0.0410	0.3559	0.2937	0.0000	0.1691	0.0837	0.3050	0.0181	0.0604	0.0718	0.0446	0.0000
-2	0.0507	3.2043	0.0410	0.3559	0.2937	0.0000	0.1691	0.0837	0.3050	0.0181	0.0604	0.0718	0.0446	0.0000
-1	0.0507	3.2042	0.0410	0.3558	0.2937	0.0000	0.1690	0.0837	0.3050	0.0181	0.0604	0.0718	0.0447	-0.0033
0	0.0508	3.2080	0.0410	0.3560	0.2858	0.1067	0.1715	0.0836	0.3047	0.0167	0.0613	0.0656	0.0462	-0.0122
1	0.0592	3.5992	0.0383	0.3699	0.3229	0.1128	0.1692	0.0841	0.2902	0.0183	0.0565	0.0732	0.0434	-0.0223
2	0.0581	3.5486	0.0386	0.3682	0.3244	0.1137	0.1682	0.0841	0.2886	0.0182	0.0564	0.0732	0.0430	-0.0270
3	0.0576	3.5253	0.0387	0.3674	0.3251	0.1141	0.1677	0.0841	0.2878	0.0181	0.0564	0.0731	0.0428	-0.0291
4	0.0573	3.5145	0.0388	0.3670	0.3254	0.1143	0.1675	0.0841	0.2875	0.0181	0.0563	0.0731	0.0427	-0.0301
5	0.0572	3.5094	0.0388	0.3668	0.3256	0.1144	0.1674	0.0841	0.2873	0.0181	0.0563	0.0731	0.0426	-0.0306
6	0.0572	3.5070	0.0389	0.3667	0.3256	0.1144	0.1673	0.0841	0.2872	0.0181	0.0563	0.0731	0.0426	-0.0308
7	0.0571	3.5059	0.0389	0.3667	0.3257	0.1144	0.1673	0.0841	0.2872	0.0181	0.0563	0.0731	0.0426	-0.0309
8	0.0571	3.5054	0.0389	0.3667	0.3257	0.1144	0.1673	0.0841	0.2872	0.0181	0.0563	0.0731	0.0426	-0.0310
.	.	.	.	.	.	.	.	.	.	.	.	.	.	
.	.	.	.	.	.	.	.	.	.	.	.	.	.	
∞	0.0571	3.5050	0.0389	0.3666	0.3257	0.1144	0.1673	0.0841	0.2872	0.0181	0.0563	0.0731	0.0426	-0.0310

[a] In the context of REV t is a generation rather than a time index.

References

1. Kotlikoff, L.J., Summers, L.J. (1981): The Role of Intergenerational Transfers in Aggregate Capital Accumulation. Journal of Political Economy 89, 706–732
2. Gale, W., Scholz, J.K. (1994): Intergenerational Transfers and the Accumulation of Wealth. Journal of Economic Perspective 8, 145–160
3. Samuelson, P.A. (1958): An Exact Consumption-Loan Model With or Without the Social Contrivance of Money. Journal of Political Economy 66, 467–482
4. Diamond, P.A. (1958): National Debt in a Neoclassical Growth Model. American Economic Review 55, 1126–1150
5. Auerbach, A.J., Gokhale, J., Kotlikoff, L.J.(1991): Generational Accounting: A Meaningful Alternative to Deficit Accounting. In: Bradford, D. (Ed.): Tax Policy and the Economy. MIT Press, Cambridge, MA, 55–110
6. Auerbach, A.J., Gokhale, J., Kotlikoff, L.J.(1992): Generational Accounting: A New Approach to Understanding the Effects of Fiscal Policy on Saving. Scandinavian Journal of Economics 94, 303–318
7. Kotlikoff, L.J.(1992): Generational Accounting, Knowing Who Pays and When for What we Spend. Free Press, New York
8. Jürges, H. (1999): Parent-Child Transfers in Germany: A Staudy of Magnitude and Motivation. Zeitschrift für Wirtschafts- und Sozialwissenschaften 119, 429–453
9. Schlomann, H. (1991): Der Einfluß von Erbschaften auf die Vermögensausstattung privater Haushalte im Jahr 1988. Discussion Paper 39, Deutsches Institut für Wirtschaftsforschung, Berlin
10. Reil-Held, A. (1997): Bequests and Aggregate Wealth Accumulation in Germany. Mimeo, University of Mannheim
11. Merkle, L., Zimmermann, K.F. (1992): Savings, Remittances and Return Migration. Economics Letters 38, 77–81
12. Ablett, J. (1996): Intergenerational Accounting and Saving in Australia. The Economic Record 72, 236–245
13. Auerbach, A.J., Kotlikoff, L.J., Hagemann, R.P., Nicoletti, G. (1989): The Economic Dynamics of an Ageing Population: The Case of Four OECD Countries. OECD Economic Studies 12, 97–130
14. Raffelhüschen, B. (1998): Anreizwirkungen des Systems der sozialen Alterssicherung. Peter Lang, Frankfurt/M
15. Barro, R. (1974): Are Government Bonds Net Wealth? Journal of Political Economy 6, 1095–1117
16. Becker, G.S. (1974): A Theory of Social Interactions. Journal of Political Economy 82, 1063–1093
17. Laitner, J. (1997): Intergenerational and Interhousehold Economic Links. In: Rosenzweig, M. and Stark, O. (Eds.): Handbook of Population and Family Economics, Volume 1A. Elsevier, Amsterdam, 189–238

18. Davies, J.B. (1996): Explaining Intergenerational Transfers. In: Mechnik, P. (Ed.): Household and Family Economics. Kluwer Academic Publishers, Boston, 47–82
19. Bernheim, B.D. (1987): Ricardian Equivalence: An Evaluation of Theory and Evidence. NBER Macroeconomics Annual 2, 263–303
20. Poterba, J. (1998): Inter Vivos Transfers and the Incentive Effects of Estate and Gift Taxes in the United States. Mimeo, MIT
21. Drazen, A. (1978): Government Debt, Human Capital, and Bequests in a Life-Cycle Model. Journal of Political Economy 86, 505–516
22. Lindbeck, A.W., Weibull, J.W. (1988): Altruism and Time Consistency: The Economics of Fait Accompli. Journal of Political Economy 96, 1165–1182
23. Bruce, N., Waldman, M. (1990): The Rotten-Kid Theorem Meets the Samaritan's Dilemma. The Quarterly Journal of Economics 105, 154–165
24. Breyer, F. (1990): Ökonomische Theorie der Alterssicherung. Vahlen, München
25. Bernheim, B.D., Bagwell, K. (1988): Is Everything Neutral? Journal of Political Economy 96, 308–338
26. Laitner, J. (1991): Modeling Marital Connections Among Family Lines. Journal of Political Economy 99, 1123–1141
27. Yaari, M.E. (1965): Uncertain Lifetime, Life Insurance, and the Theory of the Consumer. The Review of Economic Studies 32, 137–150
28. Barro, R.J., Friedman, J.W. (1977): On Uncertain Lifetimes. Journal of Political Economy 85, 843–849
29. Davies, J.B. (1981): Uncertain Lifetime, Consumption, and Dissaving in Retirement. Journal of Political Economy 89, 561–577
30. Abel, A.B. (1985): Precautionary Saving and Accidental Bequests. American Economic Review 75, 777–791
31. Eckstein, Z., Eichenbaum, M.S., Peled, D. (1985): The Distribution of Wealth and Welfare in the Presence of Incomplete Annuity Markets. Quarterly Journal of Economics 100, 789–806
32. Hubbard, G.R., Judd, K.L. (1987): Social Security and Individual Welfare: Precautionary Saving, Borrowing Constraints, and the Payroll Tax. American Economic Review 77, 630–646
33. Hurd, M.D. (1989): Mortality Risk and Bequests. Econometrica 57, 779–813
34. Kuehlwein, M. (1993): Life-Cycle and Altruistic Theories of Saving with Lifetime Uncertainty. Review of Economics and Statistics 75, 38–47
35. Friedman, B.M., Warshawsky, M.J. (1990): The Cost of Annuities: Implications for Saving Behavior and Bequests. Quarterly Journal of Economics 105, 135–154
36. Kotlikoff, L.J. (1989): What Determines Savings? MIT Press, Cambridge, MA
37. Kotlikoff, L.J., Spivak, A. (1981): The Family as Incomplete Annuities Market. Journal of Political Economy 89, 372–391
38. Desai, M., Shah, A. (1983): Bequest and Inheritance in Nuclear Families and Joint Families. Economica 50, 193–202
39. Bernheim, B.D., Shleifer, A., Summers, L.H. (1985): The Strategic Bequest Motive. Journal of Political Economy 93, 1045–1076
40. Lucas, R.E., Stark, O. (1985): Motivations to Remit: Evidence from Botswana. Journal of Political Economy 93, 901–918
41. Cox, D. (1987): Motives for Private Income Transfers. Journal of Political Economy 95. 508–546
42. Cox, D. (1990): Intergenerational Transfers and Liquidity Constraints. Quarterly Journal of Economics 105, 187–217

43. Rosenzweig, M. (1988): Risk, Private Information and the Family. American Economic Review 78, 245–250
44. Rosenzweig, M. (1988): Risk, Implicit Contracts and the Family in Rural Areas of Low-Income Countries. Economic Journal 98, 1148–1170
45. Stark, O., Taylor, J.E. (1991): Migration Incentives, Migration Types: The Role of Relative Deprivation. Economic Journal 101, 1163-1178
46. Bergstrom, T.C., Stark, O. (1993): How Altruism can Prevail in an Evolutionary Environment. American Economic Review 83, 149–155
47. Stark, O. (1995): Altruism and Beyond. Cambridge University Press, Cambridge
48. Yaari, M.E. (1964): On the Consumer's Lifetime Allocation Process. International Economic Review 5, 304–317
49. Atkinson, A.B. (1971): Capital Taxes, the Redistribution of Wealth and Individual Saving. Review of Economic Studies 38, 209–227
50. Blinder, A.S. (1974): Toward an Economic Theory of Income Distribution. MIT Press, Cambridge, MA
51. Blinder, A.S. (1976): Inequality and Mobility in the Distribution of Wealth. Kyklos 29, 607–638
52. Modigliani, F. (1986): Life Cycle, Individual Thrift, and the Wealth of Nations. American Economic Review 76, 297–313
53. Hurd, M.D. (1987): Savings of the Elderly and Desired Bequests. American Economic Review 77, 298–312
54. Ihori, T. (1994): Bequests, Fiscal Policy, and Social Security. In: Toshika, T. (Ed.): Savings and Bequests. University of Michigan Press, Chicago, 137–166
55. Abel, A.B., Warshawsky, M.J. (1988): Specification of the Joy of Giving: Insights from Altruism. Review of Economics and Statistics 70, 145–149
56. Adams, J.D. (1980): Personal Wealth Transfers. Quarterly Journal of Economics 95, 159–180
57. Sussman, M.B.,Cates, J.N., Smith, D.T.(1970): The Family and Inheritance. Russell Sage Foundation, New York
58. Menchik, P.L., David, M. (1983): Income Distribution, Lifetime Savings and Bequests. American Economic Review 73, 672–690
59. Cox, D., Rank, M.R. (1992): Inter-Vivos Transfers and Intergenerational Exchange. Review of Economics and Statistics 74, 305–314
60. Olneck, M.R. (1977): On the Use of Sibling Data to Estimate the Effects of Family Background, Cognitive Skills and Schooling. In: Taubman, P. (Ed.): Kinometrics: The Determinants of Socioeconomic Success Within and Between Families. North Holland, Amsterdam, 125–162
61. Menchik, P.L. (1980): Primogenitur, Equal Sharing and the U.S. Distribution of Wealth. Quarterly Journal of Economics 94, 299–316
62. Tomes, N. (1981): The Family, Inheritance and the Intergenerational Transmission of Inequality. Journal of Political Economy 89, 928–958
63. Tomes, N. (1988): Inheritance and Inequality within the Family: Equal Division among Unequals, or do the Poor Get More? In: Kessler, D., Masson, A. (Eds.): Modelling the Accumulation and Distribution of Wealth. Clarendon Press, Oxford, 79–104
64. Menchik, P.L. (1988): Unequal Estate Division: Is It Altruism, Reverse Bequests, or Simply Noise? In: Kessler, D., Masson, A. (Eds.): Modelling the Accumulation and Distribution of Wealth. Clarendon Press, Oxford, 105–116
65. Wilhelm, M.O. (1996): Bequest Behavior and the Effect of Heirs' Earnings: Testing the Altruistic Model of Bequests. American Economic Review 86, 874–892

66. McGarry, K., Schoeni, R.F. (1995): Transfer Behavior in the Health and Retirement Study: Measurement and the Redistribution within the Family. Journal of Human Resources 30(Supplement), 184–226
67. McGarry, K. (1997): Inter Vivos Transfers and Intended Bequests. NBER Working Paper No. 6345, Cambridge, MA
68. Dunn, T.A., Phillips, J.W. (1997): The Timing and Division of Parental Transfers to Children. Economics Letters, 54, 135–137
69. Altonji, J.G., Hayashi, F., Kotlikoff, L.J. (1992): Is the Extended Family Altruistically Linked? Direct Tests Using Micro Data. American Economic Review 82, 1177–1198
70. Altonji, J.G., Hayashi, F., Kotlikoff, L.J.(1997): Parental Altruism and Inter Vivos Transfers: Theory and Evidence. Journal of Political Economy 105, 1121–1166
71. Horsman, E.G. (1975): The Avoidance of Estate Duty by Gifts Inter-Vivos. Economic Journal 85, 516–530
72. Cox, D., Raines, F. (1985): Interfamily Transfers and Income Redistribution. In: David, M., Smeeding, T. (Eds.): Horizontal Equity, Uncertainty, and Economic Well-Being. University of Chicago Press, Chicago, 393–425
73. Hurd, M.D., Mundaca, G. (1989): The Importance of Gifts and Inheritances among the Affluent. In: Lipsey, R.E., Tice, H.S. (Eds.): The Measurement of Saving, Investment, and Wealth. University of Chicago Press, Chicago, 737–758
74. Modigliani, F. (1988): Measuring the Contribution of Intergenerational Transfers to Total Wealth: Conceptual Issues and Empirical Findings. In: Kessler, D., Masson, A. (Eds.): Modelling the Accumulation and Distribution of Wealth. Clarendon Press, Oxford, 21–52
75. Modigliani, F. (1988): The Role of Intergenerational Transfers and Life Cycle Saving in the Accumulation of Wealth. Journal of Economic Perspectives 2, 15–40
76. Poterba, J. (1997): The Estate Tax and After-Tax Investment Returns. NBER Working Paper No. 6337, Cambridge, MA
77. Modigliani, F., Brumberg, R. (1954): Utility Analysis and the Cosnumption Function: An Interpretation of Cross-Section Data. In: Kurihara, K. (Ed.): Post-Keynesian Economics. Rutgers University Press, New Brunswick, 388–436
78. Diamond, P.A., Hausman, J. (1984): Individual Retirement and Savings Behavior. Journal of Public Economics 23, 81–114
79. Hayashi, F. (1986): Why is Japan's Saving Rate So Apparently High? In: Fischer, S. (Ed.): NBER Macroeconomics Annual 1986. MIT Press, Cambridge, MA, 147–210
80. King, M., Dicks-Mireaux, L. (1982): Asset Holding and the Life Cycle. The Economical Journal 92, 247–267
81. Kurz, M. (1984): Capital Accumulation and the Characteristics of Private Intergenerational Transfers. Economica 51, 1–22
82. Mirer, T.W. (1979): The Wealth Age Relation Among the Aged. American Economic Review 69, 435–443
83. Bernheim, B.D. (1991): How Strong Are Bequest Motives? Evidence Based on Estimates of the Demand for Life Insurance and Annuities. Journal of Political Economy 99, 899–927
84. Ando, A., Guiso, L., Terlizze, D. (1993): Dissaving by the Elderly, Transfer Motives and Liquidity Constraints. NBER Working Paper No. 4569, Cambridge, MA

85. Jürges, H. (1999): Do Germans Save to Leave an Estate? An Examination of the Bequest Motive. Discussion Paper No. 98-24 (Revised Version), University of Dortmund
86. Laitner, J., Juster, F.T. (1996): New Evidence on Altruism: A Study of TIAA-CREF Retirees. American Economic Review 86, 893–908
87. Federal Statistical Office(1997): Einkommens- und Verbrauchsstichprobe 1993.CD-ROM, Berlin
88. DIW – Deutsches Institut für Wirtschaftsforschung (1999): Das Sozioökonomische Panel. CD-ROM, Berlin
89. Börsch-Supan, A. (1992): Saving and Consumption Patterns of the Elderly: The German Case. Journal of Population Economics 5, 289–303
90. Kessler, D., Masson, André (1989): Bequest and Wealth Accumulation: Are Some Pieces of the Puzzle Missing? Journal of Economic Perspectives 3, 141–152
91. Deutsche Bundesbank (1999): Zur Entwicklung der privaten Vermögenssituation seit Beginn der neunziger Jahre. Monthly Bouletain, November, 33–50
92. Menchik, P.L. (1980): The Importance of Material Inheritance: The Financial Link Between Generations. In: Smith, J.D. (Ed.): Modelling the Distribution and Intergenerational Transmission of Wealth. Chicago Press, Chicago, 273–288
93. Becker, G.S., Tomes, N. (1979): An Equilibrium Theory of the Distribution of Income and Intergenerational Mobility. Journal of Political Economy 87, 1153–1189
94. Becker, G.S., Tomes, N. (1986): Human Capital and the Rise and Fall of Families. Journal of Labor Economics 4, 1–39
95. Björklund, A., Jäntti, M. (1997): Intergenerational Income Mobility in Sweden Compared to the United States. American Economic Review 87, 1009–1018
96. Couch, K.A., Dunn, T.A. (1997): Intergenerational Correlations in Labor Market Status, Journal of Human Resources 32, 210–232
97. Dearden, L., Machin, S., Reed, H. (1997): Intergenerational Mobility in Britain. Economic Journal 107, 47–66
98. Hurd, M.D., Smith, J.P. (1999): Anticipated and Actual Bequests. Mimeo, NBER
99. Davies, J.B. (1982): The Relative Impact of Inheritance and Other Factors on Economic Inequality. Quarterly Journal of Economics 47, 471–498
100. Shorroks, A.F. (1975): The Age-Wealth Relationship: A Cross-Section and Cohort Analysis. Review of Econonics and Statistics, 57, 155-163
101. Fischer, S. (1973): A Life Cycle Model of Life Insurance Purchases. International Economic Review 14, 132–152
102. Weil, D.N. (1997): The Economics of Population Aging. In: Rosenzweig, M., Stark, O. (Eds.): Handbook of Population and Family Economics, Volume 1B. Elsevier, Amsterdam, 967–1014
103. Auerbach, A.J., Kotlikoff, L.J. (1987): Dynamic Fiscal Policy. Cambridge University Press, Cambridge
104. Keyfitz, N. (1988): Some Demographic Properties of Transfer Schemes: How to Achieve Equity Between the Generations. In: Lee, R.D., Arthur, W.B., Rodgers, G. (Eds.): Economivs of Changing Age Distributions in Developed Countries. Clarendon Press, Oxford, 92–105
105. OECD (1988): Ageing Populations: The Social Policy Implications, Paris
106. European Commission (Ed.)(1999): Generational Accounting in Europe. European Economy 6 (Reports and Studies), Luxembourg

107. Auerbach, A.J., Kotlikoff, L.J., Leibfritz, W. (Eds.)(1999): Generational Accounting Around the World. University of Chicago Press, Chicago
108. Besendorfer, D., Borgmann, C., Raffelhüschen, B. (1998): Ein Plädoyer für intergenerative Ausgewogenheit: Rentenreformvorschläge auf dem Prüfstand, Ifo-Studien 44, 209–231
109. Weil, D.N. (1996): Intergenerational Transfers, Aging, and Uncertainty. In: Wise, D.A. (1996): Advances in the Economics of Aging. University of Chicago Press, Chicago, 321–339
110. Statistisches Reichsamt (1938): Statistik des Deutschen Reichs, Band 495
111. Kaiserliches Statistisches Amt (1887): Monatshefte zur Statistik des Deutschen Reichs, Heft 11
112. Kaiserliches Statistisches Amt (1913): Statistik des Deutschen Reichs, Band 246
113. Börsch-Supan, A. (1991): Aging Population: Problems and Policy Options in the US and Germany. Economic Policy 12, 104–139
114. Bretz, M. (1986): Bevölkerungsvorausberechnungen: Statistische Grundlagen und Probleme. Wirtschaft und Statistik, 233–261
115. Federal Statistical Office (1998): Statistical Yearbook for Foreign Countries, Stuttgart
116. Bonin, H., Raffelhüschen, B., Walliser, J. (2000): Can Immigration Alleviate the Demographic Burden?, Finanzarchiv, forthcoming
117. Federal Statistical Office(1997): Statistical Yearbook for Foreign Countries, Stuttgart
118. Raffelhüschen, B. (2000): Aging, Fiscal Policy, and Social Insurance: A European Perspective. In: Auerbach, A.J., Lee, R. (Eds.): Demographic Change and Fiscal Policy. University of Chicago Press, Chicago, forthcoming
119. Federal Statistical Office (1996): Statistical Yearbook for the Federal Republic of Germany, Stuttgart
120. Sommer, B. (1994): Entwicklung der Bevölkerung bis 2040, Ergebnisse der achten koordinierten Bevölkerungsvorausschätzung, Wirtschaft und Statistik, 497–503
121. Bonin, H., Raffelhüschen, B., Walliser, J. (1999): The German Squeeze: Unification and Aging, European Economy 6 (Reports and Studies), 57–70
122. Federal Statistical Office (1991): Bevölkerung und Erwerbstätigkeit, Fachserie 1, Reihe 1.S.2., Allgemeine Sterbetafel für die Bundesrepublik Deutschland (Gebietsstand vor dem 3.10.1990) 1986/88
123. Birg, H. (1999): Langlebigkeit, Geburtenrückgang und Migrationsprozeß – Trends der Demographischen Alterung in Deutschland im 21. Jahrhundert. Mimeo, University of Bielefeld
124. Wolf, D.A. (1988): Kinship and Family Support in Aging Societies. In: U.N. Department of International Economic and Social Affairs (Ed.): Economic and Social Implications of Population Aging: Proceedings of the International Symposium on Population Structure and Development, Tokyo, 10-12 Sept., 1987. New York, 305–320
125. Bundesverfassungsgericht (1980): Urteil des 1. Senats vom 28.2.1980, BVerfGe 93, 257/290
126. Weil, D.N. (1994): The Saving of the Elderly in Micro and Macro Data. Quarterly Journal of Economics 109, 55–81
127. Disney, R. (1996): Can We Afford to Grow Older? A Perspective on the Economics of Aging. MIT Press, Cambridge, MA

128. Smith, J.D., Orcutt, G.H. (1980): The Intergenerational Transmission of Wealth: Does Family Size Matter? In: Smith, J.D. (Ed.): Modelling the Distribution and Intergenerational Transmission of Wealth. Chicago Press, Chicago, 273–288
129. Menchik, P.L. (1979): Inter-Generational Transmission of Inequality: An Empirical Study of Wealth Mobility. Economica 46, 349–362
130. Kotlikoff, L.J., Raffelhüschen, B. (1999): Generational Accounting Around the Globe. American Economic Review 89, Papers and Proceedings, 161–166
131. Raffelhüschen, B. (1999): Generational Accounting in Europe. American Economic Review 89, Papers and Proceedings, 167–170
132. Boll, S. (1996): Intergenerative Verteilungseffekte öffentlicher Haushalte: Theoretische Konzepte und empirischer Befund für die Bundesrepublik Deutschland. Diskussionspapier 6/96, Volkswirtschaftliche Forschungsgruppe der Deutschen Bundesbank
133. Raffelhüschen, B. (1999): Generational Accounting: Method, Data, and Limitations. European Economy 6, Reports and Studies, 17–28
134. ter Rele, H. (1997): Generational Accounts for the Dutch Public Sector. Research Memorandum No. 135, Netherlands Bureau of Economic Policy Analysis, The Hague
135. Franco, D., Gokhale, J., Guiso, L., Kotlikoff, L.J., Sartor, N. (1994): Generational Accounting: The Case of Italy. In: Ando, A., Guiso, L., Visco I. (Eds.): Saving and the Accumulation of Wealth: Essays on Italian Household and Government Saving Behavior. Cambridge University Press, Cambridge, 128–160
136. Federal Statistical Office (1992): Finanzen und Steuern. Fachserie 14, Reihe 8, Umsatzsteuer, Stuttgart
137. BMF – Bundesministerium der Finanzen (1997): Finanzbericht, Bonn
138. BMA – Bundesministerium für Arbeit und Sozialordnung (1996): Arbeits- und Sozialstatistik, Hauptergebnisse, Bonn
139. Federal Statistical Office (1996): Volkswirtschaftliche Gesamtrechnung 1995. Fachserie 18, Reihe 1.3, Hauptbericht, Stuttgart
140. Deutsche Bundesbank (1998): Monatsbericht Januar, 50. Jahrgang Nr. 1, Frankfurt/M
141. Bonin, H., Raffelhüschen, B., Walliser, J. (1999): The German Squeeze: Unification and Aging, European Economy 6 (Reports and Studies), 57–70
142. Bach, S. (1996): Zur Neuregelung von Vermögen- und Erbschaftsteuer. Wochenbericht des Deutschen Instituts für Wirtschaftsforschung 30, 497–506
143. Federal Statistical Office (1997): Statistical Yearbook for the Federal Republic of Germany, Stuttgart
144. IW – Institut der Deutschen Wirtschaft Köln (1999): Zahlen zur Wirtschaftlichen Entwicklung der Bundesrepublik Deutschland. Bacht, Essen
145. de Nardi, M., İmrohoroğlu, S., Sardent, T.J. (1999): Projected US Demographics and Social Security. Working Paper No. 14, Federal Reserve Bank of Chicago
146. Bosworth, B., Burtless, G., Sabelhaus, J (1991): The Decline in Saving: Evidence from Household Surveys. Brookings Papers on Economic Activity 1, 183–241
147. Auerbach, A.J., Laurence J.K. (1990): Demographics, Fiscal Policy, and U.S. Saving in the 1980s and Beyond. In: Summers, L.H. (Ed.): Tax Policy and the Economy 4, MIT Press, Cambridge, MA, 73–101
148. Wachtel, P. (1984): Household Saving and Demographic Change, 1950–2050. In: Schultz, T.P., Wolpin, K.I. (Eds.): Research in Population Economics 5. JAI Press, Greenwich, CT, 217–233

149. Raffelhüschen, B., Risa, A.E. (1997): Generational Accounting and Intergenerational Welfare. Public Choice 93, 149–163
150. Rothschild, M., Stiglitz, J. (1977): Equilibrium in Competitive Insurance Markets. Quarterly Journal of Economics 90, 629–649
151. Börsch-Supan, A., Reil-Held, A. (1999): How Much is Transfer and How Much Insurance in a Pay-As-You-Go System? The German Case. Mimeo, University of Mannheim
152. Fehr, H., Kotlikoff, L.J. (1996): Generational Accounting in General Equilibrium. Finanzarchiv 53, 1–27

GPSR Compliance

The European Union's (EU) General Product Safety Regulation (GPSR) is a set of rules that requires consumer products to be safe and our obligations to ensure this.

If you have any concerns about our products, you can contact us on ProductSafety@springernature.com

In case Publisher is established outside the EU, the EU authorized representative is:

Springer Nature Customer Service Center GmbH
Europaplatz 3
69115 Heidelberg, Germany

Batch number: 10725973

Printed by Printforce, the Netherlands